WHEE! WE, WEE

All the Way Home

WHEE! WE, WEE

All The Way Home

A GUIDE TO SENSUAL, PROPHETIC SPIRITUALITY

MATTHEW FOX

BEAR & COMPANY
SANTA FE, NEW MEXICO

To Fr. M. D. Chenu, O.P.

who has never succumbed to separating
the body
the body politic
and the spirit—
and who for that reason
remains the freshest teacher of my life
and, in his seventies,
the youngest person I know

Bear & Company, Inc.
P.O. Drawer 2860
Santa Fe, NM 87504

Cover Design: Kathleen Katz

Cover Photo: Catherine Busch, c.s.j.

Printed in the United States of America

Fifth Printing: September 1987

This book was originally published by McGrath Publishing Company in 1976.

CONTENTS

164559

PART III
Obstacles
(Small and Large Dragons)
to Experiencing Ecstasy and
The God of Ecstasy:

WEE

This little piggie went to market.
This little piggie stayed home.
This little piggie had roast beef.
This little piggie had none.

And this little piggie said . . .
"WHEE!
We
wee"
all the way home

from everyone's childhood

Where are we really going? Always home!

Novalis

PREFACE
to Bear & Company Edition

This is a practical book about waking up and returning to a biblical, justice-oriented spirituality. Such a spirituality is a way of passion that leads to compassion. Such a way is necessarily one of coming to our senses in every meaning of that phrase and in this regard this book was, I believe, anticipated by the late Catholic monk, Thomas Merton, when he wrote:

> The first step in the interior life, nowadays, is not, as some might imagine, learning *not* to see and taste and hear and feel things. On the contrary, what we must do is begin by unlearning our wrong ways of seeing, tasting, feeling, and so forth, and acquire a few of the right ones.[1]

Like any book for adults and would-be adults, there is unlearning to do, there is letting go to undergo, if one is to understand this book and its spirituality. Above all, there is the unlearning of dualistic spiritualisms that have haunted so much of western Christian thinking and acting for centuries.

In the five years since this book first appeared, much has happened in practice and in intellectual growth in our culture and in our churches to reinforce the basic guidelines to a sensual, prophetic spirituality. Three Mile Island, Love Canal, and their haunting implications point to a few of the political implications of our ignoring our earthiness and our relationship to the earth; the emergence of a stronger fight of family farmers against giant conglomerate agribusinesses as represented by poets Wendell Berry and Robert Bly points to the issue of holiness of the land; studies by Ashley Montagu and James Prescott on violence vs. sensuality reveal the issues at stake in body-spirit consciousness; feminist writers like Susan Griffin in her *Woman and Nature* and Adrienne Rich in *Of Woman Born* pursue the connections made in this book between the feminist tradition and an earthly spirituality; the renaissance in theological and church circles of creation theology as represented by writers like Helen Kenik, Claus Westermann, Walter Brueggemann, Rosemary Ruether,

Roland Murphy, and myself all point to a more holistic and therefore holier church future. Already publications like *Modern Liturgy* and the newsletter *Body & Soul* point to a growing awareness of how rich life can be after dualisms are laid to rest.

In this preface I would like to treat some areas of concern in this book that have become richer to me since I first wrote the book and have, I believe, been developed to greater depths in cultural and theological movements since 1976. Perhaps all this is to argue the truth of the opening pages of this book: that a new age—call it Aquarian or call it holistic—might indeed still emerge from the troubled consciences and consciousnesses of the West. If institutions fight it and do not care to enter into it, that only underlines the depth of the change; institutions might delay but they will never destroy that vision whose time has come. As the West begins out of dire necessity to listen finally to the Third World, one unmistakable lesson that is heard is the following: African, Asian, and Latin American peoples do not need and do not want exports of dualistic consciousness and action from the powerful western cultures. They are telling the West to put to rest the violent asceticism of Philo who declared, "We must keep down our feelings just as we keep down the lower classes." The subtle connection between repression of body and oppression of the body politic has been laid bare and is no longer subtle. The needs of the poor are human needs, universal needs, and bodily needs: food, clothing, shelter, health care, education, humanizing work. Until the global village restructures its economics and politics around these needs—which also means letting go of luxury living, consumer compulsions whether personal or social, and greed—there will be neither peace nor justice. The process of that happening constitutes a social / spiritual transformation of the fullest and most ecstatic order.

How do North Americans and First World countries become liberated themselves? That is the theme of this book: to name the liberation and the journey that godly liberation takes. I believe that the first stage of the liberation process is *Whee!* or *ecstasy.* By insisting on our return to ecstasies, I am insisting on spirituality's return to experience. Without experience we lose all trust and without trust in our experience, God and we are dead. We remain asleep, in a stupor and practicing idolatries, for when a person surrenders her or his right to ecstasy, that person surrenders to others the right to define where truth lies. Psychologist James Fowler, in mapping out stages of psychological and faith growth, talks of "images of the Ultimate

Environment"[2] which are for him images that one grasps holistically as the conditions of our existence. I ask: When does one do this grasping of images? It happens, I submit, in ecstasies.

Not all ecstasies are red or orange in color; some are quite subtle and come in blue or green-blue colors. But all ecstasy is a uniting, a forming or a re-forming of what once was or is all new. In this sense, then, a spirituality that honestly begins with ecstasy is a spirituality of God as verb. Such a spirituality parallels that imaged by Meister Eckhart when he called God "a great underground river that no one can dam up, no one can destroy." A spirituality that takes ecstasies seriously enough to meditate on them and the lessons of union learned from them is a spirituality about God as verb, about God as experienced and experiencing us; about ourselves as becoming, growing, expanding, exploding. Such a God is God who continues the beauty of creation and the sharing of it by way of justice through ourselves. We are instruments of the God-verb; and more than that, we are images of this God-verb. We, too, are verbs and not nouns. Ecstasies ourselves.

Reflections on the Word "SENSUAL":
Sensuality as a Blessing

A word that has proved a stumbling block to some persons on reading this book has been the word "sensual." One professor wrote to me that he would never read another thing I write because I dared to talk of "sensual spirituality." Another urged me to use the word "incarnational" instead of "sensual." A threatened parent told me her daughter would never attend the school I teach in because no spiritual person ought to use the words "sensual and spiritual in the same sentence." It is good news to me that there are a few words that still arouse people in our culture. Maybe we and our institutions are not as dead as we so often appear after all. I feel sorry for these fearful people who have apparently never enjoyed the *sensuousness* (no thank you—I will not relinquish this fine English word in favor of the Latin "incarnational") of a home-grown tomato or a ripe peach. Have they never wallowed in the delight of a baby's smell, squeals, or a puppy's cuddling? Of the smell of a horse's sweat or a lilac's perfume? Shame on such people! They ought to take time off from whatever they imagine they are doing that is more important and return to the basics. The sensual basics of our existence. Shame on them! Scolding me from behind their ivory-towered seminary systems and their violent academic bureaucracies. I did not make things sensual; nor did I create bodily senses by which to respond ecstatically to the sensual. The Creator made these gifts, and made them very good. Even Karl Rahner, in a moderate way, has agreed to the need to redeem the word sensual. He writes:

> As 'instinctive basis' too, sensuality is necessary and good; it is not to be extinguished (in Stoic or Manichean fashion) but more and more integrated into the whole person and its good decision and ordered to God . . . The derogatory sense of sensuality which is now its usual one has its justification, but it is worth trying to revive the first and more original sense of the word.[3]

Ecstasies are sensual experiences, I suggest in this book; they are equally spiritual experiences. The moments of nature and friendship, of dance, music, carpentry, hospitality, conversation, conviviality, sexual expression, non-violent work, non-competitive sport (jogging has become many a monk's and lay person's meditation time since I first wrote this book), unwished for suffering—all these are bodily / spiritual experiences. Goose bumps are the proof of this. Our bodies do not lie nearly as facilely as our theologies do. When we are moved, we are indeed moved: chemically, electrically, our bodies speed up, heat up, slow down, relax, give us goose bumps. No one who has admitted he or she is vulnerable to goose bumps can any longer believe in the violence that separates spirit and body, spirituality and sensuality.

But here lies the rub: If indeed there are persons and groups of persons in our culture and its institutions (religious ones very much included) who are too impervious to be moved and therefore to experience ecstasy, then there lies the explanation of much of the violence of our culture and its institutions. To repress our wonder is to kill our capacity for the divine. And this condition of spiritual torpor which in turn leads to *acedia* or spiritual boredom is the natural condition of most of us in our culture. Or at least Ernest Becker thinks this is the case.

> Most of us—by the time we leave childhood—have repressed our vision of the primary miraculousness of creation. . . . The great boon of repression is that it makes it possible to live decisively in an overwhelmingly miraculous and incomprehensible world, a world so full of beauty, majesty, and terror that if animals perceived it all, they would be paralyzed to act.[4]

If we have failed to develop in healthy and whole ways in the West, the loss of touch has much to do with this distortion. Ashley Montagu writes that "affectionate, tactile stimulation is clearly, then, a primary need, a need which must be satisfied if the infant is to develop as a healthy human being."[5] Babies will live longer without food than they will without touch. And yet, Montagu, observes, as so many Asians, Africans, and others have observed: "American culture has been regarded as a no-touch one." (p. 169) Erik Erikson, in his study of the white Anglo-Saxon male who came of age in the late forties and has been running corporate America in our time, points out that an alienation from their bodies was characteristic of such men. "Anybody who thinks or feels too much seems 'queer' to him. This objection to feeling and thinking is, to some extent, derived from an early mistrust of sensuality."[6]

Sensuality does not mean S*E*X exclusively as so many fearful persons presume it does. These frightened individuals ought to meditate on page 184 of this book. In fact, Montagu suggests that this preoccupation with sex that has, in fact, narrowed the term sensuality for us westerners, is itself a sign of the fear of sensuousness that is killing us all.

> It is highly probable that sexual activity, the frenetic preoccupation with sex that characterizes western culture, is in many cases not the expression of a sexual interest at all, but rather a search for the satisfaction of the need for contact. (p. 192)

The guilt that we tend to over-identify with our sexuality is not in fact a guilt for being sexual—we were made that way—but the guilt that comes from the fear of living and loving the way we were made: sensually. "Guilt results from unused life," warns Ernest Becker (p. 180). The flight from our sensuality is built into an educational, cultural, or religious view of the world that rewards only the left side of the brain. Psychologist Robert Ornstein points out that the neglected side of the brain in western culture since the eighteenth century is the yin side which includes darkness, night, receptivity, and *sensuousness*.[7] To recover sensuality and spirituality is to recover our psychic holness that has been lost under the influence of the En-Light-enment when truth became exclusively identified with "clear and distinct ideas" of daytime and male-dominated scientific problem-solving.

A spirituality of sensuousness and ecstasy is also a spirituality of humility in the fullest sense of the word. By "humility" I do not mean the veiled masochism of "I can't" that has so often been invoked in pious Christian circles. I mean the true meaning of the word: It comes from *humus*, meaning *earth*. To be humble is to be earthy; close to the earth; simple; in touch with the earth that is ourselves and others. Farmer-poet Wendell Berry, in his brilliant essay on "The Body and the Earth" speaks of the humility I write about.

> The Creation is bounteous and mysterious, and humanity is only a part of it—not its equal, much less its master. . . .The Creation provides a place for humans, but it is greater than humanity and within it even great men are small. Such humility is the consequence of an accurate insight, ecological in its bearing, not a pious deference to 'spiritual' value.[8]

From harmony with our bodiliness comes harmony with the rest of creation and the driving out of devils of violence and competition, Berry believes. An authentic spiritual vision ensues from such an act of humility.

> A human has no right to destroy what he did not create. . . Seeing himself as a tiny member of a world he cannot possibly think of himself as a god. . . . Returning from the wilderness, he becomes a restorer of order, a preserver. He sees the truth, recognizes his true heir, honors his forebearers and his heritage, and gives his blessing to his successors. (p. 99)

Berry has struck a theological gold mine when he talks of how humility as earthiness brings with it the giving of *blessing* to one's ancestors. A theology of blessing is what a spirituality of ecstasy is all about; it is what the creation-centered tradition in the West is all about as well: That life is a blessing and that humans are to take responsibility for their role in seeing to it that the blessings of life (or the creation ecstasies spoken of in Chapter One of this book) are indeed passed on to others. Humans are invited to return blessing for blessing. Sadly though, we are free to return curses for blessings, as so much of human history today and yesterday demonstrates.[9] For the biblical person, the term "blessing" is not an abstraction: It is a shared ecstasy, as Professor Mowinckel puts it:

> Blessing includes that which we call material as well as the spiritual. But first and foremost, blessing is life, health, and fertility for the people, their cattle, their fields. . . . Blessing is the basic power of life itself. Blessing is a capability of the soul, a power that lives in the clan and its members.[10]

As Professor Kenik demonstrates so convincingly, the entire story of faith in the Hebrew Bible, which begins with Abraham's story, is a pledge of blessing. We read in Genesis 12:

> Go forth from the land of your kinfolk and from your father's house
> to a land that I will show you. I will make of you a great nation, and I
> will bless you; I will make your name great, so that you will be a bless-
> ing. I will bless those who bless you and curse those who curse you.
> All the communities of the earth shall find blessing in you.[11]

The question comes down to whether our bodies are blessings or
curses; whether our senses are blessings or curses; whether our sensuality is a blessing or a curse. If these energy-sources are blessings
and gifts, then we are to thank God for them by celebrating them,
thereby returning blessing for blessing. We are to flex them, use them,
develop them as Jesus taught in his story of the talents, and not bury
them out of fear or guilt. Indeed, blessing is the biblical word for
pleasure. Creation—including our own—is so good and so gratui-
tous that it deserves to be called a blessing and a pleasure. The ecstasies of creation are primal sacraments meant to seal our experience
with the Divine.

One lesson that is learned when we treat creation ecstasies with
appropriate reverence and sacramental awareness is our infinity: we
touch divine depths when we commune with cosmic depths and taste
the beauty of a Mozart. However, we are also made aware at such
moments of our finitude as well. Thus, if we celebrated our bodies
instead of running from them, we would know that our bodies teach
humility just as the earth does by instructing us in our limits. If we
listened to our bodies and reverenced them, flowed with them and
treated them as gently as the Creator treated them, we would learn
important lessons of limits. For bodies do break, bend to viruses and
to collisions, speak to us from beds of flu, colds, rheumatism, and
eventually death. Is enough truth about our limitations not contained in these moments so that we have no need to stifle the ecstasies that our bodies celebrate with us as well?

The failure to let one's self go in creation ecstasy is the failure to
live, and constitutes a surrender to the idolatry of control that so
haunts our culture. Philosopher Ortega y Gasset observes that "to
live is to feel oneself lost. . . . He who does not really feel himself lost,
is without remission; that is to say, he never finds himself, never
comes up against his own reality." (in Becker, p. 89) The spiritual
journey cannot begin without the letting go that ecstasy demands.
Too many believers, remaining too uncritical of the control manias
that culture teaches and that are allowed to poison faith traditions as

well, believe that tactical ecstasies constitute the exclusive religious experience of letting go. Nothing could be further from the truth or can distort the truth more grotesquely. For the faith-fact is that creation itself is a God-given experience, a blessing, a prayer waiting to be responded to or entered into. Those who ignore the holiness of creation and the spiritual experience that natural ecstasies can be, end up distorting the faith message and confusing tactical, man-made devices, with spiritual experience. Natural ecstasies are blessings in the theological sense of that term and our living them corresponds to the *via affirmativa*; tactical ecstasies are devices for awakening us to the blessings of life and in turn allowing for a richer *via affirmativa* experience. A principal goal of this book has been to remember and redeem the *via affirmativa* tradition which has been so glibly forgotten; and in doing this, to reunderstand the *via negativa* traditions in their proper place (cc. 1-4). Dr. Weil in his fine study on drug use points out that "many people" in our culture "do not know how to get high without using a drug" and for that reason smoking marijuana becomes "an excuse for experiencing a mode of consciousness that is available to everyone all the time."[12] Yet, he warns, as I do in stressing natural ecstasies over tactical ones: "Until one notices one's own spontaneous highs, one cannot begin to develop them." (p. 113).

I have been enheartened by persons who have put into practice the lessons of creation ecstasies that I hint at in this practical guide book. When a diocese in Michigan employed my list of ecstasies as a list of themes for a year of adult education in parishes, this is what happened. Each month was dedicated to a different ecstasy. Biblical readings, story telling, discussions, and lectures were built around these ecstasies. People began to learn the connections between their love of camping, love of spouse, love of music, and their spirituality. And the single most-often repeated comment was: "Now for the first time I see a connection between my faith and my everyday life." In other words, spiritual integration was allowed to happen. And with it, a sounder theological grounding for living. For the way of natural ecstasies is the spiritual way for, by far, the majority of human persons. This is why so many have approached me in response to this book with a simple "thank you," saying that I have articulated what in fact has been their spiritual experience but which so few other theologians had confirmed for them. No wonder, too, that Kubler-Ross points out that it is these simple but deep ecstatic moments that per-

sons who die peacefully remember "with smiles on their faces"—
moments with others around a campfire or piano. Natural ecstasies,
as I indicate on pages 81f., are the stuff our memories were made for.
They fill us up and empty us and thereby constitute our deepest
prayer experiences which always culminate in Thank You. No wonder Meister Eckhart could declare with all seriousness: "If the only
prayer you say in your whole life is 'Thank You,' that would suffice."

The Biblical Tradition on a Sensual Spirituality

Jewish thinking, which is biblical thinking and which was also
Jesus' thinking, takes it for granted that the sensual is a blessing and
that there is no (spiritual) life without it. For all life is spiritual for the
biblical lover of God's creation. Jewish composer Ernest Bloch put
it this way in talking of his music which was consciously Jewish in
character. "It is the Jewish soul that I feel vibrating throughout the
Bible that interests me: the freshness and naivete, the violence, the
savage love of justice, the despair, the sorrow and immensity, the sensuality."[13] Readers ought to note that sensuality and a "savage love of
justice" go together in Bloch's estimation. Compassion is a kind of
passion for the biblical persons. "The physiological psychology of
the Bible places the seat of the sympathetic emotions in the bowels,"
observes another student of the Bible.[14] When we let go of Hellenistic assumptions about spirituality and enter into Jewish ones which
are biblical ones, we also learn that faith comes more from hearing
than from seeing. This is significant for a sensual spirituality since
eyes are more abstract than ears—we can see at far greater distances
than we can hear. This means that a hearing-oriented spirituality is
more sensual, more intimate, than a written one. Eyes touch more
linearly while ears touch more in a rounded fashion.[15] Claude Tresmontant comments that the biblical person "is not a dualist" and
therefore "has a sense and a love of the carnal because he has a sense
of the spiritual and perceives the presence of the spiritual *within* the
carnal."[16] And Paul Tillich is equally blunt about Jewish spirituality
and how it not only differs from Neo-Platonists' assumptions about
incompatibility of the sensual and the spiritual, but actually negates
dualistic traditions of the Neo-Platonic schools. He writes that in the
Bible:

> The term 'body' stands against these traditions as a token of the
> prophetic faith in the goodness of creation. The antidualistic bias of
> the Old Testament is powerfully expressed in the idea that the body

(contradicts) the Christian concept of Spirit, which includes all dimensions of being; and it is incompatible with the symbol 'resurrection of the body.'[17]

To recover a sensual spirituality is to recover a biblical one and in this sense this book is an essay on the question: What happens if the West surrenders the Hellenistic suppositions about spirituality and rediscovers the Jewish spiritual consciousness. In Part IV of this book, I have especially invoked the prophets for their sense of sensual spirituality, especially Amos and Jeremiah. Isaiah, too, had visions of the messianic times as sensual gifts shared equally. He writes:

> On the mountain, Yahweh Sabaoth will prepare *for all peoples* a banquet of rich food, a banquet of fine wines, of food rich and juicy, of fine strained wines. On this mountain he will remove the mourning veil covering all people, and the shroud enwrapping all nations, and will destroy Death forever. (Is 25.6f.)

The principle that we have found in this book concerning morality and sensuality very much holds in this instance: The rich food and fine wines are "for all peoples"—not for a privileged few. The prophet Jeremiah, in depicting the New Creation, necessarily turns to dancing as a primary image.

> They will come and shout for joy on the heights of Zion,
> they will throng towards the good things of Yahweh:
> corn and oil and wine,
> sheep and oxen;
> their soul will be like a watered garden,
> they will sorrow no more.
> The virgin will then take pleasure in the dance,
> young men and old will be happy;
> I will change their mourning into gladness,
> comfort them, give them joy after their troubles,
> (Jer. 31.12-14)

Indeed, in the Hebrew language the word "rejoice" means to "dance." The prophetic insight about pleasure and spirituality remains as I named it in this book: not that one loves pleasure less but that one loves the sharing of it as much. Pleasure is not sinful, nor is sensuousness. But the hoarding of it is, the inordinate clinging to it—the miserly building of man-made luxury and pleasures for a few while the many go away unable to subsist and thereby enjoy the pleasures of a decent, human existence, with all the responsibility and ecstasy that is implied in such a full and rich existence.

While I have chosen to concentrate on the prophetic tradition as a sensual, spiritual one, it is certain that the wisdom literature of the Bible, so steeped in creation theology, is also profoundly sensual. Indeed, Van Rad in his study of wisdom declares that wisdom in biblical literature is "almost voluptuous,"[18] and that wisdom teaches us above all else to trust creation and our experience of it. "The experiences of the world were always, for Israel, at the same time experiences of God, and experiences of God were experiences of the world."[19] A life wanting in trust of creation and the Creator behind creation is a life not yet lived. It is no spiritual life but a life of control. Professor Roland Murphy calls this "openness to experience and nature and a basic trust" one of the principal themes of all wisdom literature (p. 190). God is revealed not only in historical acts of salvation history, but also in our daily experiences—which I would submit are integrally part of history and salvation history. Writes Murphy:

> Indeed, one may pursue fruitfully the idea of God revealing himself in experience and in nature (as opposed to his revealing himself in historical acts, such as salvation history). The biblical model for this kind of revelation of God is precisely the wisdom literature of Israel. Here men and women were in contact with God through creation (wisdom) on the level of faith response. This is not salvation history with dates and notable saving acts, but it is salvific.[20]

Salvation, after all, means to make whole and healthy. Integration and holness-making is what saving is about. This can happen and indeed must happen with our integration of the sensual and the spiritual.

No scriptural book is more explicit on the union of God and sensuality than the *Song of Songs*. And yet, through the Hellenistic and platonizing tendencies of Origin's exegesis of this book, centuries of Christians have sublimated and repressed the full beauty that it contains. Scriptural scholar Marvin Pope comments on how Origin, whose influence on later commentators "was considerable," managed to "denature" the *Song of Songs*. "Origin combined the Platonic and Gnostic attitudes toward sexuality to denature the Canticle and transform it into a spiritual drama free from all carnality."[21] The *Song*, notes Roland Murphy, is a "biblical model of eroticism" and in it that:

> Sensuousness comes to the fore. In the 'embrace' refrain she describes his left hand under her head (2.6;8.3). He celebrates her lips that drip honey, while sweetmeats and milk are under her tongue (4.11). She

says that the mouth of her lover is sweetness itself (5.16), and requests his kisses (1.2). He compares her to a palm tree that he will climb in order to take hold of the branches and fruit (7.9). His scent is that of a sachet of myrrh, a cluster of henna, that rests in her bosom (1.13-14). The fragrance of her garments is 'the fragrance of Lebanon' (4.11).[22]

Moreover, notes Murphy, the very style of the *Song* is sensual. "The sensuous atmosphere that surrounds the Song. . . is heightened by the fact that the language is never blunt; it is subtle and seductive, leaving many things unspoken but nonetheless present." The senses play a "capital" role in the *Song,* he notes.[23] God's name is never mentioned in this book, for God's name does not need to be excessively invoked when believers give themselves to spiritual ecstasy: the experience is the name. Too much naming can interfere with the ecstasy and the letting go which at times must extend even to letting go of divine names. The Jerusalem Bible, in its commentary on the *Song of Songs*, offers a sad observation: "People have found it surprising. . .that a book that makes no mention of God and whose vocabulary is so passionate should figure in the sacred canon."[24] Maybe the reason the people are so surprised is that they have been mistaken as to the biblical meaning of "sacred." After all, the immense amount of Hellenistic exegesis done to the Scriptures over the centuries must surprise the prophets, the wisdom writers, and the author of *Song of Songs*.

And surely it would surprise Jesus as well. It is telling how Jesus links dancing to the prophetic vocation in Luke's version of the beatitudes.

> Happy are you when people hate you, drive you out, abuse you, denounce you as criminal, on account of the Son of Man. Rejoice when that day comes and dance for joy, for then your reward will be great in heaven. This was the way their ancestors treated the prophets. (Lk. 6.23; cf. Jer. 31.12-15)

And in a passage that strikes me as the most poignant of the entire Gospel, one that explains the violence behind the crucifixion, Jesus laments the loss of the capacity to dance. He does this speaking out of the wisdom tradition.

> What description, then, can I find for the people of this generation? What are they like? They are like children shouting to one another while they sit in the market place:
> 'We played the pipes for you,
> and you wouldn't dance;
> we sang dirges,

and you wouldn't cry.'
For John the Baptist comes, not eating bread, not drinking wine, and
you say, 'He is possessed.' The Son of Man comes, eating and drinking, and you say, 'Look, a glutton and a drunkard, a friend of tax collectors and sinners.' Yet Wisdom has been proved right by all her children. (Lk. 7.31-35)

For Jesus, as for the Jewish mind in general, there is something
wrong with persons who cannot dance to pipes—and this uptight-
ness will interfere with compassion as well. For Jesus, the Good
News is the Good Sensual News—that we are coming to our senses
and finding God there (see below, p. 157). Jesus was no ascetic. His
is authentic biblical spirituality, as Rabbi Heschel indicates:

> Asceticism was not the ideal of the biblical man. The source of evil is
> not in passion, in the throbbing heart, but rather in hardness of heart,
> in callousness and insensitivity. . . .We are stirred by their passion and
> enlivened imagination. . . . It is to the imagination and the passions
> that the prophets speak, rather than aiming at the cold approbation of
> the mind.[25]

Additional Examples of
Sensual/Prophetic Spirituality in Christian History

In the first edition of this study, I listed some models who
attempted a more biblical and therefore sensual, prophetic spirituality in the Christian past (Chapter 17). Here I would like to name a
few others who can assist us. The remarkable Benedictine nun, Saint
Hildegard of Bingen (1098-1179), was a poet, a playwright, a musician, an artist, a physician, a botanist, a pharmacist, a mystic, a
prophet and an abbess of a male/female monastery. She was also the
mother of the Rhineland mystic movement and an authentic representative of the creation-centered spiritual tradition. "She experienced one world of creation," writes one scholar.[26] For her there was
no wavering on the goodness of God's creation. She wrote: "God is
the good and all things which proceed from God are good."[27] She
insisted on humanity's creation being from the earth and in inter-
dependent relationship to the rest of creation. And about the senses
she had this to say:

> Humans grasp and know everything in creation with their five senses.
> They love with their faces, taste with their lips, analyze by hearing,
> seek with the scent that pleases them, and act with the feeling that
> makes them happy. And in doing this they have God, the Creator of
> everything, as their model. (p. 66)

As is appropriate in a creation-centered theology, Hildegard recognized the ecstasy of human love and of sexuality. For Hildegard:

> Marriage is not seen as something meaningful only through a third party, a child. What is primary is the union of husband and wife. . . . Sexuality is not seen just as the reproductive aspect of marriage but in the union of two human beings. Hildegard sees marriage as a great good and lists virginity under the sign of Christ's sufferings. (p. 88f.)

Hildegard develops a spiritual category which she calls *viriditas*. *Viriditas* is greening power; it is the power of springtime, life-freshness, germination, fruitfulness and fertility. Her images for the powerful life-force are sensual. She says, "The earth sweats germinating power from its very pores."[28] Greening power is the power of moisture that moistens the soul, preserving it from "dryness and carelessness," that is, from drying up. She warns about the loss of this sap that is a blessing. "When a person loses the freshness of God's power, he or she is transformed into the dryness of carelessness, and lacks the juice and greenness of good works, and the energies of the heart are sapped away."[29] Hildegard's is a juicy spirituality. She reveals her lack of dualism regarding soul and body when she sets up an equation that looks like this:

$$\frac{body}{soul} = \frac{earth}{moisture}$$

She says, "The soul is the freshness of the flesh, for the body grows and thrives through it, just as the earth becomes fruitful through moisture."[30] Had Hildegard's theology been studied and elaborated on by theologians with half the attention given to Augustine's, a Christian theology of relationship, of sexuality and of marriage would not be nearly as vacuous as it is today.

A sensual/prophetic spirituality of Hildegard, Francis, and Aquinas finds its theological apogee in the German Dominican preacher, philosopher, and spiritual theologian, Meister Eckhart (1260-1329). Dependent on all these forerunners (including the Beguine, Mechtild of Magdeburg), he was an original thinker in his own right. Eckhart, like Hildegard and Mechtild before him, rejects ascetic practices. "Asceticism is of no great importance," he states flatly.[31] He insists that tactical ecstasies ought not to be emphasized, and that it is in fact a sign of inexperience in the spiritual life that makes them necessary at all. For Eckhart, it is at least as important to be able to "eat with perfect propriety" as it is to fast (p. 197); those who emphasize spiritual practices are "behaving no differently than if they took God, wrapped a coat around his head, and shoved him under a bench." (p. 201) Eckhart cautions against a mentality of tactical ecstasies:

> You should not restrict yourself to any method, for God is not in any one kind of devotion. Neither in this nor that. Those who receive God thus do God wrong. They receive the method and not God. (p. 209)

Too much tactical ecstasy is in fact an expression of too much ego—it is just one more expression of control instead of the letting go that all spiritual depth experience is about.

> Those people who in penitential exercise and external practice, of which they make a great deal, hold fast to their selfish I. . . . Such people are called holy on account of their external appearance; but internally they are asses, for they do not grasp the actual meaning of divine truth. (p. 209)

Instead of ascetic practices, the finest way to insure harmony of sensuality and spirituality is by "the bridle of love." "If you wish to burden the flesh and make it a thousand times more subject, then place on it the bridle of love. Through love you will overcome it most quickly, and through love you will burden it most heavily." (p. 244) The soul does not war with the body; "the soul loves the body," says Eckhart. "Nothing brings you nearer and unites you so to God as this sweet bond of love. Let whoever has found this way seek no other." (p. 244)

Why is Eckhart so confident that tactical ecstasies are of no great significance? Because he has so well a developed theology of blessing, the blessing that creation or isness is. "Isness is God," he declares. (p. 89) Because creation ecstasies are so near to the person, God too is near and everyday. What I have called "ecstasy" in this book, Eckhart calls "breakthrough." And breakthrough for Eckhart happens not once a year or once a month but many times a day for the person who is awake and aware. That is, for the person who has learned to let go. For that person, God is everywhere and all is in God.

> If one is rightly disposed, one has God with one in actual fact, and if one really has God with one, one has God in all places, in the street and in the presence of everyone, just as well as in the church, or the desert, or in the cell. (p. 208)

Breakthrough or ecstasy is a breakthrough in our consciousness—an awareness of the unity of all things in God. It is even nobler than our creation insofar as it is our awakening to the holiness of all being, the godliness of our creation included. Ecstasy for Eckhart does not conjure up the other-worldliness of Plotinus and the Neo-Platonists, as Reiner Schurmann remarks. No elitism haunts Eckhart's spirituality.

> In Eckhart there is no appeal to a privileged experience, no regret of falling back into the body after a repose in the divine, and above all no opposition between a higher world and a lower world into which the soul is resigned to redescend.[32]

Eckhart's breakthrough is a "worldly comprehension of the instant: flight from the present situation turns into a way of being with it." In this non-elitist and creation-ecstasy spirituality, as in so much else, Eckhart follows his brother Aquinas. Aquinas, unlike his Augustinian-trained friend Saint Bonaventure, insisted that *"amor facit ecstasim,"*[33] that is, love—any love—makes us ecstatic. Bonaventure and the Augustinian schools before and after him restricted the term "ecstasy" to an experience of God and the soul exclusively. As we have seen in our treatment of the *Songs of Songs*—which never even names God—this tradition is more Neo-Platonic than it is biblical. Comments one scholar:

> Here we find the ultimate difference between ecstasy in Bonaventure's thought and that of Thomas Aquinas: ecstasy finds a universal application with the latter, it is limited to relations of the soul with God with the former. From this universalist character there derives the importance of the doctrine of ecstasy for the spiritual life in Thomas. . . .[34]

Still another contribution to a sensual / prophetic spirituality on the part of Eckhart is his theology of pleasure. He actually analyzes how a person can develop a deeper love of pleasure. He says that we enjoy ecstasies of living at three levels of enjoyment—the examples he uses are wine and meat.

> 1. First, we enjoy wine and meat *as* wine and meat. "Mmmm—good wine, delicious meat," we say.
> 2. Secondly, we enjoy wine and meat *as a gift.* A gift-consciousness, a consciousness of gratitude and gratefulness, overwhelms us.
> 3. Third, we enjoy wine and meat as "eternally-not-other." This means that no one passage of time can erase our experience of ecstasy. As I have written below, ecstasy and memory are inextricably tied together. Not only is ecstasy forever; it is also forever "not-other," i.e. we become our ecstasies and they become us. We are what we eat; we are also the eaten and consumed ones. We are ecstasy; ecstasy is us. All subject / object relationships, all relationships of dualism are pierced: oneness is recognized for what it is: the law of the universe. This is breakthrough, when "all is in God and God is in all." (p. 76f.)

That Eckhart's sensual spirituality was also prophetic and justice-oriented is without a question. He himself said that "the one who understands what I say about justice understands everything I have to say." He supported the oppressed peasants of his day, preaching to them in their vernacular language; he also supported and learned from the feminist movement of working-class women, the Beguines, and was condemned by the same pope who condemned them, thus sharing their fate. His trial was in many respects a political one; he was warned several times to quit "confusing the simple people" by preaching to them in their own tongue. His reply was that the "oppressed need to learn; for if they do not they will never learn how to live or why to die."[35] Indeed, his entire spirituality culminates in compassion which he understood both as social justice and as celebration. Yet, for this spirituality to develop, people must be at home with passion. And so he warned that "all deeds are accomplished in passion." Eckhart felt no need to resort to controlling passions. Rather, he was for directing them to creative healing of society and self. Aquinas had taught that the passions were in fact the seat of the virtues,[36] and this lesson was not lost in Eckhart. In this regard too, Eckhart's spirituality is far different from Augustine's of whom M. D. Chenu writes:

> Augustine was a temporary victim of Manicheism and moreover his whole life was coloured by an unusually sad experience of uncontrolled passion. With this background it is understandable why the disciples of St. Augustine had little place for matter in their conception of man and in their spirituality.[37]

Eckhart, like Aquinas, had no "thorn in the flesh" that haunted him and created guilt for bodiliness for other generations of Christians. It might be said of Eckhart what Chesterton said of his brother Aquinas: "He saved us from Spirituality (meaning spiritualism)—a dreadful doom."[38] It is because Eckhart's this-worldly spirituality was rooted in creation and the holiness of matter—as all authentic biblical spirituality must be—that it flowers into prophetic consciousness and activity for social justice. Eckhart comments: "For the just person, justice is his or her being, her life, her very existence." (p. 472)

Still another champion of sensual spirituality is the "first woman of English letters," the mystic Julian of Norwich (c. 1342-1415). Julian was not afraid of the body, nor did she see it or its functions as outside the realm of the spiritual. In fact, in a passage that will make many-a-modern blush for its earthiness, Julian teaches that going to the bathroom is holy. "God does it," she insists.

> A man walks upright, and the food in his body is shut in as if in a well-made purse. When the time of his necessity comes, the purse is opened and then shut again, in most seemly fashion. *And it is God who does this*, as it is shown when he says that he comes down to us in our humblest needs. For he does not despise what he has made, nor does he disdain to serve us in the simplest natural functions of our body, for love of the soul which he created in his own likeness. For as the body is clad in the cloth, and the flesh in the skin, and the bones in the flesh, and the heart in the trunk, so are we, soul and body, clad and enclosed in the goodness of God.[39]

What a beautiful and truthful expression of the holiness of matter and the holiness of our existence and the authentic meaning of humility is this passage! Julian's panentheism (see pp. 119ff.) emerges as a primary symbol for how our body and soul too are related as enclosed and not as at war with each other. There is much that is richly creation-centered in Julian, who so clearly knew the Benedictine tradition represented by people like Hildegard and who knew Eckhart as well. Of particular note for the purposes of this book is her frequent use of the word "sensual." Julian writes that to be human is to be sensual. "When our soul is breathed into our body, at which time we are made sensual, at once mercy and grace begin to work." (p. 286) Our sensuality is a gift from God; in fact, "God is in our sensuality."

> Our sensuality is founded in nature, in mercy and in grace, and this foundation helps us to receive gifts which lead us to endless life. . . . God is in our sensuality. (p. 287)

Body and soul for Julian form a "glorious union" and are to work in harmony with one another—"let either of them take help from the other." Since Jesus is fully human, he too took sensuality upon himself. "Our sensuality is only in the second person, Christ Jesus." (p. 295) In fact, it is God who forms the glue between spirituality and sensuality. "He is the mean which keeps the substance and the sensuality together, so that they will never separate." Salvation for Julian actually means the healing of dualisms: hers is truly an incarnational theology.

> As regards our sensuality, it can rightly be called our soul, and that is by the union which it has in God. That honourable city in which our Lord Jesus sits is our sensuality, in which he is enclosed. . . . For until

the time that it is in its full powers, we cannot be all holy and that is when our sensuality by the power of Christ's Passion can be brought up into the substance. (p. 289)

Our God-experience is itself sensual, bringing to completion all the capacities of our senses.

We shall all be endlessly hidden in God, truly seeing and wholly feeling, and hearing God spiritually and delectably smelling God and sweetly tasting God. And there we shall see God face to face, familiarly and wholly. (p. 255)

Not surprisingly, Julian developed a theology of the maternal side of God. God is the Mother of natures. And creation is so good, such a blessing. "God is everything which is good, as I see, and the goodness which everything has is God." (p. 190)

That goodness which is natural is God. He is the ground, his is the substance, he is very essence or nature, and he is the true Father and the true Mother of natures. And all natures which he has made to flow out of him to work his will, they will be restored and brought back into him by the salvation of humankind through the operation of grace. (p. 302f.)

When one treats oneself to these wonderfully creation-centered mystics like Hildegard, Eckhart and Julian, as well as those I enunciated on pages 208 ff. of this book—Heloise, Francis, Aquinas, Valla, Teilhard—one learns to trust one's own experience more. Ecstasy must be trusted as well as remembered. One also understands the exclamation of appreciation for the Middle Ages that the Protestant prophet and martyr Dietrich Bonhoeffer uttered shortly before his execution in a Hitler death camp. The Middle Ages was the last time that Christianity truly offered a creation-centered spirituality for its people, and Bonhoeffer sensed this when he wrote from his cell:

I wonder whether it is possible. . . to regain the idea of the Church as providing an understanding of the area of freedom (art, education, friendship, play). . . ? I really think that is so and it would mean that we should recover a link with the Middle Ages. Who is there, for instance, in our times, who can devote himself or herself with an easy mind to music, friendship, games, or happiness?[40]

Who is there indeed? There is us. Everyone who lives spiritualities of authentic ecstasy and the sharing of ecstasy has overcome this "uneasy mind" or guilt that our culture rains upon us and lives life more fully. That is, more spiritually.

Prophecy: Sensuality and Pleasure as Political Issues

Mahatma Gandhi taught that one of the great sins is pleasure without conscience. And so it is. Pleasure is meant to be pleasure shared; and this sharing is done by way of justice and love, that is, by compassion. But injustice is invariably linked to contempt of pleasure and body. As W. H. Auden warned, "as a rule it was the pleasure-haters who became unjust." Isolation of the body from the body politic only reinforces injustice, as Wendell Berry warns us:

> You cannot devalue the body and value the soul—or anything else....Contempt for the body is invariably manifested in contempt for other bodies—the bodies of slaves, laborers, women, animals, plants, the earth itself." (p. 105)

Those who cannot celebrate bodiliness are reduced to violent competition between bodies. The prophets were not introverts wallowing in their personal faith-life. Indeed, they faced the awesomeness of the divine ecstasy, as Rabbi Heschel observes. "What the prophet faces is not his own faith. He faces God. To sense the living God is to sense infinite goodness, infinite wisdom, infinite beauty. Such a sensation is a sensation of joy." (p. 143) It is the intensity of the joy—or ecstasy as we have used the term in Part I of this book—that drives the prophets to criticize injustice. Walter Brueggemann, in his study on *The Prophetic Imagination*, insists that there can be no birth of compassion without a rebirth of passion. Says he: "Immunity to any transcendent voice and disregard of neighbor leads finally to the disappearance of passion. And where passion disappears there will not be any serious humanizing energy."[41] Authentic, prophetic criticism, he argues, begins viscerally "in the capacity to grieve because that is the most visceral announcement that things are not right." (p. 20) Prophets are visceral people sensitive to the "cries" of the oppressed. The Book of Exodus is a book of crying out, as in Chapter 11: "And there shall be a great cry throughout all the land of Egypt as there has never been, nor ever shall be again." Brueggemann also reminds us of the symbolic consciousness that is integral to every prophet. Every prophet is an artist, he insists.

> We need not ask if our consciousness and imagination have been so assaulted and co-opted....that we have been robbed of the courage or power to think an alternative thought....The characteristic way of a prophet in Israel is that of poetry and lyric....The *imagination* must come before the *implementation*. Our culture is competent to implement almost anything and to imagine almost nothing....Every

totalitarian regime is frightened of the artist. It is the vocation of the prophet to keep alive the ministry of imagination. (pp. 44ff.)

"The loss of passion," he observes, "is the inability to care or suffer." (p. 46)

The passion that both Heschel and Brueggemann celebrate in the prophet comes from the senses. The opposite of greening power is the deadening power of dull senses. As we read in Isaiah:

Make the heart of this people fat,
and their ears heavy,
and shut their eyes;
lest they see with their ears,
and understand with their hearts,
and turn and be healed. (Is. 6.10)

Healing is preceded by turning or being converted; in this case, by turning from asensuality to sensuality. Of course, when I talk of the prophet I am talking of each of us. As Heschel has put it, "There is a part of the prophet in the recesses of every human being."

All injustice is a form of violence; all violence is a form of injustice. There have been several studies on the psychological origins of violence (of course, there are sociological origins as well) since my writing of this book, and all agree that the repression of body consciousness early in one's life is the major psychological reason for violence. Writes Ernest Becker: "The modern world, after all, has wanted to deny the person even his own body, even his emanation from his animal center; it has wanted to make him completely a depersonalized abstraction." The result is violence, for "if we don't have the omnipotence of gods, we at least can destroy like gods." (p. 84f.) The opposite of guilt is not innocence—no one is innocent; the opposite of guilt is responsibility. We choose to wallow in our guilt rather than to take responsibility for social justice and healing. "Better guilt than the terrible burden of freedom and responsibility" comments Becker. (p. 213) Those who preach guilt for passion and those who internalize this guilt are actively obstructing compassion. Dr. James Prescott, writing in the *Bulletin of Atomic Scientists* observes that:

The reciprocal relationship of pleasure and violence is highly significant, because certain sensory experiences during the formative periods of development will create a neuropsychological predisposition for either violence-seeking or pleasure-seeking behaviors later in life.

He cautions that body pleasure is different from promiscuity, which in fact reflects a basic inability to experience pleasure.[42] Is it little wonder that persons committed to global justice, such as those who take the Shakertown Pledge, include in their pledge the following declaration, "I affirm the gift of my body, and commit myself to its proper nourishment and physical well-being."

The moral issues of ecology are issues of our love of body or hatred thereof. If we truly loved the sun, the water, the air, the earth, we would respect them and put their preservation ahead of consumerism and so-called "development." The earth itself cries out today for hospitality; a cosmic hospitality is needed if we are to learn the lessons of Three Mile Island, of Love Canal, and its thousands of cousin situations around the country. We would heed the prophetic warning of Chief Seattle a hundred years ago, "This we know. The earth does not belong to man; man belongs to the earth. This we know. All things are connected like the blood that unites one family. All things are connected. . . .The whites, too, shall pass; perhaps sooner than all other tribes. Continue to contaminate your bed, and you will one night suffocate in your own wastes." We are nearing that dreadful time that he foresaw a century ago, of "the end of living and the beginning of survival."

The issue of sensuality lies at the heart of a violent work-world and a violent economic system. Big technology often robs persons of the most satisfying, that is the most sensual, work, as E. F. Schumacher observes:

> The type of work which modern technology is most successful in reducing or even eliminating is skillful, productive work of human hands, in touch with real materials of one kind or another. . . .Today, a person has to be wealthy to be able to enjoy this simple thing, this very great luxury."[43]

And theologian M. D. Chenu complains that it is precisely the abstraction and distance caused by abstraction in the modern marketplace's stock market and especially in multinational corporate economics that makes the capitalist economic system intrinsically violent. When capitalism is small, it is personal, he argues; and so it is a moral form of economics. But when it is gigantic, it is abstract (asensual in my terms) and intrinsically violent. The moral menace of multinational corporations—which Chenu calls perverse "moral monstrosities"—is precisely their abstraction.[44] José Miranda seconds this argument about abstraction and distance-making being the basis of economic injustice and violence. Western and Christian culture, he argues,

> has been invariably aristocratic, privileged, incapable of perceiving
> the most massive, tragic, and urgent reality of our history. Its human-
> ism was and is a humanism of thought—a mental, aesthetical human-
> ism. And its 'man' is an abstraction, a Platonic essence valid semper et
> pro semper, not real flesh-and-blood humanity, a humanity of blood
> and tears and slavery and humiliations and jail and hunger and untold
> sufferings.[45]

One reason compassion has been either rare or co-opted by sen-
timentalisms is that we have lost *touch* with the pain of humanity. We
have succumbed to asensuality. In the same current of thought,
W. H. Auden warns Americans that "the great vice of America is not
materialism but a lack of respect for matter." This lack of respect for
matter creates a void in our centers that we try to fill with consumer
goods, but to no avail. For we were made to love matter well, not to
ignore it. Ironically, by ignoring it we become victims of distorted
matter which is luxury living or the greed for luxury living, i.e., consumerism.

An entire political program presents itself in this book. Natural
ecstasies and making them available to all constitutes such a program. For politics is indeed about pleasure since it is about priorities,
and we prioritize according to what we love or think we love. The
issues of who will eat and what will be eaten; of who will be clothed,
housed, with work, with health care, with basic education for children, with safety to their person—these are bodily / political issues.
The issues of survival with which the poorest of the poor wrestle are
not abstractions—they are sensual / spiritual issues. Their solutions
and the imagination to create solutions must also be born of sensual / spiritual consciousness.

The need for a revolution in imagination and in symbolic or trans-
parent thinking has not diminished in the five years since I first published this book. In fact, it has increased in all areas of global village
survival from energy needs and conservation (for example, the imagination needed to engineer solar energy cheaply) to economic systems
that accurately reflect the global village we all now live in; to
ecumenism of world religious faiths; to putting people to "good"
work; to reindustrializing society's workplaces; to alternative and
simpler life styles; to less greedy means of transportation; etc. Only
imagination can heal our struggling planet, and imagination can
only happen when it is born of ecstasy (*Whee!*) and is applied to

social and cosmic interdependence (*We*).

Moreover, the surest way to change people and hopefully their institutions is by way of pleasure. Not by wars but by appealing to interests of persons, which is to say, by appealing to what they consider their fullest pleasure to be. A student of mine who read this book decided to do an experiment. He went to a coffee shop in the bus station in Chicago and ordered a bowl of popcorn. Then he swam with the ecstasy of each individual kernel of popcorn and took several hours to eat this one bowl. During that period at least eight individuals came up to him and asked: "Where did you ever learn to enjoy your food so much?" Does this instance not demonstrate that people are looking for greater pleasure? That people are attracted by pleasure? That people are also united by pleasure? Perhaps there has been a dearth of nonviolent social change in the West because there has been too little consciousness of pleasure and the political force that it is and can be. Pleasure obviously has a deep social meaning—otherwise the manipulators of social symbols, who, for example, advertise their wares to us, would not be so bent on forcing *their* definition of pleasure (pleasure as consumerism) upon us. The biblical tradition sings of pleasure for the many, not for the few. The pleasure of all or of none. To find true pleasure, all of us need to let go of certain ways of pleasure-seeking. This is one meaning of living a "simple life style," namely the redefining of what authentic pleasure is and where it can be found. The problem is that today even sensuality has been reduced to a consumer item. Thomas Merton foresaw this when he wrote fifteen years ago that it was raining outside and that he was going to walk bare-headed in the rain because "before long they will be selling you the rain."

Mysticism is not in itself ethics, though in all authentic instances mysticism leads to ethics and indeed a living ethic leads to mysticism. Some persons get confused when hearing of a "sensual" or a "pleasurable" spirituality and feel this is synonymous with moral anarchy, at least at a personal level. While I stress the work for justice which is the prophetic work in this book as the natural expression of ecstasy, the question often arises: How about personal ethics or ethics between individuals? Are there norms in this regard when it comes to our sensual pleasures? The norms that emerge from the biblical tradition are, I believe, two. First, for a person or a people to pursue pleasure at the expense of another or others is morally wrong. The proper name for this kind of pleasure-seeking is sadism and we engage in it whenever we fail to question the roots of our pleasures. One of the liberating elements of building pleasure on natural ecstasies as listed in this book is that these ecstasies are not much rarer or further from any human being than human being consciousness itself. Whereas, for example, tearing down tropical rain forests in Brazil for the "pleasure" of McDonald hamburgers is indeed sadistic.

The second norm regarding the morality of personal pleasure appears to be the following: When others can be hurt by my or our pleasure-making, then open discussion and dialogue are in order. Hurting others in itself is not evil—some of our deepest growing has happened as a result of hurt, whether direct or indirect. But it is not for the pleasure-seeker alone to determine whether another is hurt for his or her benefit or not—that person ought rightly to be in on the dialogue. It is by such a dialogue that a healing community is born and expands in wisdom, grace, and understanding.

Those who are uncomfortable with the thesis of this book are those who have been victims (and perhaps perpetrators as well) of anti-Semitism. It is no small thing that the loud cries of anti-Semitism in Christian history invariably found their crescendo in calling the Jews "those lustful Jews."[46] Biblical spirituality is indeed sensual. But all sensuality—contrary to the Neo-Platonic tradition in Christianity—is not sinful lust. Sensuality is among one of God's richest blessings. And those who care about justice—the effort to share sensuality and earth (as opposed to luxury) pleasure—know this. That numerous fearful persons unable to let go of dualisms exist in our midst is no secret. But more and more converts to Aquarian, holistic living are equally in our midst today. All are invited to heed the warning of Mahatma Gandhi: "Worship without sacrifice is a sin." It is time believers learned to sacrifice their dualisms and their fear of body, their distrust, their fear of cosmos and creation, their security blankets of fall/redemption theologies ("original sin made me do it"), their guilt and quest for moral perfectionism, their fear of the artist and the thinker, and finally their anti-Semitism. With this sacrifice of our dualisms and fear of the body, worship—which is celebration over the healing of God's cosmos and God's people—might actually happen once again.

Institute of Creation-Centered Spirituality
December 1980

INTRODUCTION:
Sensuality, Prophecy, and Our Spiritual Futures

T he year is 1981. The twentieth century has four-fifths run its course. When our children reach the age we are today, the year will be 2001. Does all this signify a new age? A new spiritual era? Does it require a new spirituality?

A spirituality is a way—a way of living in depth. Today, an increasing number of persons are putting into question the ways of their past and are searching for new spiritual ways, new depths that are both real enough and challenging enough to throw themselves and ultimately their world and environment wholeheartedly into. This phenomenon of the resurgence of concern for spiritualities is everywhere evident—among teenagers drifting from drugs to Zen, among businessmen reciting their mantras, among religious believers returning to their childhood traditions, among religious believers departing from their churchly affiliations, among nonbelievers of religion who seriously and considerately explore depth and deep order in their lives, among Marxist priests and liberated homemakers, male and female.

The omnipresence of this spiritual hunger and thirst—and the emptiness and vacuum that nourish it—give evidence of the universality of a common phenomenon: the changing of a consciousness. A people, once called Western civilization, are in deep spiritual torment. We are becoming uprooted. Our past spiritual traditions, which are as ignored as they are unpracticed, seem to hold only partial appeal to the new age of political and personal consciousness that we citizens of a newly discovered Global village are embarking on. There are those who say that we are indeed embarking on a "whole new spiritual age"—an age whose cataclysmic outcome will depend more than ever before on the human race getting itself together; that is, getting their *whole* lives, including their politics and war machines as well as their quests for beauty and God and their love of the earth, together.

One tradition that offers us a glimpse into our own futures (how often spiritualities train us only to look back to the past—usually someone else's past!) is the astrological tradition. What I present here is not my personal belief in astrology (I do not *believe* in astrology) but a method of seeing the human consciousness historically, where historical means both past and future. The truth of this symbolic method of seeing our futures lies not in anyone's beliefs but in the evidence available from our experience that there might be a valuable insight in this tradition. Carl Jung pleads the case for the astrologically-influenced friends in our midst by arguing that astrological wisdom is significant for what it tells us of the contents of our spiritual unconscious and, as such, needs to be taken very seriously.

In particular, Jung subscribes to the way of seeing human history in 2,000-year stages corresponding to the Age of the Bull (4000-2000 B.C.), a symbol of primitive, instinctual civilizations and represented by Cretan religion; the Age of the Ram (2000 B.C.–1 A.D.), characterized by the religion of the Jews and the emergence of conscience and awareness of evil wherein religion sacrificed rams; the Age of Pisces, the fishes, (1 A.D.-1997 A.D.), dominated religiously by the figure of Christ, who was the last member of the Ram Era (himself being slain as a lamb) and the first fish of the Piscean Era (having called his followers to be "fishers of men") Christians, who were reborn in the waters of baptism, adopted the fish as an early symbol of their belief. The symbol for the Age of Pisces, it should be noted, is that of two fish swimming in opposite directions. This symbol implies a dualistic spirituality that has so characterized Christian thinking and, in particular, Christian mysticism. It also implies a Christ vs. anti-Christ tension. Christians might take note that up to now neither they nor their institutions have ever been asked to thrive and survive in a nondualistic (i.e., a nonpiscean) period.

The Piscean Age ends in about twenty years according to this theory, and if there is some truth to it, then we would today already be feeling birth pangs of the next stage opening up before us: the Age of Aquarius, the water bearer, will be characterized by a return to the symbol of water, "the deep." In this age, evil will be made conscious to every individual who may in turn be made truly spiritual and responsible. In the Age of Aquarius, "it will then no longer be possible to write off evil as the mere privation of good; its real existence will have to be recognized. This problem can be solved neither by philosophy, nor by economics, nor by politics, but only by the individual human being, via his experience of the living spirit."[1] An age of the spiritual—where both the spirits of ugliness (evil) and of beauty (God) will be available to every person to choose his own way.

In order not to lose our spiritual ways, we are all urged (and theologians in particular) to "read the signs of our times." One of these signs is the immense interest in the sensual life. Those who made *The Joy of Sex* a bestseller or *Playgirl*, *Playboy*, *Penthouse* etc. everyday words are not necessarily voyeurs or sexual deviates; they are persons seeking a different attitude toward the gifts of sexuality and sensuousness. While many persons, myself among them, have lamented the book called *The Total Woman*, I did not understand its popularity until a reviewer pointed out that "the book has a subtle message for the not-so-sophisticated, which is that it is okay to be sexy . . . . It is not a reaction to woman's liberation but a gently encouraging book for women to be in step with the

1970's."[2] Please do not think that I am accepting *Playboy's* or *The Total Woman's* definition of sensuality in this book. I am emphasizing, however, that a quest—even a commercialized one—for sensuality is a sign of the asensual spiritual times we have been living in the Piscean Age.

Another sign of our times is the language we employ. It is striking that in the second edition of Webster's dictionary (serving our needs from 1950 to 1966) the word "spiritual" is given as an antonym to "sensual.' Fortunately for us all, Webster's third edition (1966) eliminates such a false dichotomy. Yes, the Age of Pisces, an age symbolized by two fishes swimming in opposite directions and, therefore, an age of overplayed dichotomies, is coming to an end. Dichotomies like body vs. soul, sensual vs. spiritual, male vs. female, subject vs. object, haves vs. have-nots, rich vs. poor will have no place in the future spirituality—provided persons take the new age and its consequences seriously.

A journey from dualism to wholistic spirituality can be ennervating. Such a weariness continues to plague spiritual persons as a clear-cut *spiritual energy crisis*, principally, it seems to me, because we are still dichotomized. We have yet to relate the mystical to our political and institutional lives. And the reason we have failed to relate the two is that we have presumed, in good piscean fashion, that the mystical was asensual and not sensual: that there is no necessary relationship between our attitude toward body and our attitude toward body politic. Thus, our lack of spiritual energy.

The reader who has familiarized himself or herself with my previous study on American spirituality with the unlikely title of *On Becoming a Musical, Mystical Bear: Spirituality American Style* will recall that I called therein for a return to rooting ourselves. We need our roots for all the uprooting that the future will demand of us. But our roots as human beings are—all angelic spiritual traditions notwithstanding—profoundly sensual. We are sensual-spiritual creatures made to get high, divinely so, on ecstatic experiences and on sharing these experiences.

The same reader has been led to understand the intimate and necessary connection that exists between mysticism and prophecy in a creation-centered (as distinct from a redemption-oriented) spirituality. Establishing this connection and placing it in its historical and theological setting formed the thrust of that book's spiritual way—one of love of life *and* hatred of its enemies, a way of Yes and No. In the present book I probe more deeply into the practical aspects of developing a spiritual life that is both mystical and prophetic. The most basic theological ramification of this spiritual way is that a sensual mysticism is clearly the surest route to a prophetic consciousness. And vice versa.

To be specific, a sensual spirituality is a prophetic one in our culture for at least three reasons. First, the prophetic issues of our time are, in fact, sensual issues: these include the preservation of nature and the outlawing of war. (The intimate relationship between war and rape is well made by Susan Brownmiller.[3]) The freedom of women to be themselves and operate in any of our institutions (including religion's sanctuaries) and the freedom of men to be the warm, sensitive, cuddly and humorous persons they could be, especially in domestic situations (from which our society so often excludes them, forcing them to be "breadwinners all"); the elimination, therefore, of sexism as applied to men or women, gay persons or straight persons. The elimination of age-ism whether applied to old persons (who, being apparently sensually unprovocative, become genuinely ignored) or young persons (who, being apparently provocative sensually, become objects to pander, control, repress). The issues of energy and the human race's efforts to keep itself warm, cool, moving and producing its industry. Racial fears and taboos (James Baldwin observes that "White Americans . . . are terrified of sensuality and do not any longer understand it")[4] and anti-Semitism and antisensuality go hand in hand. The issues of food and the harvesting and sharing of the earth's and sea's sensual crops to render famine obsolete. Issues of capitalism vs. alternative economic systems wherein pleasure will be derived not from stockpiling capital but from watching more and more people enjoy living. I received a letter from an ex-businessman recently and he wrote: "The inner life, ah, how it conflicts with our society. It's not exploitable, can't be sold, not materially productive. There is little therefore that encourages its coming to the fore." Middle-class Americans may or may not know that with the money it costs for a color television set they could feed an entire starving family for a year. The issue is not that bit of information (which, if left dangling, could simply create guilt) but the more global question: What means are available to alter our economic consciousness and with it our economic systems?

Do we really imagine that we can resolve any of these political-sensual issues without integrating our personal-sensual spiritual needs? A wholistic treatment of body politic presumes a wholistic attitude toward the body.

Second, the spirituality of the prophets from Amos and Hosea to Jesus Christ was, in fact, a sensual spirituality. None called for a "mortification of the senses" but for a sharing of the Creator's gifts. The prophets needed the sensual both for their own enrichment and, as a taste of the visions they entertained for the people of God.

Third, an eschatological time demands our living in harmony with our sensuousness, for the alternative to a sensual spirituality is more of what we have: more repression and with it more oppression. The route our civilization has taken us has been a route of repression of the sensual and oppression of others. Repression produces boredom in oneself and oppression of others. It is blatantly clear that America languishes from both of these symptoms today. As for the former, consider this recent survey conducted in a suburban high school near Chicago. Of 180 high school students interviewed, 178 (!) cited the number one problem for a teenager in America today as: boredom. There is no deeper malady to the spiritual life than boredom and ennui with life. A college student recently was asked why she fell asleep during a showing of Hitler's concentration camps: "Dulled by previous experiences such as the Viet Nam War, Alice Cooper and *The Exorcist*, I have developed this defense mechanism," she explained, "that allows me to endure. I simply don't react at all." These are our youth who are saying this—youth, with all its potential for energy and vibration, for creating and enthusiasm, is drying up in our very midst. Parched. Drying. Dying. We should heed the warning of e. e. cummings: "Ye! the godless are the dull and the dull are the dammed."

As for the latter symptom, that of oppression, I have already cited one instance: American adults and their adult-run institutions are rendering our youth bored with life. That, surely, is one form of oppression, but there are so many others. Studies on violence and especially violence and the media reveal what a sorry spiritual state bored America is in when our kicks must come at others' expense. The issue of displaced sensuality nowhere is more evident than in our watching of violence in crime shows, cartoons and professional football, all while we obey the commercials that accompany them and stuff ourselves with ersatz foods, beverages, automobiles, deodorants and ever stronger detergents. Our retired president, the popular choice of the American people in two elections and winner of the last one by the greatest plurality in all of our two hundred year history, has said it all for us. His remedy for America's ills, offered from his place of retirement in California, has a familiar ring about it.

> We are so cynical, so disbelieving—it may take the shock of an invasion—in Korea or in Thailand. If American lives are threatened, we may regain our sense of belief in our country and our need for strength.[5]

There we have it: America the beautiful being asked to go to war to regain its lost beauty. We are reduced by the "vision" of our highest elected official to the impotent state of war-making. Wisdom American-style, has spoken from on high. Mr. Nixon has truly laid bare our bored, repressed and oppressive American soul. Once again, only the poet seems adequate to respond:

> Then let men kill that cannot share,
> let blood and flesh be mud and mire.
> scheming imagine,passion willed,
> freedom a drug that's bought and sold
> (e. e. cummings)

Mr. Nixon is no aberration on the American cultural scene. He has been around too long and achieved too much success in that system to be considered a renegade in it. He made it in that system. Right to the top. He is a spokesman for an entire spirituality. For an asensual spirituality. For a sense-less spirituality. For a non-sense spirituality. Our culture, more than any other before it, has managed to repress the sensual and call oppression holy.

This book is about altering that spirituality at its roots. For there has long been a supposition, however unspoken, in the Christian West that salvation does not take place in the sensual and that God and the sensual are irreconcilable. In this book, I present a spirituality that is both sensual and spiritual. I write about a sensual-prophetic spirituality in the West: about enjoying and sharing the enjoyment of the goods and gifts of the earth; about creating, not destroying; about getting high on life's pleasures and on the sharing of the pleasures. And that is why this book is about our future, less dichotomized, spiritual way. For taking the future seriously means taking time and our bodies seriously;[6] and taking the body politic with its cultural institutions seriously.

Some will ask: What does all this talk of sensuality and ex-presidents have to do with a book on the experience of God in our time? I respond by citing a theologian of more repute and authority (but of far too little influence in the history of Christian spirituality) than myself. Thomas Aquinas, writing in the thirteenth century, warned us:

> They hold a plainly false opinion who say that in regard to the truth of religion it does not matter what a man thinks about the creation so long as he has the correct opinion concerning God. An error concerning the Creation ends as false thinking about God.[7]

False thinking about God is what our materialistic and antispiritual culture has been feeding us for so long. A spirituality that pretends (for a human can, in fact, only pretend) to ignore the body and the body politic is either no spirituality at all or a spirituality for the oppressor who, by instructing the oppressed to ignore bodily and political and historical questioning, reaffirms his own political position. Whether a religion calls injustice or sensuality the primary offense against the Creator (i.e., sin) will determine much in the way of both its political and its spiritual theology. (cf. R. 53) False thinking about creation leads to false thinking about God and back to false thinking about sin and creation. Or, what is worse, to no thinking at all about injustice, which is the sin of sins because it interferes with the Creator's continual sharing of the joys of the earth.

What will be necessary to bring about a genuine spiritual renewal for the Age of Aquarius? What are the implications for ourselves and our institutions and, therefore, our culture as we pass out of the Age of Pisces? What mystical and prophetic way might we follow with alacrity, enthusiasm and big-heartedness? What will rescue us from the pitfalls and the death of boredom and spiritual ennui?

The goal of our journey is much, much nearer than we usually imagine. Ecstacy is an everyday phenomenon to the spiritual "for whom all things are pure." Or, at least, this can be the case. How do we develop a sensual-prophetic spirituality? I foresee a three-stage journey to our spiritual adventures:

1. *WHEE!* (Part I): We learn to treasure and trust our experiences of ecstasies (natural and tactical) for they are, in fact, our experience of God. The experience of God is not an elitist thing meant for a few who may be intellectually, culturally or religiously privileged. Every human person is a *bearer of ecstasy* and, therefore, of God.

2. *We* (Part II): What becomes of us as we fall more deeply in love with life and its ecstasies, including the Life-giver? What changes can we expect in ourselves along our spiritual way? In one word, it is our passing from a literal, ego or "I" consciousness to a symbolic "We" consciousness. Our passion (ecstasy) culminates in compassion (sharing) and politics.

3. *wee* (Part III): What dangers should we expect to encounter along our spiritual way either from our inner selves or from our culture with its dragonesque institutions? And how might we sanely deal with such perfidious small and large dragons? All too often, books on meditation and spirituality have come to signify pacification rather than education because they see humility as merely a private, psychological struggle. In fact, humility has profound social consequences and is often best learned battling in streets or institutions rather than in our imaginations. The section on our *wee*ness will, I believe, set things right politically and spiritually so that we are not eaten up along the way of our spiritual journeys.

This three-stage journey—WHEE! We, wee—constitutes, I believe, the spiritual journey of mysticism and prophecy that the twenty-first century is asking of us. The journey is never complete: Stage 3 leads us back to Stage 1, and so forth. While this journey does constitute a future-oriented spiritual way, students of Eastern and past Western mystical traditions will detect, I am sure, many provocative likenesses with these deep and rich traditions.

Parts I, II, and III of this book constitute, I believe, a handbook, a tool, an instrument for the journey. Boy scouts and girl scouts carry handbooks; chefs rely on cookbooks: why shouldn't we who want to be serious about our spiritual journeys be provided with the rudimentary stuff for our voyage?

Part IV of this book, "Toward a Theology of a Sensual Spirituality," provides a more historical and analytic overview of the theological implications of a sensual-prophetic spirituality of WHEE! We, wee. In it, I survey the spirituality of the prophets and Jesus; Christian spirituality vis-a-vis these issues in the Piscean Age; and, finally, our spiritual futures.

This is a simple book for simple people. That does not mean, simplistic, for what makes up this book is experience—my own and as many others as I could touch or be touched by—and experience is never simplistic. But reflection on experience can be put simply and received simply in the heart. And we call this reception meditation. This is a book of meditations and for this reason the chapters are short. The reader is invited to think along with (yes, and hopefully ahead of) me, the author. The large left-hand margins are for notes, doodles, questions and insights of the meditator. For all true meditation is participation. The God we speak of in this book is not a noun or a concept or an idea—not a God who *should* be a part of our lives but a God who is in fact an experience in our lives. A shared God. A God we experience and who experiences us.

When it comes to the experience of God, there are no liberals and no conservatives; there is not "progress" in modern theology vs. "ignorance and superstition" of past ages. Indeed, tradition is most probably a better and richer source for spiritual insight than a one-dimensional present. I have been surprised, in preparing this work, how much of the medieval spiritual tradition of the West I draw on, especially the experience of Thomas Aquinas from the thirteenth century whose works have been used as weapons for ideological debates for so long that we have nearly forgotten the creation-oriented rather than repression-oriented spiritual vision that he espoused. A vision based on experience.

The trail to God is also a journey with God. This simple nearness of the goal is what is so present to children and saints but so often lost when theologians (bless their academic souls!) become too impressed with their own discipline. Theologian Hans Küng calls the results "theological jungles," and W. B. Yeats puts it more graphically when he lumps together in one potpourri theologians, scientists, lawyers, and mathematicians. "Those learned men . . . are a terror to children and an ignominious sight in lovers' eyes . . . . They have followed some abstract reverie, which stirs the brain only and needs that only, and have therefore stood before the looking-glass without pleasure and never known those thoughts that shape the lines of the body for beauty or animation, and wake a desire for praise or for display." (in CP. 106)

This is a simple handbook because a lot is left unsaid within it. I trust the reader to draw from his or her own experience to say what has to be said. But, at the same time, I respect, and know the reader will respect, silence

itself. For, as one thinker has observed. "pseudo-philoso-
phers . . . use words not indeed to conceal their thoughts
. . . but rather to conceal the absence of them."[8] God is
simple and capable of prolonged silences; and we who
strive for spirituality strive for simplicity and also, at the
deepest moments, for silence. Our ecstasies begin and, in
some way, issue in silence at some deep level of our being.

I have written this book as a practical guide to our
mystical-prophetic futures because I am convinced that
humankind can no longer afford the luxury of a privately-
oriented mysticism. We shall become ecstatic together or
extinct together. We shall either learn to enjoy the earth
and the sharing of its simple, sensual gifts, or we shall
prolong the pleasures we now take in the pain we inflict on
one another. The options are lessening; choice is everywhere in the air. With this book as with the living out of its
implications, I can only wish the reader a deep, fun,
shareable—that is, an ecstatic—experience. I believe that
that is the only reason a writer writes or a reader reads or a
theologian theologizes—or any of us bothers to live at all.

Please allow me to thank friends who are everywhere
present in these pages because they teach me ecstasy and
prophecy. In particular, Elizabeth and Dan Turner,
Brendan Doyle, Mary Kay Hunyady and the Sacred Heart
Sisters of Barat College, who have encouraged me and
many others.

List of parenthetical abbreviations used in this text
(Alive) *Alive*, Piers Paul Read.
(Castaneda) A Separate Reality: *Further Conversations
with Don Juan*, Carlos Castaneda.
(CP) *The Creative Process*, Brewster Ghiselin.
(Fox) *On Becoming a Musical, Mystical Bear: Spiritual-
ity American Style*, Matthew Fox.
(Hesse) *Siddhartha*, Hermann Hesse.
(Hesse, *Journey*) Journey to the East, Hermann Hesse.
(Laing) *The Politics of Experience*, R. D. Laing.

(LB) *Love's Body*, Norman O. Brown.

(M) *Marx and the Bible*, Jose Miranda.

(N, Naranjo) *On the Psychology of Meditation*, Claudio Naranjo, Robert Ornstein.

(R) *New Woman, New Earth*, Rosemary Ruether.

(Rilke) *Letters to a Young Poet*, Rainer Maria Rilke.

(Solz) *The Gulag Archipelago*, Aleksandr Solzhenitsyn.

(Terkel) *Working*, Studs Terkel.

(Tillich) *The Shaking of the Foundations*, Paul Tillich.

(Traherne) *Centuries of Meditations*, Thomas Traherne.

(TTE) *Touch the Earth: A Self-Portrait of Indian Existence*, T. C. McLuhan.

(Watts) *Nature, Man and Woman*, Alan W. Watts.

PART I
The Experience of Ecstasy as the Experience of God:
WHEE!

What is spiritual is better experienced than spoken about. Precisely because experience nourishes its truth in us, we have difficulty formulating concepts about spirituality. One way, however, of agreeing on a spiritual meaning is to go to its opposite. Here we have a statement by a person who knows from experience (is there any other way of knowing?) the opposite of ecstasy. He is "Joey," a professional killer who has murdered thirty-eight men in his lifetime, all but three on mob contracts, and has earned about $4 million in the process. "To carry out an execution with the cold knowledge of what you're doing, you have to believe in nothing but yourself. Most people have the fear of reprisal; I do not. Because life and death don't mean anything to me. I don't care if I live or die, and I don't care if anybody else lives or dies. I have no emotion. None. It's all long gone."[1]

"To believe in nothing but yourself" and "not to care if I live or die"—these are the exact opposites of the ecstatic experience. For an ecstatic experience is one of forgetting oneself and of being turned on in a full and deep way. Our ecstasy is our getting outside ourselves (the word comes from two Greek words meaning "to stand outside of"); our forgetting ourselves—if only for a second, a minute, an hour, a day . . . or a lifetime. Ecstasy is our getting high. For this very reason, because ecstasy is a forgetting, it is also memorable. Ecstasy is a memorable experience of forgetting oneself, of getting outside of oneself. Our ecstatic experiences, then, are the memorable experiences of our lives.

CHAPTER 1
Natural Ecstasies:
how we all get high all the time
on nature, friendship, sex,
the arts, sports, thinking, travel,
and involuntary deprivations

What are some of these memorable and ecstatic experiences in our lives? In listing some ecstasies that practically all of us share in common and might find recognizable, we see that they are integral to our relation to creation and nature so I call them *natural ecstasies* or *creation ecstasies*.

The first of the natural ecstasies we can all recognize from our experience is nature itself. How often, how easily, we can fall into forgetfulness (and therefore ecstasy) while sitting by the sea learning to vibrate with it; or walking barefoot on an earthen field with sunshine on our backs; or finding a lone spot with the pine trees at the peak of a mountain; or catching the fragrance of lilac bushes in our neighbor's lawn at springtime; or gazing up at lightning-bug-like stars flickering in a black summer night sky; or listening to the rain; or the forest. One can go on and on detailing experiences of nature that are ecstatic ones. For our spiritual lives begin and end in the refreshment of the sea and the earth, the mountains and the skies, the flowers and the sunshine.

Our ecstasy or standing outside of ourselves is so real in nature that we truly come to believe what is the fact: that we *are* the sea; we *are* a part of the stars; we *are* of the earth. "You never enjoy the world aright till the sea itself floweth in your veins, till you are clothed with the heavens and crowned with the stars; and perceive yourself to be the sole heir of the whole world, and more then so, because men are in it who are every one sole heirs as well as you." (Traherne, xvi)

I recall listening once to some young men who enjoyed hunting and fishing. When I pushed them to articulate more fully what it was they loved about these sports, they explained that it was not the actual gaming of the prey so much as the communion with nature. "Getting up before dawn, stalking in fields, where only you and early morning dew and the animals exist"—in short, hunting and fishing become occasions for nature ecstasy for many in our culture.

This truth our spiritual ancestors, the North American Indian, knew so well. The following testimony is from Walking Buffalo of the Stoney Indian Tribe in Alberta, Canada. "You whites don't understand our prayers. You didn't try to understand. When we sang our praises to the sun or moon or wind, you said we were worshipping idols. Without understanding, you condemned us as lost souls just because our form of worship was different from yours.

"We saw the Great Spirit's work in almost everything: sun, moon, trees, wind, and mountains . . . . Did you know that trees talk? Well, they do. They talk to each other, and they'll talk to you if you listen. Trouble is, white people don't listen. They never learned to listen to the Indians so I don't suppose they'll listen to her voices in nature. But I have learned a lot from trees: sometimes about the weather, sometimes about animals, sometimes about the Great Spirit." (TTE, 23)

A second ecstasy familiar to us all is friendship. The mutual attraction and sharing that reaches to a point of forgetfulness of self, whether it takes place between two persons of the same or opposite sex, is an experience of ecstasy built into our everyday lives. The wisest test for its reality is probably the laughter test—can we laugh not only

with a friend but even at one? And can that friend laugh at
(as well as with) us? Has our friendship penetrated
sufficiently to that depth of experience which is forgetfulness of the self and all the roles we play and all the
kingdoms we must play for during our less ecstatic hours?

Surely the ecstasy of friendship is an experience of
prayer for many persons who say, "I pray best when
talking to others." For in friendship we are relaxed enough
to experience something greater than ourselves. And that
experience some call God and others, love.

The ecstasies of sexual enjoyment also constitute a
forgetfulness of self, an experience beyond oneself, a taste
of the divine. Or at least they can. This kind of ecstasy is
in no way reserved for the young alone (and, as a matter of
fact, when the young dissipate themselves too early in a
single-minded pursuit of it, it seems to lose its ecstatic
power for them). Sex seems to find its fullest joys as a
combination of the first two kinds of ecstasy—as an
experience of nature and of friendship. The respect that
sexuality requires to maintain its ecstatic character appears
to be rarer and rarer in our culture. "Physical pleasure is a
sensual experience no different from pure seeing or the
pure sensation with which a fine fruit fills the tongue; it is
a great unending experience which is given us, a knowing
of the world, the fullness and the glory of all knowing.
And not our acceptance of it is bad; the bad thing is that
most people misuse or squander this experience and apply
it as a stimulant at the tired spots of their lives and as a
distraction instead of a rallying toward exalted moments."
(Rilke, 36)

The squandering or misuse of sexuality is such a cruel
and wasteful way of depriving ourselves of beautiful
experiences of ecstasy. It is almost as if we would prefer
controlling our ecstasies to enjoying them. "You gain
power over sexuality precisely by the role of unlimited
expression. Sex becomes our tool like the caveman's
wheel, crowbar, or adz. Sex, the machine, Machina

Ultima," comments the American psychiatrist Rollo May.[2]

But neither ecstasy nor sex are about control. They are about participation, which is forgetfulness of control. They are about being intermediaries and, in that sense, receivers of a power "which is given us," as Rilke has said. They are not about control; far less are they about proving something. "But when the mounting excitment is accepted rather than grasped, it becomes a full realization of spontaneity, and the resulting orgasm is not its sudden end but the bursting in upon us of peace." (Watts, 158)

Who has never lost herself, stood outside and beyond himself, while listening to a Mozart sonata? or while delighting at the dance that beautiful bodies express? or at reading a favorite novel? or taking in the colors of a Matisse, the shadows of a Rembrandt? or in admiring the handiwork of a dressmaker, glass blower or the craftsmanship of a cabinet maker?

Not only as receivers of the arts but also as doers do we taste the delights we call ecstasy. For who has not forgotten self when striving to write or to paint or to sing or to dance or to construct cabinets or sew or make music? Michelangelo speaks from the perspective of an artist. "True art is made noble and religious by the mind producing it. For those who feel it, nothing makes the soul so religious and pure as the endeavor to create something perfect, for God is perfection, and whoever strives after perfection is striving for something divine." And Nietzsche speaks of the artist's inspiration when explaining his writing. "One can hardly reject completely the idea that one is the mere incarnation, or mouthpiece, or medium of some almighty power. The notion of revelation describes the condition quite simply; . . . One hears—one does not seek; one takes—one does not ask who gives: a thought flashes out like lightning, inevitably without hesitation—I have never had any choices about it. There is an ecstasy. . . ."[3]

Thus the gifts of reading and writing, of making music

and appreciating music, of painting and of responding to paints, of craftmanship take their place alongside a list of natural ecstasies.

Another familiar ecstatic experience in our lives is that of sports. Who does not forget himself, stand outside of himself, when careening down a slope on skis? When diving into water and marrying her skin to the water in swimming? in ice skating, jogging, playing tennis or ball, horsebackriding, etc. In ecstasies of sport, we experience again our communion with nature: our bodies and whole selves are once again immersed in our origins—water, sky, earth and, because excellence is demanded of us, fire. Consider the surfer's union with the waves, the sea, sky and wind.

Not all sports qualify as ecstatic, however. Norman Jewison, director of the film *Rollerball*, is clearly frightened by the organized violence that so much of sports has become. "The trend to increasing violence among players and fans alike is shocking to all true sportsmen," he comments. And this is especially the case in "the physical body-contact sports that attract the largest television audience . . . . We are only a few steps away from designing sports to accommodate the medium and to generate further advertising revenue" from selling items of comfort while watching games of violence.[4] Indeed, those sports which are engaged in primarily for competition's sake fail the first test of ecstasy. When winning becomes a goal we set for ourselves, we are no longer involved in ecstatic experience but are ego-tripping. But when we engage in sports for the sake of excelling and experiencing, then we taste ecstasy if we care to. Sports as competition with oneself or as a pursuit of excellence or perfection—this is sport as ecstasy.

The experience of thinking, of marrying two thoughts so that a child thought is born, is also an ecstatic experience—one wherein we forget ourselves, enjoy ourselves so fully that we say, "This is fun!" and want to do it again. And again. And again. Thinking as ecstasy: we see it in fourth and fifth graders and, it seems, in a decreasing number of persons from that age on. Why is this so? Is formal education the opposite of education in thinking which would truly be education in ecstasy? For anyone who has ever thought for himself or herself, given birth to an idea, thinking needs no defense as ecstasy. Only a nod of recognition. Everything spiritual is like that. You taste it or you don't; you recognize it or you miss it.

Alas, when thinking becomes thinking to control or manipulate and exclusively this, then we have lost thinking as ecstasy which is always thinking for the sake of giving birth. Thinking for truth's sake (and truth is always newly born) not for the sake of engineering or problem solving. Of course, we need the latter kind of thinking, but when it takes over as our exclusive way of thinking, people quit thinking. They tempt boredom and usually lose. Instead of forgetting ourselves in ecstasy, we forget that thinking itself is fun and freeing, an end in itself. "What a deliverance it is to be able to *think*, and thereby remain multidimensional," exclaims Dietrich Bonhoeffer.

Visiting or traveling is everybody's experience of forget-fulness of self. Families dashing on a Memorial Day holiday weekend to team up with other families; the joy of vacation strikes deeper than the admission of "no work today": it means ecstasy today! Forgetfulness of our everyday world of problem solving and concerns for self-survival. In visiting relatives or friends, we immerse ourselves in the world of joys and sorrows; that is, the ecstasies of others.

Travel to other cultures is simply an extension of this home visiting carried out by families desirous of reunions. The ecstasy of nature in its different forms from the fjords of Norway to the beaches of the Mediterranean; of the dances of the Basque to the chantings of the Buddhists. In short, an excursion, an education in how others experience ecstasy. Of course, this experience is itself another ecstatic one. No wonder we look forward eagerly to our vacations, our weeks of ecstasy. Ecstasy shared is ecstasy re-experienced.

Some suffering, some losses, some deprivations also present themselves as occasions and, indeed, experiences of ecstasies. You know this by visiting a hospital or a home for mentally (though seldom emotionally) retarded persons; or getting to know some physically-handicapped persons. An accident or a crippling disease seems to strike the recipient in one of two ways: making that person more self-conscious and self-pitying than we all tend to be anyway; or, and this is more often the case than we might be aware, allowing the person to forget a certain striving, a certain need to prove oneself, a certain self-interest. In other words, ecstasy results. But never, never is this the case in wished-for suffering (which is a controlled kind of suffering). Only involuntary suffering or our natural suffering—the loss of a loved one or of a cherished dream or of an organ or a limb is ecstasy. The ecstasy here is not the act of taking pleasure in the pain but the experience of standing outside of oneself, perhaps for the first time, as a result of an unwished for deprivation. Persons who deal with others in crisis situations, for example, those who observe the approaching death of others, report how often the nearness of death alerts ecstatic moments of vision and joy in a patient. Sometimes these persons aware of their own death leave behind a taste of what they have experienced as in this instance of a young man dying after a plane crash in the Andes: The night before he died he prayed a rosary and afterward he was asked why he was crying: "Because I am so close to God," he replied. And he wrote a farewell note to his girl friend and parents.

In situations such as this, even reason cannot understand the infinite and absolute power of God over man. I have never suffered as I do now—physically and morally—though I have never believed in Him so much. . . . Strength. Life is hard but it is worth living. Even suffering. Courage. (*Alive*, 154f.)

Many who have been suddenly and accidentally deprived of a limb or have come near to death return with similar visions and a new perspective on life. Indeed, non-sought-after experiences of finiteness and one's limits can themselves bring about ecstatic experiences.

I was once stressing this point in a lecture and afterwards a woman came up to me with the following story. She had had a mongoloid child and had watched him die over a six-month period several years previous. Relatives, neighbors, friends and clergy tried to comfort both during the ordeal and after her son's death. "None of them, however, knew what they were talking about," she insisted. "For once I accepted the reality of my son's death, sitting holding his hand for six months was the most profound experience of unity—unity with all things, life, death, self, others, God—that I have ever experienced before or since," she declared.

Who among us has not forgotten himself and broken into a bigger world in lively occasions of celebration. Folk dancing, music, laughter, games and parties: joyful moments shared by doing celebrating together. Egg-tossing and sack-racing; space-walking and clown-gazing: all are occasions for forgetting oneself and being turned on. For celebrating is, by definition, a forgetting in order to remember: a loss of ego for the sake of a greater communion: an ecstasy shared by many.

Surely the summit of all ecstasies, for those granted the gift of a life long enough to carry one into adulthood, is the ecstasy of sharing by way of serving. Parents who genuinely pass on the joy of living to children; teachers who authentically arouse the ecstasy of thinking in their students; musicians who touch people to the depth of weeping and rejoicing—surely such persons live blessed lives. For their *work* has become their ecstasy. And their efforts and sleepless nights, their mistakes and moments of success, indicate how sincerely they strive for the ecstatic by striving for perfection in their work or profession. Yet this striving is never fulfilled. Stretch, yes; grasp, never: that is the rule for God-seekers. Michelangelo confessed the same on his deathbed: "I regret that I have not done enough for the salvation of my soul and that I am dying just as I am beginning to learn the alphabet of my profession." Everyone's work can be an ecstasy to the extent that it performs a bonafide service of passing on ecstasy to others. But so many, many person's are slaves in their work; for what they perform and strive to perfect is not a worthy expession of the ecstatic. Sometimes we need to quit work and resist the allurements of pseudoecstasies camouflaged as impressive salaries or titles in order to recover how our striving in our profession can be a spiritual experience. Other times, out of necessity of survival, we need to endure work. Work endured is never work as ecstasy. The fundamental question becomes: How do we create a society where work is ecstasy? How do we pass this on through our economic and educational institutions? How indeed if we have not been involved in such work ourselves?

And so we have completed a list. But this listing of natural ecstasies will never be completed; what we have presented is only a sampling of some of the experiences we might all recognize as our own and as properly ecstatic. All natural ecstasies presume that we (all of us) are instruments and not controllers. Instruments of nature and of the earth and sky, the seas and the sun, the human body and human wit. Instruments, too, of chance as well as of one another. In our ecstasies of nature and friendship, sex and the arts, sports and thinking, travel, deprivation, celebrating and work, we are a channel through which beautiful, memorable experiences flow; and we forget ourselves as we become that channel.

CHAPTER 2

Tactical Ecstasies:
some strategies old and new for
bringing about ecstatic experiences,
including chants
(rosaries and litanies included),
fasting, abstinence, drugs, drink,
celibacy, Yoga and Zen exercises,
TM, biofeedback

In addition to our common experience of natural ecstasies, the human race has devised other means for forgetting ourselves, for getting high, for experiencing divinity. We shall consider some of these means in this chapter, and the overall title I give them—*tactical ecstasies* —should be taken seriously. For, unlike natural ecstasy wherein we are recipients of ecstasy, these experiences are tactics or strategies or means (i.e., consciously devised plans) for taking ourselves out of the everyday world onto a more spiritual plane.

Just how these ecstasies work is best explained with a simple psychological diagram which I offer with apologies to Jung, trusting he would not disagree with my simple explanation.

The unconscious, Jung says, is God. A theologian would have to be more precise in his terminology at this point and state that God plays in a special way in the unconscious. The unconscious is God's playhouse. Prayer, psychologically speaking, is the release of God from our unconscious or our depths so as to permeate our consciousness.

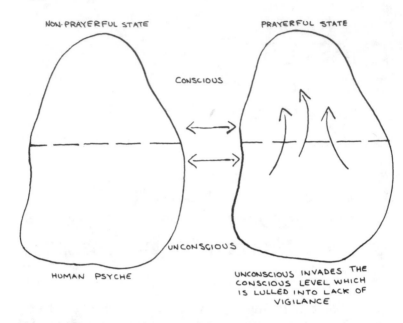

NON-PRAYERFUL STATE

PRAYERFUL STATE

CONSCIOUS

UNCONSCIOUS

HUMAN PSYCHE

UNCONSCIOUS INVADES THE CONSCIOUS LEVEL WHICH IS LULLED INTO LACK OF VIGILANCE

What prevents this release of spiritual or root energy? It is, according to this picture of ourselves, our conscious, everyday existence and attitudes of survival and problem solving. These resist our efforts to experience God, harmony, integration and synthesis. The conscious level of existence puts up a block to our ecstatic states of consciousness.

How to overcome this block? How to relax the conscious level of existence so that the unconscious might play more fully? That is the question that sages of the world's great religions—Islamic and Buddhist, Hindu and Christian, Jewish and African and Indian tribal religions— asked themselves and which they devised deliberate methods or strategies to achieve. These strategies we are now going to look at from the perspective I have indicated. I call them, appropriately I think, *tactical ecstasies*.

Chanting is a simple, yet effective way of numbing the conscious level of our lives. Like novocaine, a chant with a steady rhythm repeated over and over begins to lull one level of our minds so that a different one might flood over ourselves. For the purposes of chant, simple phrases might be used; the content of the phrases is not overpowering in itself. Some traditions that employ such chant, for example, would be the following: the Jesus Prayer (repeating over and over "Jesus mercy") used especially in Russian Orthodox Christianity; the prolonged humming for several minutes of the Hindustani "OMM-MMM" (meaning universe) with people standing with hands clasped in concentric circles produces a hypnotic, trance-like effect that is deeply moving and spiritual. To experience it is to experience the power of tactical ecstasics; Hare Krishna chant of the Krishna people; the rosary as used in Islam, Buddhism or Roman Catholicism (the "Hail Mary" that is repeated at least fifty times in a short version of the Catholic rosary was less important for its content than for the rhythm that its repetition set up. For this reason, a practitioner of the rosary was invariably instructed to meditate on matters other than the words of the chant, subjects such as Jesus' life or death); the litany as employed in medieval Catholicism or in Islam or Hinduism (again, in Catholicism, it was the repetition of the refrain "ora pro nobis," chanted by a large group in unison, that provoked spiritual power of a community kind among its practitioners. The same effect is gained today in Jesse Jackson's "We are beautiful" refrain that he so effectively invokes with his PUSH organization). The primary purpose, after all, of daily ritual and formalized prayer is not to please a deity (as magic incantations do) but to lead persons to an intuitive experience of a deity; that is, it is a tactical device for an ecstatic experience.[1]

We see then that the use of chant is an age-old devise restricted to no religious tradition in particular but common wherever the effort to bring about a prayerful state is taken seriously. In many instances, as for example among African and North American Indian religious rituals, the natural outcome of the hypnotic state brought about by chant was a ritualistic dance. This dance then added to the trancelike experience and the subsequent ecstasies of the participants. (In Eastern and Western Catholicism, this dance tended to take the form of processions, such as one can still appreciate in Latin cultures in our day.) Ritual too can be an effective tactical ecstasy when it is freely entered into for a specific purpose. I recall attending a Japanese tea ceremony with an interested though very diverse group of participants, and each of us afterwards reported a deep and memorable experience deriving from the seriousness and skillfulness of the woman who performed that ritual. More everyday rituals that may be a part of our lives—from lighting a family Christmas tree to blowing out birthday candles on a cake—also reveal the power of ritual and ritualistic traditions.

Another device for relaxing our everyday consciousness so that the unconscious might assert itself is fasting. Whoever has truly fasted in his life ("truly fasting" means choosing to do so by one's own deliberate decision) is aware of a primary result that is just about universal. It is usually referred to as "lightheadedness." Fasting (besides rendering one at first hungry and then not caring about hunger or food) invariably renders one light in the head. This is its primary purpose as a spiritual tactic, and its effectiveness to bring about ecstasy of a tactical kind is attested to by the immense breadth of its usage in just about every major religious tradition, West and East.

Close to fasting (which is doing without food altogether for a specific period) is abstinence, which is doing without certain foods. A vegetarian, for example, chooses deliberately to deny himself meat and meat products. This practice is becoming increasingly more recognized in America today, and the motives of the practitioners are by no means exclusively economic. Rather, those who try it speak of "needing less sleep" or "not feeling so heavy," of better digestion, circulation of the blood, etc. Again, abstinence (in particular from meat and its products) is an age-old spiritual tactic (monks of the West and the East still practice it today) to ensure a certain lightness and, therefore, a certain vulnerability to ecstatic experience. The great gurus of abstinence in present day culture are, of course, our nutritional experts who, for good reason and with startling results, recommend resistance to artificially preserved foods or foods with excessive sugar or fatty cholesterol content. A movement to eat more natural foods as a reaction to what technology has done to the human diet is a contemporary adaptation of the tactic of abstinence.

Another form of tactical ecstasy is the taking of drugs. Recently, Americans have become so uptight about the abuse of drugs and subsequent legal and moral issues about them that the spiritual dimension is seldom considered. But here again, if one considers the peyote of the North American Indian ceremony (cf. Castanada) or the incense of the Hindu or of Eastern and Western Catholicism, one realizes that the use of drugs for spiritual effects is an age-old religious tradition. Because there are abuses in its use, and devastatingly lethal abuses, does not erase the wisdom of religious sages throughout the centuries as to the tactical efficacy of drugs in teaching us to see and not just look. What ex-altar boy of the incense era of Catholicism is not a witness to the Yes-saying qualities of incense, say at a solemn High Christmas Mass? Like the other means to tactical ecstasy, drugs can render one level of our consciousness numb and relaxed while conjuring up other depths of our unconscious. As one serious investigator of mystical phenomena, Arthur J. Deikman, reports, "nature and drugs are the most precipitating factors" in mystical experience. "If paranoid reactions occur during the drug state, they are inimical to an ecstatic experience. On the other hand, when drug subjects lose their defensiveness and suspiciousness so that they accept rather than fight their situation, the 'transcendent' experience often ensues."[2] More authentic spiritual masters were into drugs before Timothy O'Leary; and more authentic ones since.

Perhaps the most commonly employed tactic for ecstasy in our culture is alcohol. When William James observed half a century ago that "alcohol was the poor man's symphony" in the United States, he was offering a profound commentary on a prime motivation in the alcohol dependency in our country. When the natural ecstasy, such as the arts afford, is stifled for financial, psychological (such as the Andy Hardy syndrome), or other reasons (for example, the stifling or nonencouragement of talent or inability to make a living in the arts), we can expect a flight to drink as a tactical substitute. For at least drink allows the unconscious to perform a bit in what is otherwise a humdrum or a compulsively-paced existence. It is no coincidence that Jew and Christian alike choose wine and not soda pop for their religious banquets: a tactical device of employing alcohol to loosen the Yes-faculties.

Another tactical device for encouraging an ecstatic experience, though one far less in vogue than drink or even drugs, is celibacy. A voluntary and deliberate decision to abstain from sexual experience for a definite period of time does not derive its efficacy from any fear of sex or abhorrence of the body. (When it tries to, it is utterly useless as a tactic for ecstasy and becomes a weapon for controlling others and thereby satisfying unfulfilled needs for power and control.) Rather, it derives from fundamentally the same psychospiritual insight that the other means we have listed presume: a putting to sleep of one area of a person's desires and consciousness that will allow another area to express itself. Like any other of these tactics, the only "proof" of its worth is in the results and when one meets a celibate who is truly (i.e., deliberately) so, one does sense some results. Call it lightheadedness as in the case of fasting (which celibacy so closely resembles) or call it vulnerability. Jesus and Gandhi, Thomas Aquinas and

Mother Teresa, testify to a certain ecstasy that *might* follow on a celibate decision and lifestyle.

The basic principle behind exercises of Yoga or Zen meditation is that the individual is encouraged to listen to and become in harmony with the vibrations and, indeed, music within one's own body. By concentration on the bodily chant or rhythm, the everyday consciousness is lulled into relaxation and a person is more apt for ecstatic experience.

Transcendental meditation is not unlike a Yoga or Zen exercise, being in fact a westernized version of Yoga minus the physical calisthenics demanded by Yoga. The stillness brought about by concentration on the mantra (itself a chanting device) is evidence of the efficacy of this particular exercise in ecstasy. As is the lowered blood pressure and metabolic rate (so low that it registers a deeper sleep in twenty minutes than most of us experience in our seventh hour of sleep) and the consequent feeling of energy that practitioners confess to.

Other forms of meditation (candle-gazing, light-watching, word-concentrating, mandella-gazing, Ignatian exercises) are also forms of tactical ecstasy. So are formal retreats or deliberate efforts to withdraw temporarily to another place for an altered state of consciousness awareness and experience. "The practice of meditation, then, can be considered an attempt to turn off conceptual activities temporarily, to shut off all input processing for a period of time, to get away for a while from the external environment." (Ornstein, 193) The turning off effort leads to an active practice of opening up as well. The act of combining formal meditation with renunciation produces "deautomatization . . . , a very powerful effect," comments one psychologist. (Tart, 37)

Technology's efforts in the field of tactical ecstasy, though late coming, will prove very substantial. As a beginning, we have the measurement of alpha, beta and theta brain waves by various biofeedback apparatuses. More than merely measuring for states of very great relaxation (alpha, beta or theta) that are states of extreme vulnerability to ecstatic experience, these machines are being used with effective results to actually train persons so that they may slip into such states when they want to or feel the need. While use of biofeedback machines to test alpha wave consciousness might put a lot of monks out of business, its employment in developing such wave control may well launch an entire generation of laical monks.

In this chapter, we have been examining the forms of tactical ecstasy that are available in our culture either through recent efforts at building strategies (e.g., TM, biofeedback) or through more ancient traditions (chant, fasting, abstinence, celibacy, drugs, drink). In each instance, we have a deliberate attempt to bring about an ecstatic state of consciousness. But, for these means to be truly effective, certain rules need to be observed. These and other important matters we will discuss in the following chapter.

CHAPTER 3
How the practices of natural and tactical ecstasies differ and the difference this makes

In discussing our experience of ecstasy, I have distinguished between natural and tactical kinds of ecstasy. This distinction is not for the sake of convenience or chapter divisions of a book; rather, it corresponds to a profound and far-reaching contrast between the two kinds of ecstasy. To ignore these differences, as religions tend to do when they get flabby, is to invite spiritual disaster. Before we treat the differences, let us recapitulate what we have said by reproducing the lists side by side. Most readers, I am confident, will recognize the differences on seeing the activities in list form.

ECSTASIES

Natural	Tactical
Nature	Chant and ritual dance, processions, ritual
Friendship	
Sex	Fasting
Arts and craftsmanship	Abstinence
Sports	Drugs, Drink
Thinking	Celibacy
Travel and visiting	Yoga, Zen exercises
Involuntary deprivations	TM, formal meditations, retreats
Celebration	
Work	Biofeedback

The most fundamental contrast between natural and tactical ecstasies is that a natural ecstasy is an end in itself while a tactical ecstasy, as the name implies, is only a means. How simple and basic is this rule, yet how frequently violated! By calling natural ecstasy an end in itself, we mean that God is directly experienced in these actions. In tactical ecstasy a person is rendered vulnerable for a God-experience, but the tactic itself is no guarantee of God's presence—it is a preparation for an event but not the event itself. The natural comes first because first, spiritual man receives. The tactical is second because it is man-made, a strategy devised by man and his religious cultures. The personal experience of creation needs to precede cultural experience, and when this basic rule is violated, an act of repression risks being canonized a sacred act. The tactical, then, presumes the natural and should build on it. Tactical divorced from natural ecstasy is an invitation to danger. For example, celibacy without first knowing the sexual; or fasting without first knowing the joys of eating; or drugs without friendships or highs from nature.

There are also significant differences among tactical ecstasies themselves—namely, the difference between an external stimulus (as in the case of drugs or drink, for example) whereby a person receives aid from outside his body and personality, and an internal asceticism (as, for example, in fasting or celibacy or Zen meditation). While dangers abound in each of these ways, at least those that are internal are not as severe or as potentially upsetting to the operation and chemistry of a person as outside stimuli can be. Nor are the internal tactical trips as habit-forming or as hard to break away from once the ecstasy from this strategy is achieved. Both kinds require a guru or at least a group to encourage and support when the trip gets dark or lonely.

We call one who exercises in tactical ecstasy an 'ascetic.' The word "asceticism" comes from a Greek word meaning exercise or training. Appropriately enough, the term was originally used by persons of a Stoic or Cynic philosophical persuasion. Significantly, however, though the term is never once used of Jesus' spiritual practices in the New

Testament, it has reigned for centuries as the paradigm of spiritual perfection among Christians who claim to follow Jesus.

There are many implications to the term "ascetic," in particular the connotation of holiness or sainthood. And, in some instances, ascetics have indeed properly been called saints. However, there still hangs over the consciences of many the false connotation that ascetic practices, because they appear to be "harder and more strenuous" than natural ones, are thereby more efficacious or enriching or saintly. Nothing could be further from the truth. For asceticism or tactical ecstasy, since it is secondary to natural ecstasy, is engaged in *only out of necessity*. Or, one might even say, out of failure with natural ecstasy. It is never engaged in for its own sake, recall, but only as a means. This is why, to be effective, tactical ecstasy demands a deliberate and personal decision by the individual embarking on such a path. (The idea that *any* tactical method, whether fasting or celibacy, can accomplish spiritual experience merely by making it a rule or universal norm is absurd, and the results of such legislation—or lack of them—demonstrates the truth of this observation.) Not least among the dangers involved in tactical ecstasies is that of self-delusion and ego-tripping. "Denying yourself is an indulgence and I don't recommend anything of the kind," advised Don Juan to Carlos Castaneda. "It forces us to believe we are doing great things, when in effect we are only fixed within ourselves." (p. 146)

But is asceticism or tactical ecstasy more difficult in fact than the exercise of natural mysticism? The word we use for the latter, in contrast to asceticism, is *discipline.* Think of the discipline it took you to learn to play the piano or the guitar; to learn to paint or dance; to build a living and loving relationship with another; to learn to play tennis or to swim; to think; to cook; to be a mechanic: it is simply a lie built into our uncritical spiritual attitudes that asceticism is "harder" than discipline. Each way is difficult. Each takes genuine desire of a personal kind. To call natural ecstasies "natural" does not imply that they come to us naturally like falling off a log. "Natural" does not mean "easy." It means they are there for the asking, the effort, the expressed desire—with discipline.

Moreover, it is clearer and clearer that industrial and technological society has rendered the natural ecstasies rarer and rarer. Call it the "eclipse of God" (Buber) or the "death of God" (Altizer) or the end of the Age of Pisces and Christianity (Jung) or just the common malaise that persons recite so frequently today: "I don't pray or experience God like I used to." There is ample evidence that natural ecstasies which could once be taken for granted by much of a population are now exceptions, not the rule, for a growing number of persons.

What would be some examples of this dearth of natural ecstasy? There is the rape of nature: the loss of the sun due to pollution (the three most polluted cities of the Western hemisphere—Rio de Janeiro, Buenos Aires and Mexico City—all being polluted by *North* American industrial wastes, were not long ago the paradises of the hemisphere, places where, if nothing else, sun and body met with the sea); rivers and streams so filthy that fires start regularly in them; smelly and contaminated lakes; abandoned mines where once there were vegetation and wildlife, etc. The kind of discipline (and asceticism) it will take to refresh what man has done to nature will not come easily. Yet, the task is a sacred one; every bit as sacred as building a monastery ever was.

Examples abound for the law of other natural ecstasies as well: sex as a commodity or as an exercise in ego-proving; the usefulness of friends and the lack of communication between spouses, parents or peers; the lost pride in one's craftsmanship and productive work (cf. Terkel); education as schooling in education instead of in thinking; the opiate of professional sports passing on values of violence and winning for winning's sake over values of excellence and striving in one's own participation in sporting activities; the outrageous and obscene cost for experiencing the fine arts and, at the same time, the meager opportunities for many with artistic gifts ever to develop them; the prostitution of visiting other countries by way of oases of one's own country (Hilton Hotels, etc.) that effectively prevent the spiritual purpose of travel, which is participation, integration and vulnerability.

Nor should we be deterred from the pleasures of natural ecstasies because we fear what the hedonist within us might do and what lengths he or she might go to. This fear breeds more rules, more limits, more fear. Instead, we need to keep our heads about us and realize that the Creator has implanted certain limits within all natural ecstasies. A setting sun sets; a vision from a mountain top ceases; lovers do not stay in bed forever; a symphony has an ending. I have an aunt who loves opera and cries each time she leaves one, saying, "Why did it have to end?" Life itself has its ending and its limits, as do all the joys within life. We do not have to play patrolman or God and project our puny limits onto the Creator's beauties.

The hedonistic fears we harbor are invariably manufactured fantasies. As such, they tell us more about the repression within ourselves than about the way to experience the beauties of life. If we were to live our fantasies more and manufacture them less, we would become realists overnight. And far less fearful. And much more loving of life. And willing to allow others to enjoy the pleasures of living.

The road back to sanity, to everyday experience of God by natural ecstasy, will not be an easy one. But is there any other route?

What we learn from this brief listing of some obstacles in our culture to natural ecstasy is the old adage repeating itself: "Corruption of the best is the worst." For each and every of the natural ecstasies can be abused—instead of ecstasy, which is a forgetfulness of self, we can indeed manipulate sex or friends, the arts, or nature itself to assert one's ego. Ego-tripping on the most spiritual of pathways instead of losing ourselves on these same pathways—what pathetic animals human beings can become!

Since the sixteenth century, there has been a trend in the West away from tactical ecstasies to natural ones. The Protestant spiritual traditions eliminated fasting, celibacy, chant, drugs and drink in great part. The Second Vatican Council marked a transition in Roman Catholicism from a great deal of tactical mysticism (chant—in the Latin language even, an especially effective means for chant to take effect covered as it would be by an otherwise "dead" language; rosaries; processions; incense; fasting; abstinence; heavy on celibacy) to acknowledging the role of natural mysticism (celebration is in; one's work in the world is a spiritual work; sexuality is God's gift; music can be sacred even when 'profane'; etc.). This trend is very much in line with the last three centuries of Protestant spirituality.

Yet, there is a danger in this trend for the West. The danger is the age-old one of substituting one extreme condition for another by overreacting to the failures of the former. It is one thing to say, for example, that Latin is a dead language and is inadequate for public worship on a grand scale. But it is another to ignore completely the mystical strategy behind the Latin chant and thereby render all chant as out-of-date or old-fashioned. Surely, the appeal of much in oriental religions, from chant to fasting to drugs, as well as the appeal among our youth to the occult is, in large part, a judgment on an older generation of believers who have barely escaped throwing out the ecstasy with the excesses.

Once we in the West have reinstated the proper role of tactical ecstasies as means and not ends, we need no longer fear them but may use them to our advantage should we feel the need. We should be aware, for example, that tactical ecstasies engaged in for a certain period can actually heighten our appreciation of the natural ecstasies. This was the experience of Aleksandr Solzhenitsyn, for example, who comments from his prison experiences how "a prisoner's heart is so inclined toward mysticism that he accepts precognition almost without surprise" and himself, on being allowed to see a courtyard for a mere thirty seconds exclaims: "Never had my eyes seen the green of the leaves with such intensity as they did that spring! And never in my life had I seen anything closer to God's paradise than that little Butyrki Park." (274f.) Meditation can, for some, improve their enjoyment of nature or sexuality, friendship or the arts. In this context, tactical ecstasies can serve the function of "purifying our senses"— which is an almost lost function in the West where, in the process of becoming ends in themselves, they have tended to repress the senses and the sensual.

Moreover, a new kind of commitment to a new kind of asceticism is required of us today—one based as much on the forgotten sense of a God of justice as on a desire for a mystical experience of God. This asceticism will be of a different kind because it will be for everyone, not just for a monastic caste ("the democratizing of asceticism" one might call it). It will be characterized by a voluntary and necessary giving up of certain consumption patterns of luxurious living and will be felt especially poignantly by people, institutions and governments of Western Europe, the United States and Japan.[1] This asceticism will be of a prophetic kind more than a mystical one. It is urged upon the luxurious cultures by that majority of the global village who can barely survive. It is decidedly not about purging the senses but about building compassion, the capacity to suffer and share with others. This is 'prophetic asceticism'.

Some people ask about silence: What kind of ecstasy, natural or tactical, is silence? Silence is not so much an ecstasy as an attitude one brings to ecstasy and takes home from ecstasy. Consider our list of natural ecstasies, for example. Silence is presumed in a deep nature experience, an act of love, a playing of a violin, a perfect pitch. Silence is not, of course, the absence of communication; it is more an attitude of being wholly present. And silence follows on a consummate experience of the stars, another person, a deeplyfelt movie—up to and including that ultimate ecstasy before which we shall all stand in awe and silence: our death.

To safeguard against a dreadful loss of ecstasy and, therefore, a loss of the experience of God, I propose the following simple rules that may be applied to one's personal life or to an institution's to encourage and build up the experience of ecstasy:

1. Tactical ecstasies are *always* a means. A spirituality that treats them as ends is thereby admitting its own materialism and control-oriented spirituality. To treat such devices as ends is idolatrous and blasphemous and can lead to even nastier things.

2. Embarking on tactical ecstasies should be preceded by experience of authentic natural ecstasy whenever possible.

3. Since the tactical ecstasies are means, the sole valid question for using them is: Do I genuinely feel, at this time, a need for this strategy? The sole valid criterion for ceasing them is: How effective are they? Have I outgrown my need for them? Truly spiritual persons can go through a whole lifetime without tactical ecstasies (though never without natural ones).

4. Embarking on tactical ecstasies demands personal commitment. Since they can never be regulated by rule or fiat, a good guru for the tactical journey is recommended.

5. Natural ecstasies, and they alone, are ends in themselves. This means that God is experienced directly in the experience of them. It follows, then, that the personal and cultural pursuit of them constitutes the truest and most timeless path of God experience. One is reminded of the Buddha, who, after seven years of trying gurus, masters of Yoga, and all the tactical apparatus that Hinduism had evolved over the centuries, finally relaxed under a tree and

there experienced his enlightenment. 'The Middle Way' he called it.

This same motive is found in Herman Hesse's celebrated novel *Siddhartha*, where the main character begins his mystical search with tactical ecstasies and complains that "we learn tricks with which we deceive ourselves, but the essential thing—the way—we do not find." (Hesse, 15) Foregoing tactical ecstasies, he resolves that "I will learn from myself, be my own pupil; I will learn from myself the secret of Siddhartha," and he immediately discovers the dimensions of natural ecstasies. "He looked around him as if seeing the world for the first time. The world was beautiful, strange and mysterious. Here was blue, here was yellow, here was green ... and in the midst of it, he, Siddhartha, the awakened one, on the way to himself." (32) By pursuing the ecstasies of creation for a lifetime, Siddhartha finds peace, while his friend, who spent a lifetime at tactical ecstasies, did not find peace. And significantly, it is from the river that spiritual knowledge came most deeply to Siddhartha.

Jesus, too, was not a tactical mystic or ascetic but immersed himself in natural ecstasies. We know this above all from his parables wherein the falling of rain is a spiritual matter. It is God who makes the rain to fall on just and unjust alike, and the love of God is present in the forgiveness of a father for his wayward son. "This sense of the divineness of the natural order is the major premiss of all the parables,"[2] we are told by scholars of the Gospel.

And so we see that the "Middle Way,' the way of natural ecstasies, was the surest way. And surely, it still is.

CHAPTER 4
How we can all agree that our experience of ecstasy *is* our experience of God

The thrust of this handbook, as examples in the early chapters illustrate, is that the experience of ecstasy is very near for each of us or at least can be in a viable society. God is as near as our experiences of ecstasy though by no means limited to them. For religious believers of the West—Judaism, Christianity and Islam—"the God we believe in *is* the God we experience." (Laing, 141-43) If only we can learn to trust our experience and the God tasted therein. In this chapter, I present some evidence why the nearness of the experience of God parallels the nearness of our experiences of ecstasy.

The first reason is that, when all is said and done and the stripping away of burdens to faith is accomplished (rational burdens which assign faith to the "head" exclusively as well as emotional burdens which assign faith exclusively to *my feeling* of being saved—an ego trip if there ever was one—and which logically express themselves in the desire to proselytize; i.e., to be a savior of others), faith can be simply, surely and adequately understood as: *an abiding trust that life is a gift.*

What does this mean? That a faithful person is one who abides in her trust that life is a gift? First, to see life as a gift is to see life as enjoyable, beautiful, pleasurable in itself—like any other nicely wrapped gift we receive from a friend. It takes one back to the first page of Western sacred Scripture, where in Genesis we learn that creation is good in the Creator's eyes and humans are even "very good." indeed, the belief (for who can prove it?) that life is a gift is a sacred affirmation made by all religions.

But to call life a gift is to suggest that we (the human race, you and I) never possessed it and never really will; that is, that we have received life. That we are finite recipients. "Gift" implies gift-giver, a giver of life, a creator. But it also implies that the gift-giver has truly put herself into the gift (for who gives a gift that is not representative of himself?). Thus, to know the gift is to know the giver behind the gift. To know creation is to know the Creator. And this knowledge we call 'ecstasy' as the biblical meaning of 'to know' is to know intimately, as husband knows wife and wife husband, carnally and wholly.

Trust and confidence do not come easily, especially these days in the demise of Western civilization. Can we trust anyone today? Even ourselves? Can we at least trust life itself? To do so implies faithfulness—the 'abiding' aspect of faith. In spite of and fully cognizant of the uglinesses, the unjust sufferings, the slaughter of the innocents, the problems and the pathos of life, one still believes and clings, one refuses to despair—one abides in faith. One trusts that life is given, freely given, as a gift to be enjoyed and passed on for others' enjoyment. As Abraham's faith was a "hope against hope," so ours is a trust against all apparent evidence to the contrary. "The mystic must return no less a lover of men, but rather a lover in more intense and human fashion, because it is only the true worshipper who can find the world genuinely loveable"[1] and thus sustain the myth or belief that living truly is a beautiful gift.

But a gift, even the gift of life, demands a thank you. Traditionally, prayer has been understood as praise or as thank you to God. Our thesis is not divorced from such a tradition. But do we know how to thank any longer? We say thank you for some gift by enjoying it and allowing a gift-giver to witness our enjoyment. A friend who gives me a record is pleased when he learns of my delight at playing the record. After all, my delight was the very goal he intended in giving me the gift. The creator can be no different. Our thank you for creation, our fundamental prayer, therefore, is our enjoyment and delight in it. This delight is called ecstasy when it reaches a certain height, and it is also prayer. Like all prayer, it touches the Creator and we are touched by the Creator in that act of ecstasy and thank you.

What we see unfolding is a spirituality that finds its origins in trust, in thankfulness for creation. Such a spirituality contrasts sharply with those more fundamentalist movements such as Manichaeism and its present-day expression in some forms of Pentecostalism which emphasize not the beauty of life but the Fall, sin and the need for redemption. With these two lines of spirtual tradition—creation spirituality and redemption spirituality—we can trace the entire history of Western spiritual struggles. The greatest weakness of redemption spiritualities is that in them human persons are never given credit for cooperating with the Creator but instead are told that "the Lord did it." But there are still additional reasons why our ecstatic experience of creation is also an experience of the Creator.

The medieval theologian, Thomas Aquinas, dares to say that "God is in all things and intimately so." And he elaborates how intimate this presence is: "Nothing is so distant from God that it does not have God in itself"; "God is said to be absolutely present" in natural things; "God is in every place which is everywhere"; "just as a soul is in every single part of a body, so God is wholly in every single thing"; "God is present in all things by power insofar as all things are subject to his power; He is present in all things by his presence insofar as all things are nude and open to his eyes; He is present in all things by essence, insofar as He is present in all things as the cause of their existence." And "God is present in a special way in man who knows and loves God by act or habit. And because man possesses this love by grace God is present in holy people by grace."[2]

If God is as near and vitally present in all that exists, all of life, as this medieval thinker suggests, then we see why ecstasy is the experience of God. God is intimately in mountains and the sea, sunshine and the human personality, sexual activity and music, painting and good food. To know these things is to know their omnipresent Creator. The Giver is present in his gifts in an extraordinary way, an 'intimate' way, Aquinas insists. To delight in those gifts is to delight in the presence of the giver of them. The experience of ecstasy *is* the experience of God.

Another reason why ecstasy is God-experience is that, in fact, life's greatest and freest and cheapest and most plentiful gifts are the very natural ecstasies we have considered in detail in Chapter 1. Life would not be a gift without them but is a gift with them. Thus, to experience them deeply, ecstatically, to the extent of forgetting oneself in their pleasure, is to experience the object of faith, the Gift-giver. What a forgotten truth it is that God is present in every flower, every person, every blade of grass and every note in a song—to recover the certitude of this is to experience God.

In experiencing ecstasy, we are experiencing what our forefathers in spiritual traditions called 'grace'. By 'grace' they meant the following experiences: "divine help for doing or willing something that is good"; "man having a certain spiritual society with God"; "the eternal love of God"; "the very participation or expression of divine goodness"; "a participation in divine nature"; "the principle of any good work in us."[3] "There is a special way which belongs to the rational creature, in which God is said to be in them as something known is in the knower or something loved in a lover. And because, by knowing and by loving, a rational creature touches God himself in these operations, according to this very special mode God is said not only to be in the rational creature but also to dwell in him as in his own temple."[4] This, says Aquinas, is what grace does to a person—it makes a person the home of

God. As Jesus said, "I am the Temple" and early Christians followed up by reiterating, "We are the Temple."

The very purpose of this dwelling in man is enjoyment: that man may enjoy God, not *use* him. "The divine person himself is enjoyed."[5] A religious person tends to want to use God; a spiritual person enjoys God. Science and technology tend to diminish the useful need for God; but in no way can they replace the enjoyment of God—in fact, they can allow persons greater leisure and opportunity for such pleasure.

But God alone is the cause of grace as "fire alone can cause fire."[6] If this is so, and only experience demonstrates the experience of grace, then this same experience, ecstasy, is God-caused. God, through and along with creation's natural ecstasies, is the cause of our experiences of being graced, of gracefulness, of divine life. Grace then becomes an action of God's presence that is caused by God through the gifts of her creation.

What we have been saying can be put into theological vocabulary by saying that revelation happens through creatures and our experience as creatures of nature, music, love, sex, dance, suffering, thinking, and working. This is another way of saying that revelation, "the veritable speech of God" occurs far more broadly than merely in books (however sacred) or through church authorities (however insistent). Everything that is, is holy, and our experience of ecstasy can be our recognition of this fact. "The world is not only a good world," warns the philosopher Joseph Pieper, "it is in a very precise sense *holy*" and "if existing is not only good but also holy, then the rejection of existence is not only evil but also sacrilegious, antigodly . . . . Wherever we encounter something that has flamed anything real, anything existent in any way whatsoever, we encounter something that has "flamed up' directly from God."[7] The revelation of the Creator is available in many forms to many people—to all those who can admit "WHEE!" and be moved by the

Creator who is in his/her creation. How loudly the Creator shouts to us through creation's beauty; how deaf we so often are.

For all these reasons plus whichever others the reader would like to add, we can agree that our experiences of ecstasy *are* our experiences of God. And we do not make this statement nor, more importantly, perform such activities oblivious of their import. God and the very action of God is ours to experience if we care enough to treat ourselves to the ecstasies of living.

PART II
Becoming Like God:
WE

When we associate closely with something or someone, we learn to love that thing or person—the sea or a mountain, a favorite piece of music or a painting, a classroom of eager learners, our children, our spouse, our lover. And when we love we begin to conform in some ways, perhaps to smell just a little bit like, to laugh a little bit like, to anticipate the needs of our partner just a little bit. In short, in the process of being reborn by ecstatic experiences we are to some degree remade.

It follows that when we spend time with ecstasies of creation, we become like the Creator and take on the Creator's characteristics. We recover what it means to be "made in the image and likeness of God" as Judaism and Christianity boast of in the first book of their sacred Scriptures. If we are made in God's image and if we experience that image every day through ecstasies great and small, as we have demonstrated in the first part of this book, then we should expect that there will be a process to our becoming like God. For there are degrees to it. Ten years ago, we were like the Creator in some ways; but today in others; and tomorrow, hopefully, in others. Or, as Paul put it, "When I was a child, I prayed like a child, but now that I am a man I have put away the things of a child." What paths and routes might we travel in the process of becoming like God? This is our subject for meditation in the next six chapters. We need to explore the obvious question- what is God like?—in order to recognize the image to which we are becoming more and more conformed, more and more similar, though always remaining our unique selves. How will we know when we are becoming like God? "By their fruits you will know them," we are instructed—but what are these fruits? What does ecstasy do to us?

CHAPTER 5
How God is like an elephant— learning to remember and not forget our ecstasies

A mong our many joys in experiencing ecstasy is our experiencing a time lapse, a forgetfulness of the kind of time-orientation that clocks give us. When we wait for them to strike 4:30 for our workday to end; or when we study our watches dashing to catch a plane on time. Ecstasy is a forgetfulness of everyday problems, an immersion into another time frame. "Timelessness," some might call it; "a taste of the eternal," other would say. Ecstasy is the experience of forgetting oneself and one's time for a second, an instant, an hour, a day, a lifetime. A hermit living close to nature runs his life by nature's time, not his own and not any other man's time; a musician at her piano is lost in a new sense of time. Creation has its own times and our ecstasy baptizes us into these times. The time of the full moon; the time when a child is due for birth; the time for making and receiving love; the timing of a musical piece expertly sung or performed; the timing of a good joke. Forgetting ourselves long enough to get in tune with another time, creation's time, is one of the joys of ecstatic experiences.

But if timelessness is so special and such a joy and so closely married to our ecstatic experience, then it is also memorable and unforgettable. The experience of forgetting oneself, of getting outside of oneself, is itself a memorable experience. Indeed, ecstatic experiences *are* the memorable experiences of our lives.

Dr. Elizabeth Ross, commenting on her experiences with dying persons, observes that "a sunset together or sitting at the river, at a campfire, or moments when a family sang together—glimpses of experiences, always with other human beings. It's a silent, meaningful companionship that had meaning and that lasts for decades. Those are the moments dying patients remember and with smiles on their faces. They think of these moments. These people die peacefully."[1]

People who cannot remember, who have no ecstasy to recall or refer to, are a sad people indeed; a people without experience of forgetfulness of self and, therefore, without experience of God.

For God remembers. God is like an elephant. What does God remember? The creator remembers, not objects (such as, "I can remember my report card") but moments of participation (such as my acts of love, my lost moments by the sea, my turning people on with a joke or a thought). The Creator remembers her creation—remembers as a constant participant in it. The creator cherishes creation. As vivifier and breather and sustainer and beauty-maker—that is, as a lover remembers her beloved.

But memory, like any spiritual power, is highly risky and dangerous, with immense capacity for destruction buried within it. "The weakness of memory is its self-centeredness," warns Stephen Spender; "hence the narcissistic nature of most poetry" (or religion, we might add). (CP, 122) Another danger to spiritual memory are the imposters that assert themselves in memory's name and who, like wolves in sheep's clothing, in fact, kill all spiritual memory. Nostalgia is an example of such bogus memory.

God's kind of memory is not memory as nostalgia— "remember when in high school we did such and such to so and so"; "remember the good old days"; etc. This is not spiritual memory; for the spiritual rememberer does not escape to the past but remembers to re-participate, to re-experience *now* the immense joys of the past. Such memory is not flight from the present, as in nostalgia, but a hallowing of the present. As when one visits a cemetery to remember one's loved ones and, in the process, communes even with those whom we never knew to love but who, because we participate in the same struggle of life as they, are memorable to us.

A spiritual person, a God-like person, does not forget spiritual experience and ecstasy but remembers with intense participation the ecstasies of life. He remembers sadness as well as togetherness, as the poet Rainer Rilke observes, speaking from memory. "Even if you were in some prison the walls of which let none of the sounds of the world come to your senses—would you not then still have your childhood, that precious, kingly possession, that treasure-house of memories?" (20) Yes, a kingly possession is our past for it is a treasure-house of ecstasies. And to be alive (which is to be spiritual) is to call upon that treasure-house, as Rilke later encourages. "Enjoyment of (creating) is so indescribably beautiful and rich only because it is full of inherited memories of the begetting and bearing of millions. In one creative thought a thousand forgotten nights of love revive, filling it with sublimity and exaltation. And those who come together in the night and are entwined in rocking delight do an earnest work and gather sweetnesses, gather depth and strength for the song of some coming poet, who will arise to speak of ecstasies beyond telling." (37) Yes, ecstasy builds on memory; ecstasy on ecstasy. And God, who is the ecstasy of them all, does not forget. Dare we?

People who we call spiritual giants have always urged the rest of us to forget in order to remember. What were the prophets of the Hebrew people doing shouting and running about naked with warnings if not to say to their own people: "Remember the law you have forgotten." "Return." "Forget not." and Jesus, who saw himself in that same line of rememberers (called prophets), chose to concentrate on memory in what were, in effect, his final actions on earth. Conscious as he was the night of his betrayal that his life of ecstasies and sorrows was running out on him, what did he do and say? "Do this in memory of me," he said. "Memory." The most sacred of trusts. And yet, how often have institutions claiming to speak in Jesus' name made a nostalgia piece of his memorable last meal, reducing it to an unspiritual and literal, a forgotten, event. What a pathetic instance! A man urges us to spiritual memory, and we reduce his words and actions to nostalgia. Urged to participation, we make rules, prescribe sanctions, and kill a possibly living memory.

People who become like God and cultures that allow and even encourage people to become like God do not forget. Is that what celebration and festivals are about? A birthday; a procession; a folk dance; a family reunion picnic and outing; home movies or pictures attempting to record the events. A memory of our roots; of our past; of, therefore, our deepest present and of our only future. An alive and spiritual society is one wherein the past is honored—not with nostalgia (as in the epitaph "America, love it or leave it") but with participation (as in a true Fourth of July picnic and outing); where all are equal again, the children and the adults in game playing, people tumbling on the grass, and good, home-cooked food and drink. A celebration is a sharing of common memory and, therefore, a forgetting of private memory. All become one again. The past is present; the present past; the future forgotten yet here: this is the way God thinks on time. God, after all, is oblivious of the future, yet present fully to all times.

A people without memory are a lost people; an uprooted and rootless one; a spiritless one. "Without history, without art, with a memory that begins with each morning's waking and ends with the night's sleep," warns Gore Vidal, we are in danger of achieving "a numbness far more comforting to the spirit than the always dangerous and sometimes fatal exploration of self and world which was the aim of our old culture, now discarded."[2] We call spiritual memory "tradition." And no so-called advances

of academicians, scientists or institutional Yes-men can
eradicate our need for, our desire for, yes, our ecstasy in
traditions. Just as the sea and the mountains and the forest
teach us to forget, they also teach us to remember. And so
do a people's traditions. So do people. The greatest
traditions we have to remember are in our people.
Especially those who have lived the longest and, hopefully,
experienced the most "unforgettable," that is, ecstatic
experiences. A culture that honors its old ones can make
some claim to being spiritual; one that forgets or tries to
forget them is already dead though it may not know it.

Hermann Hesse has warned of the alternative to
developing our spiritual memories: "Humanity's most
powerful and senseless desire the desire to forget."
(Hesse, *Journey*, 8)

Some people are afraid of the past, some, in an effort to
be liberal, cut themselves off from awareness of tradition.
Others, bent on conserving the past as an object, actually
destroy true memory by erecting nostalgia as an object of
memory and distorting the past. But all this is idolatory,
the worship of gods as objects. The living God is
remembered in spiritual memory which is never of objects
but of life. Ecstasy becomes cherished. What we remember
is life, our responses to it, our ecstatic moments of living
joys and tragedies; in short, we remember radical responses
to life, that is, prayer. (cf. Fox) Our memories are made to
remember prayer. Experience. Feelings. Insight. Caring.
Tenderness. Forgiveness. Tears. Play. Promises. This is why
a spiritual person can never be a liberal or a conservative
but must be radical. For true rootedness means not being
afraid of the past (or, if we are, of facing up to the fear);
not preserving the past (the conservative) and not decrying
it (the moralizing liberal) but living the present more
deeply. The superficial person flees from the past or tries
to manipulate it, for such nonspiritual persons have to
manipulate everything into their own image. But the deep
or spiritual person treats the past with the same reverence

with which he treats oceans and earth and sunshine and children and music; he lets the past wash down on him. He receives the past as he does any other gift. And his motive is the same: to enjoy himself. Ecstasy. God-experience.

Truly spiritual religion always honors the past by doing honor to the memory of past ecstasy. Thus, for example, the Hebrew people who remember the Exodus experience of their ancestors' liberation from Egyptian bondage do honor to the past, and thereby give honor to the ecstasy in the present. And only from this reverence is ecstasy born into the future. Dying and unspiritual religion does not honor the past but dishonors it by manipulating rather than reverencing the past. This manipulation is carried on by nostalgia (inciting people to wish for romanticized past time instead of living in the present) or by objectifying the past (such as erecting monuments—which are objects—as if they can preserve the ecstasy for us). Jesus recognized such manipulation of the past by religion in his day: "You hypocrites! You who build the sepulchres of the prophets and decorate the tombs of holy men, saying, 'We would never have joined in shedding the blood of the prophets, had we lived in our fathers' day.' " (Mt. 23.29f.) Plaster of paris images of holy persons and a systematic depoliticization of them is another example of manipulation of the past. Every saint has been more filled with blood and sweat (often suffered at the hands of his or her own church institutions) than of antiseptic camouflage and the kind of cleanliness that resembles television soap commercial actresses. Neither the experiences nor the ecstasies of good men and women are antiseptic.

The real world, the whole world including the spiritual one, is woven in paradoxes, as we have seen in this meditation on God as elephant. True and spiritual memory is of time lapsed and time forgotten; yet, only out of this forgetting arises authentic remembering. And the future is not born by staring at the future but by passing time with our roots, which are our past and the depth of the present.

We only remember what we forget. So, God is like an elephant. And we, through trusting our ecstatic experiences, might also grow to become elephantlike. As the poet T. S. Eliot prayed, "Teach us to care and not to care." We might add, "Teach us to remember and not to remember. Teach us to forget ourselves in order to remember our real self. Teach us to cherish. Teach us to be God-like, like an elephant."

CHAPTER 6
God as Pleasure-seeker:
the forgotten pleasure of believing
creation and the Creator are pleasures

Question: What Does God Do all Day (and Night)?

Answer: He (or She) Enjoys Himself (Herself).

We Westerners have made the gods and especially *the* God over into our own image so often—at least with the gods we always maintained a respect for the diversity of the deity. But monotheism (heavy-sounding word, isn't it?) tends to strangle the *only* God we presumably have left in order to fit him (always a him) into a particular custom-made straight jacket. For example, we've manufactured the Peeping-Tom God who plays a role in bedrooms and the back seats of cars—a role that we would hardly consider honorable even for a private investigator. We have God keeping little black books for the awful times of "judgment"—as if we were incapable of releasing our egos long enough to be honest, at least once in a while, with ourselves. We have dressed God in a long, white beard much like Father Time and as such have disposed of him as easily as we do most of the other elderly citizens of our compulsively youthful society.

So, let's just pause here for a moment and ask the obvious question. Who is God? What does God do all day and all night? The surest answer I can offer is that, judging from the creation she has given birth to, the Creator is a pleasure-seeker. God the pleasure-seeker. But what do we know of pleasure-seeking? We, who spend our waking hours working and our vacation hours preparing to work more efficiently, do we know anything at all of pleasure? Are we knowers of pleasure? The purpose of ecstasy, like the purpose of living, is for the fun of it. We learn this in prayer and the communion with the pleasure-seeking God. But do we? Do we any longer "walk with God in the garden in the cool of the evening" as Adam did? And do we encourage others to do the same? Just where has all the pleasure gone? Is it only for childhood times? Can only children play amid lost time? Must we always guard time, save it, control it because to lose time is to lose money? Or self image?

If we are ignorant of pleasure we are ignorant of God. It is no wonder that as pleasure has dwindled for us so has our image of a pleasure-loving God. No wonder the perverse kinds of pleasure we have dreamed up—our chemicals that can truly eliminate vegetation, our bombs that burn or tear only human flesh, our violence-ridden entertainment—so fully occupy us today. Our sadism is the price for lost pleasures of ecstasy; for man always seeks pleasure, and a creation-oriented kind that is frustrated or repressed is sure to find an outlet in sick, death-oriented pleasures. It follows logically that the God we have invented in our own image is necessarily a vengeful, sadistic deity—peeping and judging, denouncing and spying; a God of guilt, not of the joys of the gifts of living. A God who more closely resembles a wiretapper than a lover.

In the midst of these man-made sadistic gods who take pleasure in man's guilt and suffering ("if it hurts, it's God's will"), we have lost sight of the pleasure-seeking God of Western spiritual traditions. Such was the God of the medieval mind for whom ecstasy with God was recreation (our being re-created) with God, our becoming like the divine playmate with whom we had chosen to pass our time. "The divine person himself is enjoyed" by graced man, Aquinas insists, and all persons are capable of profound participation in the company and good pleasure of God. The experience of thinking is itself "loveable, desirable and delightful" and incites us to the "very vision of God" according to Aquinas, who, drawing on Aristotle, sees the goal of everyone's life as "that in which the enjoyment is the greatest, and that which he finds most attractive." The two trends in life-style that Aquinas recognizes in his culture, the active and the contemplative, offer him a simple choice based on the consideration of which direction will provide the greater pleasure for a person. Thus, human life for Aquinas is actually divisible according to how we derive pleasure in it!

For those masochistic spiritualists who consider a contemplative's life as one of "giving up" pleasure, Aquinas makes some startling observations. "The goal of the contemplative life," he insists, "is pleasure, which is in the affective appetite: and from this love comes about." The end product of our ecstasy will be joy and peace, goodness and kindness, and these fruits of the spirit are also meant for our and others' good pleasure, for "the fruit of man is said to be the ultimate end of man, *which he should enjoy.*"[1] While Aquinas shared suspicions about sexual pleasure that many Christian theologians from the fourth century on entertained, and which we cannot agree with today, one can sense in this brief glimpse into his thinking on spirituality that he had indeed constructed an entire spiritual theology on the reality and availability of pleasure. God's and humans' pleasure—a direction to religion that clearly has been lost in so many instances of repression and flight from pleasure in the late medieval and modern ages.

Jesus, too, speaks out on behalf of a pleasure-seeking God. His entire preaching is summed up in the Kingdom Parables where, we are told, he who finds the kingdom of heaven will "for sheer joy" sell everything he owns to buy the field where it lays. Jesus was speaking from his own experience for the "sheer joy" motive surely explains Jesus' experience with the Father, an experience of intimacy and pleasure. One remembers the pleasure Jesus took in the mountains and gardens, the lake and the desert, the star-filled nights and the sunny Palestinian days where he fled so frequently to spend time with the Creator. And his prayer was to an intimate father—"Abba" as in "Papa." Surely a father on "papa" terms with his son is overflowing with pleasure—pleasure he experiences in his baby's presence and pleasure that he wishes and projects onto the living of his son. What kind of parent is not a wisher of pleasure for his child? Then surely God's pleasure for us is no less.

But the Gospel's richest story of the pleasure Jesus wanted to share in God's name is the Martha-Mary story. We recall how both women were friends to Jesus, but when he came on an unexpected visit, only one spent time, the natural ecstasy of friendship, with him. The second, Martha, was too busy doing things, washing dishes and preparing the meal. Jesus' advice was addressed to Martha: "Martha you worry and fret about so many things, and yet few are needed, indeed only one. It is Mary who has chosen the better part; it is not to be taken from her." (Lk. 10.41f.) So it goes. The true pleasures of God's creation are unforgettable and cannot be taken away. More than that, they are "the better part." Just sitting with a friend, wasting time with him, insists Jesus, is the truly contemplative act. Our worship of God is a pleasure to all concerned. For surely, in this story, Jesus was himself enjoying fully the company of his friend Mary, her attentions and affection. So it works both ways: pleasure given (by Mary) is pleasure received (by Jesus) and vice versa. Moreover, and here lies the thrust of the incident as a spiritual story, the same experience can be applied to God. The pleasure she gives us is the pleasure she wants in return.

The 'abide' theology of John's Gospel, wherein God is said to have set up his tent in humankind's midst and in the midst of each person, also argues to the pleasure-seeking of God. "Your hearts will be full of joy, and that joy no one shall take from you." (Jn 16.22) The glory Jesus has experienced with his father—yes, the *glory* of the ecstasies on Mount Tabor in the Transfiguration and elsewhere—is now the disciples' to experience. "I have given them the glory you gave to me" and "I say these things to share my joy with them to the full." (17.21, 13)

The pleasures of Jesus' life—his friends, male and female, his meals, the successes of his friends, the children whom he met and who delighted him, his parents, his study of the Law, his party going, and his times in nature and in solitude, his caring and success in caring for suffering persons—all bear down on him as he faces death his last night on earth in the Garden of Gethsemane. How little he looks forward to the perverse pleasure, the masochism and the sadism, that will be dealt him the next day. How thoroughly he rejects it, flies from it, desires it prevented. "Let this cup pass from me." Yet he fails and the crucifiers have their way. Still, however, his last act becomes itself an experience of natural ecstasy for it is unsought-for suffering. And, in a final act of trust, he commits himself (by way of hope only, for he cannot feel it) to a pleasure-loving Father, "Into your hands I commend my spirit."

Having preached a God of pleasure "who makes his rain to fall on the just and the unjust" and who "clothes the lilies of the field in the splendor of a Solomon," he now exits life in so ugly a condition of death and despair that only hope and the most abiding trust can suspect a hidden beauty. What a strange—but a real—paradox it is to see this preacher of "sheer joy," of Mary's ecstasy over friendship with him, of God's joy at people's joy, of the parable of the talents (where we are reprimanded when we fail to multiply our pleasures and joy)—to see this preacher die, being tested for his belief that life is a gift. He did not lose faith. Life, even at this extreme end, we are told, was in a curious and invisible way a pleasure.

And what of the ancestors of Jesus? Were they, too,

believers in a pleasure-loving God? The Creator is said to call creation "good" and even "very good." And the God of the prophets seeks the pleasure of mankind. They seek—in God's name—a land wherein "Justice flows like water and integrity like an unfailing stream," (Amos 5.24-26) a place where all people will drink, and drink deep. "This is the covenant I will make with the House of Israel when those days arrive—it is Yahweh who speaks. Deep within them I will plant my Law, writing it on their hearts. Then I will be their God and they shall be my people.... They will all know me, the least no less than the greatest – it is Yahweh who speaks – since I will forgive their iniquity and never call their sin to mind" (Jer 31.33f.)

And what of this knowledge of Yahweh? How pleasurable is it? To describe it, the Jews needed excellent poets, as in the Song of Songs.

> My beloved is mine and I am his.
> He pastures his flock among the lillies. (2.16)
> I found him whom my heart loves.
> I held him fast, nor would I let him go
> till I had brought him
> into my mother's house,
> into the room of her who conceived me. (3.4)
> You ravish my heart. (4.9)
> my sister, my promised bride,
> you ravish my heart (4.9)
> I come into my garden,
> my sister, my promised bride,
> I gather my myrrh and balsam,
> I eat my honey and my honeycomb,
> I drink my wine and my milk.
> Eat, friends, and drink,
> drink deep, my dearest friends. (5.1)
> Set me like a seal on your heart,
> like a seal on your arm.

For love is strong as Death,
jealousy as relentless as Sheol.
The flash of it is a flash of fire,
a flame of Yahweh himself. (8.6)

Whoever composed these songs of the heart, of Yahweh,
and of man and woman was no stranger to the ecstasies of
creation. Nor could he have expected his listeners to be
strangers to the ecstasies of which he sings.

The psalmists, too, wax high on the pleasures of the
God of Israel.

Shouts of joy and gladness for all
    who take pleasure in my virtue;
give them a constant cause to say,
    'Great is Yahweh,
who likes to see his servant at peace!' (35.27)

They feast on the bounty of your house,
you give them drink from your river of pleasure;
yes, with you is the fountain of life,
by your light we see the light. (36.9f.)

You visit the earth and water it,
    you load it with riches;
God's rivers brim with water
    to provide their grain.

This is how you provide it:
by drenching its furrows, by levelling its ridges,
by softening it with showers, by blessing the
    first-fruits.
You crown the year with your bounty,
abundance flows wherever you pass;
the desert pastures overflow,
the hillsides are wrapped in joy,
the meadows are dressed in flocks,

the valleys are clothed in wheat,
what shouts of joy, what singing! (65.10-13)

Who needs additional evidence of the profound roots of Western spiritual traditions in a pleasure-loving, pleasure-seeking, pleasure-providing Providence? Who dares to measure what God's pleasure might be, having tasted of the depths of nature's pleasures in so many kinds of natural ecstasies? How many greater pleasures await humankind? And with what even more profound joys and peaceful experiences? How can we begin to fathom the depths and the beauties that the Creator has in store for her creation? For those committed to the experience of ecstasy, a new commandment is in store: pleasure first. But take pleasure not only in your own pleasure but also in others' pleasure. The way God does. The way the Creator does with her creation. Become like this pleasure-loving, pleasure-sharing God.

CHAPTER 7
Thinking Symbolically: how spiritual voyagers reject literal thinking for symbolic playing and how our symbolic thinking is our God-consciousness

Question: How does God think?
Response: Neither literally nor by signs but
          symbolically.
Question: What in God's name does that mean?
Response: Read on and find out.

F ollowing our familiar method of approaching an understanding of spiritual terms first through their opposites, we will begin our reflections on symbolic consciousness by considering its opposite: literal thinking.

We think literally about things: about books and words (exact ones, not the meaning behind them), laws (their letter, not their spirit), money in the bank, property owned, the past as separate and not part of the present, buildings, titles, pigeon holes, bureaucracies. All these thoughts are thing thoughts and are literal thoughts. "Literal" comes from the word "letter," yet a letter by itself, alone and apart from a word, is isolated. To isolate is to think literally: we reduce great events, such as people who are bearers of ecstasy, to the level of isolated objects, letters or things. Even living beauties like people and their ecstatic moments and memories become problems to be classified and pigeon-holed and controlled. A literal mentality exclaims that people are for the Sabbath (a law), not the Sabbath for people (which would prove to be a celebration).

We have all had experiences of literalism. Legalism is such an experience. I can narrate an incident, for example, that is small but is typical of a literalist mentality. Recently, a group of Roman Catholics was interested in recovering that tradition's Gregorian chant (not, I hasten to add, for nostalgia purposes but for the beauty contained therein). A priest who envisioned himself a guardian of the letter refused to announce the event in his parish bulletin because "he doubted whether the group had permission for such a Mass." Permission-seekers are literalists. What an irony that this same priest ten years previously had no doubt declaimed that groups did not have permission to worship God in the vernacular tongue. This is typical of literalism—it swings pendulum-like from one law to another, never stopping long enough in between (where people are) to be able to incorporate (symbolism incorporates) both extremes in one event.

Another example of literal thinking in our culture is what we have done to death. We have presumed that the reality of death can be dealt with once in our lifetime. One grand exit disguised as an illusion of continued life (painting the corpse, preserving it, buying it more plush satins and bedsprings than we ever did the individual when he was living)—this is our literal notion of death. With such an isolated and singular sense of death, it is no wonder that Dr. Ross and others complain of how persons in our culture (including doctors and clergymen) cannot deal with the dying of another. They chatter on; they talk of the streets of heaven or hell (as if they have been there); they run from it altogether.

Here is a prime opportunity wherein symbolic thinking would rescue us from literalism's strangulation. For we can learn how to deal with one's death in the full sense of our demise from this form of living by dealing first with our experience of death in its symbolic sense. We all die many times in our lives—when we say good-bye to someone or some place we love; when we go to prison; when we become sick and enter a hospital; on bad trips of drugs or alcohol; at the death of a loved one; a divorce; a loss of a friend or a breaking up with a friend; a quitting of one way of life for another—all of these are examples of *symbolic deaths*—they are tastes of the meaning of the fuller death that awaits us all. If we were persons who insisted on taking these symbolic deaths seriously, letting them change us, then we would be able simply to hold hands with the dying. We would understand something of death in the full sense. If our culture would moralize less about symbolic deaths and encourage the common expression of them more, then we would become spiritually minded, that is, symbolic about death. We would become the kind of caring persons whom Dr. Ross yearns to meet in hospitals and homes where persons are dying.

For what one learns from symbolic deaths is what one learns of the depths of living from any experience of symbolism—that the literal is not what counts; it is not what is true in life. As Aleksandr Solzhenitsyn puts it, reflecting on his prison experience: "Very early and very clearly, I had this consciouness that prison was not an abyss for me, but the most important turning point in my life." (Gulag, 187) To see prison as a turning point; death as life; silence as communication; the void as fullness—here lies a symbolic and therefore a spiritual consciousness. This, truly, is becoming alive.

One element of literalism that makes it so appealing to many in our country today is control. A literalist can control his and usually others' destinies—or so he thinks. Take, for example, the trial of Maurice Stans where we were told that he and Mr. Vesco sat down to have "one of those conversations that never takes place." The arrogance of the human race—that we imagine we can make what is is not; and what is not is! In this compulsion to control lies the essence of lying and falsehood. It is pure literalism carried to its logical conclusion.

Literalism is a disease that particularly invades religious

traditions. It is a way of trying to control with letters instead of with spirit. Fundamentalist sects, for example, insist on the "letter" of the Scripture books: in the very letter and strict obedience to it will be found salvation (as if it were even possible to obey every letter of such books which are as filled with paradoxes and contradictions as life itself is). Then we have more "liberal" (because they are intellectual) religious thinkers who assure us that salvation will come if we adhere to the exact and newest scholarly study of these same holy books. Scholarship which, we are assured, is establishing the definitive test will save us. This delusion also arises from literalist thinking. It is no wonder that so much scholarship misses the forest, concentrating (letter-like) on the trees. And, finally, we have the literalists who look not to the letter of a holy book but to the letter of papal decree as if enshrined dogma or authority saves, as if from sucking the exact meaning from such texts we might become alive.

All stereotype thinking is literal thinking: literal thinking is the ordure from the wastebasket of prejudice. Thus, shibboleths such as "women belong in the home" or "black people are lazy" or "the free world vs. the socialist world" are literal thinking. Sterotyping epitaphs become the language for demagoguery because of the intrinsic relationship between the control that literal thinking accomplishes and the politcal control that demagogues seek. Until one breaks through stereotyped and literal thinking, life is not living but a prison whose walls are made of literalism and whose captives are the mind, heart, head, and body.

The fundamental error in any of these mentalities is the presumption that literal thinking is ever capable of giving life. "The letter kills," warned Paul, "but the spirit gives life." (2 Cor. 3.6) Literalism does kill: it kills us and it kills God for "God is a spirit." A literal way of thinking is the opposite of a spiritual way of thinking. "Literalism is the ministration of death, written and engraved in stones;

tables of stone and stony heart." (LB, 223)

Spiritually-minded persons invariably consider literalism their enemy. Thus Jesus, who insisted on "letting the dead bury the dead," condemned the literalism that stood for worship among religious leaders of his time. "Alas, for you, scribes and Pharisees, you hyprocrites! You who pay your tithe of mint and dill and cummin and have neglected the weightier matters of the law—justice, mercy, good faith!" The "weightier matters" are all symbolic, not literal. No one ever defined nor legalized justice, mercy or good faith. It is (and was) so much easier and more controllable to settle for the literal in religion—the tithing of even the tiniest plants, such as mint, dill and cummin—rather than to pursue the symbolic.

Jesus had more to say of his experience of literalism. "Alas for you, scribes and Pharisees, you hypocrites! You who clean the outside of cup and dish and leave the inside full of extortion and intemperance." Another insight on the literal: it is always external. "Alas for you scribes and Pharisees, you hypocrites! You who build the sepulchres of the prophets and decorate the tombs of holy men, saying, 'We would never have joined in shedding the blood of the prophets, had we lived in our fathers' day. So! Your own evidence tells against you." Here, another insight into the literalist mentality: enshrine the past. Build. Buildings, pyramids, institutions—anything, so long as it is material and, therefore, external to the inner, spiritual self. And, what is more, having built, then manipulate. Manipulate the inner lives of others by means of nostalgia (instead of memory), by means of sentimentalism (instead of mystical experience). And, for those who do not worship at your graven building, kill. Kill the symbolist sons of bitches! Crucify them! Crucify him!

Literalism must end in killing. It is the product of death and "a dead tree bears dead fruit." Those who bring life, the spiritual and symbolic mentality, must die. Both mentalities cannot coexist. Life seeks more life; and death more of its own.

But what is this symbolism? How is it so powerful that it draws death down upon itself? How is it that God thinks this way? A symbol is not manufactured. No man "makes" a symbol but only uncovers one. Therefore, a symbol is not about control, for it does not begin as control nor end in control. A symbol begins with an experience—an ecstatic experience. An experience that is too big for a single (i.e., literal) exclamation. A symbol is the language of ecstasy. Thus, tears are a symbol (whether of joy or sadness); laughter; a kiss; an embrace; a smile; a groan; a cheering and applause. One who has been moved responds in symbols (not in letters). A symbol never stands for one thing as a letter does but for a plurality of things. Who would dare say exactly what single meaning lies behind a smile or a laugh or a tear? Does an act of love between man and woman stand for just one thing (e.g., for procreation or for conquering or for a release of libidinal energy)? Or does it stand for *many* things, including pleasure and affection and life and death and immortality and finiteness and ecstasy and void. Only the literalists would say it stands for one thing. Symbols stand for many—though always ecstatic—experiences.

The experience of language begins with ecstasy and with symbol. The baby who first learns to cry "Dada" is not indifferent or nonecstatic (and certainly not literal) about his cry of "Dada." The symbol "Dada" expresses the ecstasy the child feels in the presence of a loving parent, his first experience of standing outside of himself. No wonder the appearance of the sought-after ecstasy, the parent, so often results in cooing and gurgline—symbols of the pleasure the child takes at fulfillment of ecstasy.

Children appear especially adept at symbol-consciousness, as spiritual leaders have warned. "Unless you turn and become like a child you will not receive the kingdom." Children practice symbols when they play games. "Let's play house. You be mommy and I'll be daddy." "Let's play cops and robbers." This is symbolic thinking—you are not you but someone else. The child relates to his toys not as to objects of possession (literalism) but as occasions for ecstacy and symbolism. A child's truck is not just a foot-high metal object: it is an occasion for dreaming that she in fact is the driver of a huge van as her father might be. A doll is not a literal object for a child but a symbolic child while she or he plays the symbolic mother. "The incarnation of symbols gives us a new heart, a heart for the first time human, a heart for the first time, or is it the second time, made of flesh." (LB, 223)

Norman O. Brown instructs us that symbols are adult toys as well. What would be some experiences adults share that are symbolic ones? Like the young, we symbolize when we play. And we play when we love. Running and laughing, conversing and whispering, playing at games and playing at making love, we are involved in symbolizing. The experience of love is a symbolic—not a possessive or literal—experience. An experience that I am not just I; I am also you. And you are not just you. But also I. This is symbolism. And to see one person die for another (and people do, you know; parents have been seen to die for their children and a soldier for his buddy) is to see a truly symbolic, a truly loving act. "No greater love has a man than this—to lay down his life for his friend." Jesus knew the symbolism of which he spoke. And acted.

A symbol is not manufactured and not controllable nor oriented toward control. Neither is it external but internal. It comes from within our deepest selves, unlike the literal (such as the cleansing of a dish or the giving of money) which can be merely external.

The end product of literal thinking is signs. The end product of symbolic thinking and playing is more ecstasy. The literalist thinks in signs. The spiritual person in symbols. A sign is an object, a numberable, quantifiable, material object. Something outside of myself. The golden calf was a sign. A sign can, if it manipulates the soul or inner person, produce ecstasy but always of a perverse kind. Other signs we are more familiar with today are money and status ("Doctor this," "Professor that," "President this," etc.). Some signs, like some objects, are a necessary part of survival—stop signs or street signs, for example. Principalities and powers of literalism continually seduce us into looking for signs—signs of femininity and masculinity, signs of wealth and opulence, signs of sexual prowess, signs of achievement, signs of progress, signs of power, signs of piety, signs of justification (church going, for example). A nation of signs is a nation of thing-worshippers. We call this idolatry. For only materialism is communicable by sign. Once having communicated, signs manipulate, for they invite the soul to sell itself; that is, to whore with an object—like the nation Moses found on returning from the burning bush, God's symbol, on the mountain. Is there any distinction between a nation that whores after a golden calf and one that whores after a black Cadillac?

Symbol-people are different from sign-people. Like God is different from Baal. Like participation is different from possession. Like the experience of We is different from the experience of I. A symbol is not a sign: there is no status attached.   That is one reason why spiritual realities are eminently shareable. Signs and the realities they signify are not. They need to be hoarded and we all know it: my money cannot be your money; it is either mine or yours. Not both of ours at once. But my joy can be yours; and my music; and your painting can be mine; and your love; and your ideas. And your suffering. And, what is more, yours plus mine produces a third, a birth, a new reality. For a symbolic consciousness, one plus one does not equal two; one plus one equals three. A literal consciousness always exists as *one's* (isolated letters) or *two's* (comparisons). There is a divide and conquer strategy about literal consciousness ("you obey me"). If we allow ourselves to internalize such thinking, we become reduced to isolated *one's* or in competition in *two's;* and we are already divided and have lost our inner unity and integrity. A spiritual consciousness does not seek the neatness of *one's* and *two's* but the giving birth that *three's, four's, five's* are about. A literal consciousness asks: Do you live up to my norm? The symbolic asks: How can your uniqueness and others' uniquenesses give birth to still more uniqueness? It asks about extending ecstasy, not controlling it.

And this is the way God thinks. God thinks wholly, God thinks unity, not division, for all—not just a piece—of creation is present to the Creator. And present *now.* All, past and present and future, is present now to God. God's thinking does not insist that all is one and that there are no differences between things, only that the unity of things is more important than their diversity. This is symbolic thinking for "symbolism is mind making connections (correspondences) rather than distinctions (separations)." (LB, 81)

In spite of what Buick ads tell us—"something to believe in"—belief is never in a thing, not even in a Buick. Believing is learning to think on the same wavelengths as God. Thus, faith can never be about signs. Faith is a trusting thing, a giving of the self kind of thing, a rendering vulnerable kind of thing. Signs protect; behind the closed steel doors and rolled up windows and air-conditioned and stereoed environment of a Buick is the opposite of vulnerability. Signs secure and offer security. Symbols endanger us all. Risk, vulnerability, crucifixion awaits all symbolizers.

People who are committed to signs (and each of us is potentially such a person) will project this commitment onto others, even onto symbol-people. And this projection logically ends in death. So Jesus came into Jerusalem for the last time, riding a donkey—a symbol of Messiahship and of simplicity. And the crowds cheered and welcomed the symbol (or was it a sign to them) that day; but before the week was out the same crowds shouted, "Crucify him! Crucify him!" The tendency to reduce a symbol to a sign is as perverse as reducing God to oursleves; the alive to the dead. It is making God over into our image and likeness. It is refusing to receive—the only unpardonable sin. A practical and somewhat threatening application of this section on signs and symbols is the following: Do parents see their children as signs? Or as symbols? And are children able to see their parents as signs or as symbols? (Here was clearly Jesus' contribution to the issue.) In answering these and similar questions, we would be uncovering many familial frustrations.

How pitiful the sign-thinkers are. They can go through all of life never having participated with self, with others, with creation, with God. What is a life without participation? Without ecstasy? To spend one's life making a sign of God or a god of a sign: what a forlorn existence that is! What is worth replacing the everyday ecstasies of God in simple events—the seas and the storms, babies and old people, blades of grass and tears of orphans? Certainly not signs.

While I have spoken out clearly in favor of a symbolic over a sign-consciousness, I want to caution the reader that I am not saying that there is no room for sign-thinking at all in our lives. I would want the pilot of a plane I was flying to have a well-developed sign-consciousness, similarly, the bank that balances my checking account. What I am saying is that ours is a culture swamped in sign-consciousness at the expense of symbol-consciousness; and that, of the two modes of thinking and acting, the symbolic alone is deep and spontaneous enough to be called spiritual activity.

To learn the difference between the way God thinks and plays and the way literal people (as distinct from God-like or symbolic people) think, reflect on the following list of contrasts.[1]

Literal Thinking	Symbolic Playing and Thought
isolates one thing	unifies many experiences
manufactured	spontaneous
control	play
protects	endangers
external	internal
kills	gives life, resurrects
controllable	tends to extremism
produces signs	produces more and more ecstasies
about things	about people and their ecstasies
language for problem solving	language for mystery experience
superficial	radical (meaning "root")
a piecemeal consciousness	a cosmic consciousness
exactness of precision counts	insight and creativity count
$1 + 1 = 2$	$1 + 1 = 3$ (or more)
the way some men think	the way God thinks

Which way of thinking shall we choose to travel? The way of literalism? Or the way of symbolism? Theologically speaking, the way of literalism is the way of idolatry. The sin of idolatry is an adverb—it is looking at the gifts of life literally instead of symbolically. In contrast, the graced-life is one of symbolic consciousness. Instead of clinging to objects, things, and idols, the graced person learns ever more deeply from ecstatic experiences that she is a symbol. One of God's toys or play things. A symbol of God—the Logos, the Temple, the child of God dancing unendingly before a Creator of symbols. That is, of us. For those who are true to their ecstasies, there can be only one way, the way of symbolic thinking that God plays at. God who is not one but three; not three but one; but . . . but . . . but . . .

CHAPTER 8

Acting Symbolically:
God and ourselves as extremists—
how spiritual voyagers
stretch their souls to be God-like
and in the process appear to be
"extremists"

The Creator is surely an extremist. What else can we conclude from looking at her handiwork? The vastness of the mountains and the sea; the puniness of the amoeba and the ant and the atom. The beauty of a sunset and an act of love; the ugliness of children dying and evil triumphing. We would like so much to teach God how to re-create the universe—one without ugliness, without pain. A one-sided universe. A sheltered universe. Like ourselves. No extremes. Only a middle. Only conformity; mediocrity. No surpises. No mountains and valleys, only plains; no oceans—only swimming pools. After our own image.

But those who experience God know with certitude (Aquinas maintains that such intuitions cannot be in error—a 'first principle' of our spiritual lives, he says) that we are made to be like God, not God like us. That our becoming like God means just that—our changing from human to divine-like. That God is an extremist is evident not only from what is created but from the fact of creation at all. Why is there something and not nothing? Must it not be intuited as an act of outpouring so great that all the water pouring over Niagara Falls is only a drop in comparison? God pouring herself/himself out all of himself, the heights and the depths, the deserts and the oceans of himself, into existence. "Love diffuses itself."

An overflow—an extreme case of love—seems the most real explanation for there being creation at all.

God is an extremist and has symbolized us after her own image so that he can charge us with the following heavy counsel: "I would that you were hot or cold but because you are neither I shall vomit you out of my mouth." "Hot or cold." Is the human race hot and cold—or is it something closer to lukewarm? Does our race seem burdened with a certain gravity towards mediocrity, a flight from spiritual depths of hot and cold, high and low, bigness and smallness? Our race seems so much more at home (or imagine we are) in our own man-made images of our feelings and actions. Yet the prayers we utter (perhaps never knowing their sense) could remind us of our more divine leanings. Such as, "Your will be done on earth as it is in heaven." Earth and heaven: the extremes of it. And then there is hell too. We have all visited hell. The place of the damned, the dead, the condemned (self-condemned, that is), the unloving and uncaring, the powerful and controlling spirits, the reign of Satan and evil, of killing and stench. Why flee from hell? Or from heaven, for that matter? "No tree can grow to heaven," warns C. J. Jung, "unless its roots reach down to hell."[1] Did not Dante instruct us that a voyage through hell must precede a tour of heaven like darkness before light; death before rebirth; pain before pleasure. "Love," says one psychiatrist, "that has never faced the demonic is stale and flat and submissive and self-righteous."[2]

Do we find our lives stale, flat, submissive or self-righteous? Perhaps we have never touched the hot and cold of love. The ecstasy of beauty *and* the unforgettable pain. Perfection *and* injustice. The Yes *and* the No. The Father *and* the Son. The mysticism *and* the prophecy. To care *and* not to care. To remember *and* to forget; to love *and* to hate; to despair *and* to hope; summer *and* winter; ecstasy *and* the void; fullness *and* emptiness; justice *and* mercy;

treble *and* bass; male *and* female; talk *and* silence; life *and* death.

What we need to avoid is not the extremes but the limiting of ourselves to only one extreme and neglecting its contrary. "All emotions are pure which gather you and lift you up; that emotion is impure which seizes only *one* side of your being and so distorts you." (Rilke, 74) The remedy to fanaticism, which is one-sidedness, is not to play only the middle (where mediocrity is born) but to risk touching other extremes of creation as well. One does not stay alive and develop into a true symbol of the Creator by loving one facet of creation less but by loving others as much. Gore Vidal laments how rarely a television-bred generation appears capable of comprehending "the doubleness of things, the unexpected paradox, the sense of yes-no without which there can be no true intelligence, no means, in fact, of examining life as opposed to letting it wash over one."[3] To be spiritual is to stretch oneself. "Stretch yourself, then to the breaking point. . . . To be stretched is to be crucified; it is the crucified body that is the measure of all things." (LB, 187. cf. Fox, 73-6, 153-6)

Religions that endure are about extremes, as Wilfrid Sheed confesses when talking of his Catholic upbringing. Catholics he insists "were raised on extremes, real flesh in the host and a real God in heaven; we had beliefs and not opinions."[4] Would not a belief that creation is a gift, that pleasure is of the essence of being spiritual, that the fruits of the earth belong to all its inhabitants, that God is present in people and that is heaven, and that eternal life is now also be a spirituality that is based on "beliefs and not opinions"? A spirituality of extremes.

A spirituality of ecstasies is also a spirituality of encountering the void. The void and ecstasies go together for they are like convex and concave—one experience with two sides. The person big enough to seek a spirituality of ecstasy is also going to be plunged into the void. Presence with absence. Mountains with valleys. Fullness with emptiness.

Being spiritual is about being an extremist- like God is—but is not about being a one-sided extremist. Rather, it is about stretching oneself in several directions, as God does. As Pascal observed, "a man does not reveal his greatness by being at one extremity but rather by touching both at once." A fanatic extremism is really another show of literalism for it is man-made and man-controlled. But a divine extremism is always of a receptive, receiving kind. One stays faithful to the deep-rooted faith in life as a gift of which we are recipients. The stretching of our heart, souls, and bodies that is required of us in spiritual experience is a divine stretching. If our souls are not stretched how will God enter to dwell there? We are involved in a spiritual muscle-building complete with the cramps and pains and rationalizations for ceasing that come with any challenging workout. And the most lethal rationalization of all is security.

Our God is not secure but free. Not predictable but surprising. Absent one day; present overwhelmingly another. A void and an ecstacy. So in becoming like that God, we too become stretched in many directions at once. We learn to welcome it. It is good for the soul. It is being true to our spiritual memories and ecstasy. It is ourselves become ecstasies.

The journey from literal thinking to symbolic playing, the development of God-consciousness, is a journey for extremists. Every spiritual leader has been labeled an extremist and with good reason, touched as they are with divine madness. They are women and men who dream dreams and entertain visions. For them, imagination is more sacred than regulation, as Ezra Pound puts it: "The greatest charity is to be found among those who have not observed regulations." Prophets of old were well developed in their symbolic consciousness. Whether running about the city naked (streaking, as we would call it today) or sitting on human feces or burning draft records with napalm, they were uttering a word that was repressed and forgotten in a culture that had gone literalist. The whoring after a golden calf was a whoring after a literal (i.e., material) object. The prophet had to "root up and destroy" in order to "build and plant" (Jeremias). And Jesus. How keenly developed was his symbolic consciousness? How much like God's thinking was his own? Hear him out on the most familiar of our experiences. First, on our parents. Everyone has parents; and we all know what a parent is. We can point to them, go home to them, recall their memory. Isn't that right? No, according to the symbolic insight of Jesus. "Call no one your father but your Father in heaven." "I must be about my father's business." "Pray after me" 'Our Father who art in heaven.' "

What is this man saying? Is God so powerfully symbolic that he is to take over from my own father? Yes, says Jesus "For if a man does not leave father and mother, brothers and sisters and lands for my sake, he is not worthy of me."

Well, at least the mother is sacred. Secure. As we know her. We all know, after all, how "devoted" Jesus was to his mother. At least our devotional literature has taught us so. Jesus speaks. "And one said to him, 'Behold, your mother and your brothers stand outside, desiring to speak with you.' But he answered and said, 'Who is my mother? And who are my brethren?' And he stretched forth his hand toward his disciples and said, 'Behold my mother and my brethren.' " (Mt 12. 47-50) But we all know, it is a *literal* truth, that our mother is the one who bore us in her womb. Not really, insists Jesus. A woman cried, "Blessed are the breasts that nursed you and the womb that bore you!" No, said Jesus. "Blessed are those who hear the word of God and keep it." Is Jesus doing away with parenthood? Almost, for he is seeing it symbolically (always, we recall, a tearing down and building up process). "Amen, amen, I say to you, 'unless a man be born again, he cannot see the kingdom of God." (Jn 2.3f; 3.3) We have, then, many mothers; many more births; many more fathers and many more deaths than we have ever dreamed of. (Or, to be more precise, as many as we have dreamed of. As many as we have ecstasies, periods of rebirth.)

Let us look at the medieval mystic again. This time to Francis of Assisi. Let us listen to his song on his brothers and sisters. "Thank you, mi signore, for mister brother sun, in especial, who is your symbol; and for sister moon and the stars; and for brother wind and air and sky; and for sister water; and for brother fire; and for mother earth! .... with all our hearts we thank you for sister our mother Earth and its fruits and coloured flowers!" On his deathbed he added a thank you for "Sister Death." Has there ever been a saint who did not breathe with a symbolic consciousness? Of course not. (Cf. Pope John: "I am Joseph, your brother.") Because there has never been a person who experienced God who did not thereby take on the symbolic consciousness which is like God's.

A parable is a story, often an acted-out story. Like any symbolic expression, it is ambiguous to the literal minded. A parable arrests "the hearer by its vividness or strangeness, and leaves the mind in sufficient doubt about its precise application to tease it into active thought."[5] People who think symbolically leave stories behind for others to think symbolically wherever they go. Take Francis, for example. A spiritual brother to Francis sought a psalter of his own. Francis replied: "After you have got the psalter, you will covet and want a breviary; and after getting the breviary, you will sit on your throne like a bishop, (sic) (notice the political consciousness implied in a saint's symbolic consciousness such as Francis') and will say to your brother: "Bring me the breviary!'" Then Francis did a symbolic thing—he acted out a parable. "While saying this," the story goes on, "Francis, with great vehemence, took up a handful of ashes and spread it over his head; and moving his hand about his head in a circle as though washing it, said: 'I, breviary! I, breviary! and so kept on, repeatedly moving his hand about his head: and stupefied and ashamed was that novice."

"I, breviary," shouts Francis. Foolish? Like God is. Is this any more symbolic than his master's statement about the one thing (if not our parents) we are sure is what it is: bread and wine. Saying, "This bread is my body." "This wine is my blood." What kind of talk is this? Is this symbolic mentality to destroy parenthood and food and drink—all we hold sure and possess so totally?

Jesus, too, is a compulsive parable teller. About the plants and the fields; about seeds and about the rain; about fishermen and fishes; about kings; about virgins on their wedding night; about parties and robbers and spendthrifts and playboys. Always *this* stands for more than this. Why does he burden the imaginations of his hearers so? Why does he pour out story upon story upon them? Why so disturb them? Does he not know that the literalists "might go away confused" and plot literal thoughts like that of a predetermined trial and condemnation? And death? Why does he keep stirring up trouble and life with his symbols? Why not let matters lie. And die. And lie.

Jesus is himself a parable. "I am the truth," said Jesus, but "truth is not in safety or in the middle." (LB, 184) Jesus' death proved how right he was. Each of us is a parable of God. A parable we act out to the extent that we take on the God-like process of thinking symbolically. The parable is the opposite of repression. No wonder the repressors must kill the storyteller. For repression covers instead of uncovering. As Jesus explained, "The reason I talk to them in parables is that they look without seeing and listen without hearing or understanding." To look *and* see; to listen *and* understand—the reason for symbolic stories.

With symbols you lose your self-worth. You die into a

symbol with the hope of rising again. As Jesus lost himself to say, "Bread is my body; wine my blood." As a musician spends himself on her notes, the painter on his colors, the dancer on her muscles. Everyone with symbolic consciousness loses himself—as did the Creator in her creation. And so, we hear Jesus saying, "Lord, when did we see you hungry and feed you; or thirsty and give you drink? When did we see you a stranger and make you welcome; naked and clothe you; sick or in prison and go to see you?" And the King will answer, "I tell you solemnly, in so far as you did this to one of the least of these brothers of mine, you did it to me . . . in so far as you neglected to do this to one of the least of these, you neglected to do it to me." (Mt. 25.35,46) Significantly, this heightened level of symbolic consciousness that Jesus reached comes, in Matthew's account, as the last parable he uttered before his arrest and murder. Every hungry and homeless and sick and thirsty person becomes Jesus. Jesus is lost. He is nowhere to be found yet he claims he is everywhere. Is he mad? Or just forgotten.

And each of us. Is each of us lost? Is the "I" of us, like the "I" of Jesus, also lost? Lost in the persons of the hungry and homeless and sick and lonely? Have we made the spiritual journey Jesus and Francis and the prophets of the Israelis did—*the journey from I to we?* If materialism and literal thinking has us concentrate on a piece, surely the most powerful temptation we are subjected to is to substitute the piece called "me" for the whole called "us." We need to rise from "I" to "We"; we need to plant the "I" in order to grow the "We," and the fruit will be God-consciousness which is symbolic consciousness. The seed is the I; the plant is the We. "The resurrection of the body . . . but the body of mankind as one body." (LB 83) All symbolism is a baptism into such a unifying way of seeing reality—"the unconscious is collective . . . symbolism reconstitutes the lost (hidden) unity." (LB 210) And who knows, besides God, the limits to such spiritual expansion of our minds, hearts and bodies? "Symbolic consciousness is cosmic consciousness. ... This is my body." (212)

Passing from an I-consciousness to a We-consciousness means making the most spiritual and awesome of journeys. For it means our re-experiencing pain—not our pains, but others' pains (which become ours). It means joining that fraternity that Albert Schweitzer spoke of, the "brotherhood of those who bear the mark of pain." Pain, like any symbol, is shareable. Surely this is why literalists run from it; want to isolate pain and its sister, death. But where the spiritual walk and work and live, there is pain shared. "I have come to heal the sick," said Jesus. The sharing of the brotherhood and sisterhood of pain is a certain fruit of one's experience of God. It is becoming like God, like a God who suffers when we do; a God who dares say, "I was hungry and you fed me; in prison and you visited me; homeless and you took me in." Like other symbols, pain is not manipulatable. It is respected. And pain is everyone's—especially every spiritual voyager's, as Hesse comments: "Despair is the result of each earnest attempt to go through life with virtue, justice and understanding and to fulfill their requirements." (Hesse, *Journey*, 106)

Our ecstasy and passion culminate in compassion. We learn to suffer with others by first celebrating with them. The political, like the sensual, is collective. It is for the many, not just one. The end of ego-tripping. Indeed, "to hate" in the New Testament means to lack compassion. (M, 128) And to experience God is ultimately not to swoon in mystical ecstasies but to share the Creator's joys as the prophet Jeremiah insisted. "To know Yahweh is to do justice."

While I have spoken at length of ego loss and burial of the I for the We, I do not want to leave my reader with any false impression that such an ego loss absolutely excludes all ego development. Just as there is a child in the aware adult, so is there an adolescent and ego in the adult.

I stand against all ego loss as strongly as I stand against all loss of childlikeness in adults. Indeed, it takes a well-developed ego to be able to effectively lose one's ego for the service of others (compassion) and not merely out of mushy feelings for others (sentiment). I am saying, however, that the goal of adolescent ego development is to lose the ego ecstatically and compassionately in adulthood. Not totally and all the time, but more often than we do.

Our capacity to symbolize is our capacity to become like God, to think as God thinks. This means putting We ahead of I. Such as in *"Our* Father" which sees God not only as *the* father but, what is equally symbolic and disturbing, the father of all of us, not of one of us. Such thinking is truly public thinking. It is political in the full and truest sense. For it is symbolic and the spirit gives life. We ask to give *us our* daily bread—not a particular class of people or a ruling caste or an elite. But us. And symbolic thinking asks that *we* might be forgiven *our*—that is, our collective or public or political—sins. Especially the sins of thinking literally and dividing the earth's resources, which are everyone's, in a literal way; i.e., according to the highest bidders with signs of power and money and influence. We call this symbolic acting, distribution by the We instead of the I, 'justice.' And spiritual, symbolic persons know it by its name. "As a man," said Pablo Casals, "I seek justice. As an artist, perfection." And one might add: "As one who becomes like God, I seek justice and perfection."

But the God of justice is an extremist. "That all might be one"—what kind of common sense thinking is that? Who would dare to act so ... symbolically, so ... fanatically?

CHAPTER 9
God as a panentheistic God and ourselves in that image

Question: Where is God?
Answer: God is everywhere. (from the *Baltimore Catechism*)

An intellectual monotheism has erected a God that only philosophers and academicians can understand or worship; some churches have erected a monotheistic God that only churchmen and loyal subjects can listen to and obey. Monotheism has become a weapon for keeping people away from the experience of the everywhere God. For God is, simply, everywhere. As is the experience of God, as we have seen. God is truly Emmanuel, God-with-us. Monotheism is to God what a trunk is to a tree. We deceive ourselves if we imagine that the tree is that trunk or that the trunk, being the most visible element of the tree, is therefore the most vital. The tree is nothing (in fact, it can even be dead and trunk-watchers would never know it) without the diversity of its roots. The roots of a tree literally go everywhere. They are the life-blood of the tree.

So God too is diverse. In many directions. Attuned to the Buddhist here, the Jew there, the Christian here, the baby there. All are bathed in God. And to believe this is to be a panentheist (which means, literally, "all is in God or God is in all"). There is nothing heretical about being a panentheist.[1] Indeed, it is heretical not to be one. Yet, how seldom our monolithic institutions of academia or churchliness want to encourage any of us to experience a God that is any different from themselves. Making even God into their own image, they are piously drawn to a monotheistic, monolithic God. But such a God lacks symbolism. It is literal. It is no trinity at all. For God is not a single God, but a multiple one—or so says the Trinitarian belief. The latest effort at such manipulation of the multifaceted God is a person hang-up, where we are all to sit around and imagine God as some "overbig" person. Such a watering down of God's transcendence is happening everywhere because the psychology of person and personhood is so all-pervasive a fad (Laing calls it our modern "heresy," this search for identity). Thus, when we cling to the concept of God as person, we are encouraging this detranscendence of God. In fact, Jewish and Christian Scriptures declare that "God is Spirit," not person. It was with a metaphysical tradition of personhood in fourth century Greek theology that calling God analogously "person" took on some meaning. But we today, few of whom are metaphysicians of that tradition, would be better off dropping the notion of the personhood of God and finding a deeper understanding. For example, that God is in many persons and through many and through all the personal experiences of ecstasy that there are (and are not yet).

Not only is God everywhere to us like water to a fish, but also God is nowhere. Not here. Nonperson. The void. The distance. The silence. The pain. Jesus is said to have "linked man with nature in one order where each level could be illuminated from another, and God was to be traced in all. At every level man meets his Creator, the Lord of heaven and earth, supreme in goodness and power."[2] Such is the "God in whom we live, move and have our being." (Acts 17.28) "One God, Father of all, who is above all, and through all, and in you all" (Eph. 4.6), a God who is "all in all." (1 Cor. 15.28)

To emphasize God as panentheistic and play down God as person is not to deny the personal interest of this God in his/her people. We can celebrate a personal panentheistic God without falling into the psychologizing of God as a person.

How does panentheism affect our personalities? By
demanding more of our powers of awareness. By seeing
more than the trunk when one looks at a tree. By seeing
God in a grain of sand; and in a towering mountain; and in
a crippled old man; and in an act of love; and in a tragic
happening. To see God and, moreover, to experience God
everywhere is truly to believe that God exists—not as a
monolithic object "exists," such as the Empire State
Building, but as the living live and breathe and move and
suffer and dance and rest. It is to believe in a living God, a
God living everywhere. And the believing is the experiencing, the trusting of our experiencing of God. Becoming a
panentheistic people means experiencing God everywhere.

Another demanding feature to our experiencing a
panentheistic God is the democracy of it all. A God who is
everywhere is everybody's. A truly democratic God.
Available to the least as well as the greatest. Are we
practiced enough in democracy to know what such a God
wants of us? The God of panentheism, the everywhere
God, is not a God of power-control: a sort of commander-
in-chief of the universe's ecstasies. That is a description of
a monolithic God. No, a panentheistic God has shared the
fun, the ecstasy, the joy, and the pains and has shared
them not only with other powers (which would mean
divinity by conglomerates, a sort of godly fascism), such as
churchmen and editors of great newspapers and wealthy
business leaders and army chiefs—the God of panentheism
has shared the divinity with the littlest among us. That is
spiritual democracy. And to internalize it (make it our
own), to reflect on it, and to live with it, learning to
breathe the truth of it—this will make new people of us. A
people truly rooted in the spiritual attitude of sharing. Of
democracy. Of becoming like God. Of appreciating the We
over preserving the I.

It will render us, as it renders our God, terribly fragile
and vulnerable. So available that our time might not even
be our own. So insecure, so trusting. It might make

crucifixion a real possibility in our lives instead of an object for romantic or nostalgic longing. It will make us enemies (yes, real enemies)—powers and principalities bent on instructing us in the experience of hate and hell. For our God, too, has enemies and real ones, steeped in power and armed with powerful opinions of their own worth. "Do you not know that I have power over life and death?" warned Pilate to Jesus at his trial.

But one's awareness and one's community built on democracy will sustain a believer— "do not be afraid of those who can wreck only the body." Witness to a panentheistic God is an aware, a democratic and a vulnerable and fragile witness. As a flower is, or a baby, or a butterfly. Or anything or anybody that truly lives and thrives on receiving rather than controlling life. And if the present time clouds and does not reveal the truth of our panentheistic experience, the end time will at least uncover a God who is in all and cherishes all in himself with a sureness that the world, and all of its pieces, is ultimately a manifestation of God.

CHAPTER 10
God as artist, not master:
how God shares the creating so that
we are not creatures under God
but fellow creators with God

We call God Creator. We call ourselves made in that image. The Maidu Indians of California put the equation this way.

Earth Namer took some red-colored dirt. He mixed it with water. Very carefully, he shaped a man and a woman.

First Man and First Woman were very beautiful. But their hands were not finished.

"How shall I make their hands?" asked Earth Namer.

"Make their hands like mine so they can swim," said Turtle.

"Make their hands like mine so they can run fast," said Coyote. Earth Namer thought and thought.

"No, they must have hands like mine. They must have fingers so that they can make things," said Earth Namer.

Earth Namer made the hands of First Man and First Woman to look like his own.

Then First Man and First Woman were even more beautiful. They could do many things the animals could not do.[1]

How accurate this picture is of an inventive act: the artist seeking advice, weighing a variety of possible routes, and, finally, deciding on creating after his own image, his own dream. The Earth Namer's creations are his toys, his symbols. We are God's toys, fashioned after his own fantasies and playfulness and formed into that same likeness. Bearers of the Creator's stamp, ourselves destined to be co-creators. Not creators set apart and distant from the creator, but creators with the Creator. Like father, like son. As the poet Rilke suggests when thinking on God, "what keeps you from projecting his (God's) birth into times that are in process of becoming, and living your life like a painful and beautiful day in the history of a great gestation? For do you not see how everything that happens keeps on being a beginning, and could it not be *His* beginning, since beginning is in itself always so beautiful?" (49)

A creator is always a beginner. The bearer of beginnings. A child; a marriage; a painting; a poem; a story; a tale to tell; a meal; a social movement; a hospital; a business; a garden; a cabinet; a mechanical invention; a world; a universe. Beginners all. Creators all.

In contrast to a creator, a creature is merely a servant, a slave, a Yes-man, an obeyer of persons and not of creativity. "I no longer call you servants but friends." Co-creators made over into the image of their Creator with "hands and fingers so they can make things," like the Earth Namer himself. Creatures are easily manipulated by creator-less persons, persons who want to control rather than undergo the pains of giving birth. The fruit of an experience of God will always be the need and the willingness to create.

God the Creator. As artist, she painted the painted desert, the shades of the sea which change with each day, the pastels of the sunset, the black of a stormy night, the silver of a clearly seen Milky Way, the red of blood, the green of the earth, the yellow of grain in ripe fields, the blue of a French Impressionist sky. As musician, she composed the whistles of rustling trees, the hollering of a wind in winter, the choruses of the birds, the chattering of wee animals, the silence of space, the typanum of the heartbeat, the symphony of bird and breeze and sea orchestrated together, the opera of human cries and shouts and promises whispered in dark nights. "Is the inventor of the ear unable to hear? The creator of the eye unable to see?" (Ps. 94.9) God the poet has written straight with crooked lines, making persons of words instead of words of persons, calling to be poets in action the humblest and the lowliest. From Abraham to Moses, Mary of Nazareth to Mozart, Francis of Assisi to Buddha, Gustav Mahler to Martin Luther King, Martin Luther to Malcolm X, Joan of Arc to Mother Teresa, and all the beautiful people, God's poetic words, whom we know but do not read about.

God is also, and in a special way from humankind's perspective, a potter. This is evident not only in the Maidu Indian story of events but also in the Jewish mentality. "The Lord God formed (the verb *yásar* is the technical verb for the action of a potter) man from the clay *(áfār)* of the ground." (Gen.2.7) Isaiah repeats the picture of God the potter who threw humankind, the pot; man is one of "the potsherds (made of clay) of the ground." (Is. 45.9) Pessimists urged on by a negative spirituality want to drive into persons' heads that "dust they art and dust they shall return." But, in fact, we are not dust but clay: sometimes of a dry kind (cf. Job 10.9), but, primarily, we are the creative results of a creative potter who is the Creator.

It is this grace in responding to the Creator's artistry that characterizes the non-Puritan spirituality of American Protestants like Edwards, Emerson, and James, according to one scholar. "In America, esthetic spirituality involved not so much the appreciation of beauty attributed to or inhering in objects of artistic creation but rather a consciousness of the beauty of living in harmony with divine things—in a word, being at home in the universe."[2]

To become God-like is to become like this creator, this artist of the universe and of the atom. Like every other creator, we learn awareness. We see *and* perceive. Thus, Henry Moore in his "Notes on Sculpture" talks of that frequently inherited malady, form-blindness. "More people are form-blind than color-blind," he insists. While many persons comprehend flat form, few "make the further intellectual and emotional effort needed to comprehend form in its full spatial existence." Enter the artist we call sculptor. "This is what the sculptor must do. He must strive continually to think of, and use form in its full spatial completeness." He teaches us "to feel shape simply as shape, not as description or reminiscence. He must, for example, perceive an egg as a simple single solid shape, quite apart from its significance as food, or from the literary idea that it will become a bird." (CP, 73f.) As creators, we are ever seeking awareness, growing into the multiple dimensions of seeing, hearing, touching —and, therefore, of being seen, listened to and touched in an infinite variety, a kaleidescopic variety of ways.

If you have ever lived with an artist, you know how "differently" they perceive the world about them. Different only because more sensitively, more vulnerably. It is like living with a sensitive plant. You cannot hide your moods and negative vibrations from such a plant. A plant seeks truth and responds to it alone. Nor from the keenly tuned apparatuses of an artist for whom every vibration bears the thought or message of God. God is everywhere to the artist: true panentheism. Less and less escapes the artist. More and more is allowed to enter. The artist fills up with creation before he can properly express it. So that, like a primitive instinct, the creation must burst forth in self-expression, refusing to contain itself; the artist cannot not create. He is too full. Must empty himself. Like the Creator did. And does.

An artist is a child, a player with symbols, his toys. The musician playing with notes and chords, harmonies and counterpoints; the painter playing with colors and the impressions they leave; the actor playing with roles and life-size themes and persons to portray; the chef playing with foods and combinations of them—children all, playful playmates. The artist is ever changing, ever seeking, ever stretching, ever eager to learn and be told of new ecstasies that exist for his enjoyment. Discover, be spontaneous, shed self-consciousness: this is the beckoning of Creator to creator, of every artist to himself. "Writing, like life itself, is a voyage of discovery," observes Henry Miller about his craft and his gamey livelihood. A wanderer, the artist is. From subject to subject, color to color, note to note, word to word: has he no stability? Take the storyteller, for example. "The storyteller makes many a station, roving and relating, but pauses only tentwise, awaiting further direction, and soon feels his heart beating high, partly with desire, partly too from fear and anguish of the flesh, but in any case as a sign that he must take the road, towards fresh adventures that are painstakingly to be lived through, down to their remotest details, according to the restless spirit's will." (Thomas Mann in CP, 18) It almost sounds like Jesus, doesn't it ("the Son of Man has no place to lay his head")? This wandering, this anguish of flesh and spirit ("the spirit is willing but the flesh is weak"), his painstaking paths ("I must go to Jerusalem and there the Son of Man will be put to death"), and the restless spirit's will ("Into your hand I commend my spirit"). But not only Jesus; Buddha too was a wanderer; and Francis; and Mohammed; and Moses and the whole tribe of Israel.

There is no distinction between the artist and the person who has experienced God. No experiencer of God is not an artist. Every artist is, in James Joyce's words, "a priest of the imagination." But, if the imagination is the playhouse of God, as we discussed earlier in this book of meditations, then there is no real priest who is not also creative. A priest who is not an artist is no priest at all. Here indeed is the fullest sense of a "lay priesthood"—in our artists.

Wandering fills one with respect and respect gives birth to reverence. Why does wandering with awareness engender respect? Because respect is the opposite of control; manipulation; invasion of freedom and privacy. Perhaps we have lost reverence in the West because we have forgotten wandering. Jetting over oceans and continents is not wandering. Speed and the control and conquest of space is not wandering. It is just more control. But the artist in us wanders, if only with an eye, a thought in the imagination, an ear, a hand, a fantasy, a foot. And in this way, the artist experiences reverence not as a command to be obeyed but as a desire to fulfill. This reverence extends to one's own creation, to the creations of others and to God's creation. And from this reverence faithfulness is born.

Stephen Spender speaks of the faithfulness of the poet. "I have always felt that a poet's was a sacred vocation, like a saint's ... for the saint renounces ambition ... In poetry, even the greatest labor can only serve to reveal the intrinsic qualities of soul of the poet as he really is. Since there can be no cheating, the poet, like the saint, stands in all his works before the bar of a perpetual day of judgment ... ultimately judgment does not rest with oneself. All one can do is to achieve nakedness ... and then to stand before the judgment of time." (in CP. 122f.) Such a description applies to any creator, any artist, any of us.

The creator who shares the Creator's life, divine life, shares also the Creator's desire to symbolize. But to symbolize from the experience of one mind and one heart—from the one image and likeness into which creation is made: the creator is everywhere but in one place only. Like God, a panentheistic creator. "Art is a form of supremely delicate awareness and atonement—meaning atoneness, the state of being at one with the object." (D. H. Lawrence, CP, 71) Art becomes an "integration to the whole cosmic process" (Henry Miller). A cosmic, a God-like consciousness is common to all whose souls have been stretched by the experience of a panentheistic God. For we are touching God when touching all that is of God and bathed in God. "The divine isn't only good, it is all things." (D. H. Lawrence)

We conclude that our process of becoming like God is one of becoming creative. Everyone may not be an artist, literally speaking; but we are all creators or potentially such. To realize our creativity is to recover our spiritual sense for democracy, for the omnipresence of God, for expansion of God's creation in time and in space. A time that begins with forgotten time-ecstasy—in a space that is ecstatic space—our inner experience. And this is, as the Earth Namer says, what makes God delight: sharing the fun of creating.

PART III
Obstacles
(Small and Large Dragons)
to Experiencing Ecstasy
and the God of Ecstasy:
WEE

In the town of Selina, in a deep lake as large as an ocean, there dwelt a horrible dragon, who many times had put to flight the men who came armed against him, and who was wont to prowl about the city walls, poisoning all who came within the reach of his breath. In order to appease the monster, and to keep him from destroying the whole town, the burgesses had been offering him ... one sheep and one human being. The name of a youth or a maiden was drawn in a lottery, and no family was exempt from this lottery. And the day that Saint George reached the city, well-nigh all the young folk of the town had already been eaten up, and the lot for that day had fallen upon the only daughter of the king.

Saint George, passing that way, saw her all in tears, and asked her the cause of her trouble. And she replied: 'Good youth, get to horse and away with all speed, lest thou die the same death that awaits me!' 'Fear not, my child,' answered Saint George, 'but tell me wherefore thou weepest ....'

While they were in speech, the dragon reared his head out of the lake. All atremble, the maiden cried: 'Away, sweet lord, away with all speed!' But George, mounting his horse and arming himself with the sign of the cross, set bravely upon the dragon as he came toward him; and with a prayer to God he brandished his sword, and dealt the monster a hurt that threw him to the ground. And the saint said to the damsel: 'Fear naught, my child, and throw thy girdle about the dragon's neck!' Thus she did, and the dragon, setting himself erect, followed her like a little dog on a leash.

But when the people of the city saw him drawing near, they fled in panic up to the hills and into the caves, certain that they were all about to be devoured .... And Saint George, drawing his sword, slew the dragon, who was carried out of the city upon a cart drawn by four yoke of oxen. And the king caused a great church to be built in honour of the Blessed Virgin and Saint George, and from within there flowed a spring whose waters cured all languors. And the king offered a very large sum of money to Saint George; but he, taking nothing for himself, gave all to the poor.

From *The Golden Legand* by Jacobus de Voragine, O.P. (13th century)[1]

How does one fight a dragon? First, we must learn to recognize dragons when we experience them: some will be small, others large. Then too, not every dragon need be an enemy for life; some can be tamed to "follow like a little dog on a leash." These and other serious matters will be dealt with in the next five chapters.

CHAPTER 11
Some species of small but insidious, unfriendly dragons, such as bloated egos, exaggerated he's and she's, and moralizing, that lurk to devour us along our spiritual journey

A mong the most sinister and dangerous of dragons (though it is small, not giant in size) is the one that seduces spiritual travelers by proclaiming the ego. "Your ecstasy," so this dragon's con-game goes, "is this ego trip that I will offer you" (always at reduced and bargain basement prices). We all know what an ego trip is. We have made them; we watch others make them. It is I-consciousness asserting itself. When the goal of a trip is to inflate the I (ego); when the test of the success of the trip is deeper and deeper strokes for the I (e.g., fame, publicity, acknowledgment of the self by others); when the means used are I-inflating: that is an ego trip.

The dragon called "the ego" seduces the spiritual voyager by offering ersatz ecstasy, like crowds waving or stock reports bulging, when all the while one's roots fasten deeper and deeper about a narcissistic concern with one's own image and identity and self-worth. If people can become convinced that living is about inflating their egos, they are as trapped into nonexperience of ecstasy as a miner in quicksand. All becomes reduced to and controlled by their own egos; there is no more room for ecstatic experiences. It is so very easy to sell one's soul to the ego dragon. By buying your ego, he has already convinced you to sell your soul.

Inflated egos invariably get their highs and forms of ecstasy (however perverted) from talking about themselves, usually in forms of chatter we call bragging. What sort of bragging does one hear at conventions or business-men's graduations or ego-oriented parties? Among the male sex, usually it centers around the conquest of "broads" (instead of sexual enjoyment) and the results of contests of competition whether physical or financial— never sports as excellence. "That Championship Season" sort of party. What we have in such instances, all too familiar and so often repreated, is a pseudo-ecstasy—a perversion of the ecstasies with which we began this meditation on God-experience. For once you know you can make love or win a game, then *what else counts?* This is the question with which the spiritual life begins; it is also where the ego dies.

True ecstasy is the very opposite of an ego trip—it is our forgetting ourselves, our losing something or at least risking the loss as St. George did in assisting the maiden. True ecstasy urges us to stand outside of ourselves, to let the ego go. Spiritual leaders of many ages and places testify to how sharply this ecstasy contrasts to the ersatz ecstasy that the ego dragon offers: "Anyone who wants to save his life (also: soul or person) will lose it; but anyone who loses his life (or soul or person) for my sake will find it. What, then, will a man gain if he wins the whole world and ruins his life? Or what has a man to offer in exchange for his life?" (Mt. 16. 25f.) Solzhenitsyn describes a ringleader of thieves he knew in prison—but the descrip-tion would apply as well to any power-hungry ego fearful of ecstasy who lurks among us: "His little eyes were exactly large enough to see all familiar objects and yet not take delight in the beauties of the world." (548) There lies an intimate connection between ego-tripping and lack of ecstasy.

Ego-bloating is the opposite of a We-consciousness. It is thinking not Us but Me; not We but I. It is literal thinking. It is even refusing to think You. It is an especially conspicuous dragon towards the ends of civilizations when everyone senses a loss in the air, and they scurry like mice for their share of the remaining pieces of the cheese. Thus did the musician Gustav Mahler comment as a young man on the decline of Austrian society in 1885: "Back to waiting upon their lordships! Those faces! Those bone-dry people! Every inch of their countenance bearing the marks of that self-tormenting egotism which makes all men wretched. Always I, I—never you, you my brother!"[2] When the powers-that-be sense their own demise, there is a scurrying to the ego. "Save the I!" becomes the chant. It is a flight from brotherhood; a flight from sharing, from the you; a flight from symbolic thinking and the We. And this, above all, is the death of the soul. For it is an attempt to control the soul; to call it one's own; to own and possess it, not to experience its birth and rebirths. So Brown warns us: "The soul that we can call our own is not a real one. The solution to the problem of identity is, get lost." (LB, 161)

A dragon that is just as insidious and all pervasive in his attempt to kill our souls and their experiences of ecstasy is the exaggerated He or She dragon. Such a dragon would convince us that our fragile egos can best be placated and made content by our playing out roles according to a sexually predetermined definition of how we should feel and act. Men don't cry or express emotion; women don't think logically or become engineers. When a soul succumbs to such simplistic stereotyping, it is already condemned to the nonexperience of God, for it is a divided and, therefore, a conquered soul. It is divided in the worst possible way: against itself. For the healthly soul, whether a man's, a woman's, or a culture's, is equally male and female, as Jung insisted: the Yin and the Yang; the animus and the anima; the male and the female; the sun and the moon—these elements of our psyches are meant to work together within each of us, not at odds. Let us line up some of their characteristics.

His	Hers
order	creativity
control	respect unique differences
aggressiveness	relaxing
logic	rejoicing
competition	intuition
giving	receiving
reason	feeling
logos	eros

To live with the tension—to invite some order and search for unity with feeling and waiting for harmony to come; to allow receiving with some giving: this kind of tension is a requisite for making a spiritual journey. For this kind of bisexuality is the kind of soul that God is. And our experience of God will, in a way, be only what our capacity for this experience allows God to become in us: one such capacity being our recognition of dual sexual responses to life.

Moreover, when one or another of these sexual directions dominates in our lives, the exaggerated he or she dragon offers us more ersatz ecstasy. What is sadism if not an unbridled desire to control the freedom of another? Solzhenitsyn comments on torturers in the Soviet prison system who were possessed by "greed for power and greed for gain."

> But to the human being who has faith in some force that holds dominion over all of us, and who is therefore conscious of his own limitations, power is not necessarily fatal. For those however who are unaware of any higher sphere, it is a deadly poison ... It is intoxication! (147f.)

This observation applies to white-collar torturers and presidential egomaniacs no less than it does to prison torturers.

Does not the repression of creativity result in its making its way to the surface (like a cork held under water) in another form—as a tool for aggressiveness? Is this not the sense of warfare and the creativity that goes into devising such monsters as antipersonal weapons? Or into the prostitution of artists and creative minds for the sake of selling (and winning) the financial competition contest? And, on the other hand, is not the manipulation of the masculine by cunning seduction not a perverse kind of female receptivity? These sorts of ecstasy smother the soul.

Is bisexuality of God not what spiritual leaders like Buddha and Jesus and Francis have preached? What is Jesus if not a revelation of the anima side to God—the intimacy, the lovingness, the mercy, the smiling side; and who is Jesus if not a man with a fully developed anima side to his character—as poet, as story teller, as weeper over dead friends and live ones: a man with deep, therefore spiritual, feeling who preached compassion, thereby revealing a profound side to the nature of God: the feminine side.

> "Until you make the male female
> and the female male
> you will not enter the kingdom" *Gospel of Thomas*

Is an excessive animus, the kind that perverts creativity for its own aggressive ends, not the sense of "anti-Christ" in our time? A kind that would convince us that ninety billions of dollars should be spent for war while countless persons with untapped artistic powers who are born every day will die never having had an opportunity to share their beauties; and the artists who do perform in large metropolises of five to ten million persons do so before affluent and well-heeled audiences. In short, the fear of death far outweighs our enjoyment of the ecstasies of art and life. The God and gods of aggressiveness, Mars, Hermes, and others, can no longer rule in a global village. There is no room for their favorite sport—war. They are a vanishing breed. The wrong God at the wrong time. Only a resurgence of a sharing God—one that respects the differences of persons and that knows the beauty and fun of receptive ecstasies—has anything spiritual (i.e., living) to say to people of today and tomorrow. The age of the aggrandizement of the masculine ego and soul is ended. Mars rests; Constantine is buried. The empires are footnotes in history. The anima has proven her ultimate strength.[3]

Spiritual symbols play a very heavy role, consciously or unconsciously, in every person's efforts—whether man or woman—to develop an androgynous inner self. For religious symbols can contribute immensely to the prolongation of stereotyping or the guilt for breaking through the stereotyping. The liberty of the "he" in the woman; of the "she" in the man; of both he and she (especially the latter because it has been so forgotten for so long) in God: all this becomes a continuum, a sort of packaged and unified way of relating to the whole universe within and without oneself newly. The liberation of God from stale, stifling, hierarchical categories of maleness is a spiritual liberation for God herself—but also for every man, woman, and child. When God will no longer settle for sexual stereotyping (how great a disservice we have done her by calling her "him" for so long), then neither need persons. And when persons rebel against such stereotyping, God becomes possible once again.

Lest we think that the hyperactive machismo animus is not still prowling about American souls and the soul of America, we should reflect on the "famous" Mayaguez incident. In that incident, which America applauded so heartily, our leaders (all male) crowed because they spent forty-one American lives (no one counted the Cambodian ones) to rescue thirty-nine American seamen.[4] How blood-thirsty a famished animus becomes!

Another dragon that lurks ready and very able to disrupt our spiritual voyage is the dragon called Moralizing. You can recognize a moralizer by several characteristic traits: first of all, by the puniness of his soul and imagination. A moralizer is a sort of spiritual bureaucrat who has a pigeon-hole and category for every human act, thought, fantasy and dream. He would reduce even mysteries to pigeon-hole-able problems, a truly "perverse" mentality as Gabriel Marcel says. Moralizers are always looking for scandal and judgment—and thus testing others. Such were the "judges" of Jesus who were appropriately scandalized by his spontaneous friendships with those society called sinners. Eating and drinking with them, visiting their homes, receiving their love—a morality test that Jesus flunked and flunked badly. Moralizers, being incapable of living with a spiritual sense, reduce all human activity to a neat series of "do's and don'ts." They even project such literal thinking onto spiritual teachers like Jesus and try to reduce his spiritual teachings, for example, his words on the Mount, to a modern list of commandments.

Spiritual sense is just what the moralizing dragon drives out of the persons it possesses. For a moral reaction lacks a wide, symbolic or life-giving significance. The moral, as Rilke points out, is only "a segment of life." (72) Morality, we can say, is about rules for living; but spiritual experience is about reasons for living at all. With what quality of living can one survive? What moralizing does is to shrink the soul into piecemeal thinking, into legalistic and literal thinking; the soul becomes shrunken from being big enough for an experience of God to being small enough for the ego to be content merely with itself. In its nonspiritual state, the moralizing soul is blind to the fundamental spiritual fact that "the gifts of the spirit are more excellent than the moral virtues."[5]

A moralizer, up to his neck in ego-consciousness, busies himself with what is just about the opposite of forgetting oneself (as ecstasy and the experience of God are). The moralizer seeks the perfection of *one's own* perfection—defined, brought about and preserved by oneself. Thus Rilke warns the spiritual voyager: "Do not reproach yourself too much . . . otherwise you will too easily look with reproach (that is, morally) upon your past." Moralizers so overvalue victory that a moment of conversion becomes more significant than a lifetime of attitudes, creative activities, and decisions.

The opposite of moralizing is not amorality or, in the contemporary jargon, being value-free. Moral neutrality in the midst of decisions of life and death, of love and hate, is no virtue. Dante reserved the lowest place in hell for such persons who refused decision making. Rather, the opposite of moralizing is living because when you truly listen to the message of the moralizing dragons in our (or any) culture, you listen to them saying: cease living and start justifying yourself. A truly moral person feels no need to justify his existence. He is never a moralizer ("Judge not that you be not judged"; "who will cast the first stone?"). So deeply are his roots thrust into the experience of God and creation's ecstasies that there is never a need to judge about anything except the sharing of pleasure. True morality is concerned with the "weightier things of the law—justice, integrity and mercy." True morality is about justice, which implies the distribution of creation's pleasures; it is never about limiting pleasure and labeling those limits "sacred."

True morality does not limit ecstasy; true morality is about survival. But survival of us all, not just of a privileged party or class or group. Justice is a blindfolded lady who is unrespectful of persons with rank and privilege; who with sword is tough and hard nosed; who with scales can accurately measure immorality which is a lack of proportion in our lives or culture. Injustice—the only immorality—is about the relation between two or more parties. Thus, when placed on a scale, injustice becomes measurable; immorality becomes visible.

Cynics among us say "injustice is everywhere" and "it always has been." These same people tend to moralize (or, in the latest fad, to psychologize, which is the same kind of external judgement on a person that others used to make in the name of morality). It is ego-judgment by persons with souls too shrunken and too cynical (i.e., dried up) to recognize the experience of God in persons and in society. They are people without hope, without ids, without imagination; clinging to their egos and judging those of others as the ship sinks all about them.

The truly moral person, who can see life and its ecstasies as well as culture with its injustices, has no need of moralizing. Moralizing is a bad habit; a past thing; a heavy temptation. There is only living and the sharing of living. That is enough for the spiritual—and moral person.

It is important to realize that these three dragons we have just examined, as well as the three we will consider in the following chapter, are very much interrelated. (There is a rumor that dragons are an incestuous species.) At any rate, a spiritual voyager is well alert to how the dragon of bloated egos is clearly a brother to the exaggerated He and She dragon who is also a brother and sister to the moralizing dragon. These siblings support one another and share a mutual goal: to prevent the spiritual voyager from experiencing ecstasy.

CHAPTER 12
Some additional species of small but insidious, unfriendly dragons, such as sheltering, vicarious living and shortcutting

Still other small but insidious dragons lurk to intercept us on our spiritual journey through the land of ecstasies and voids. One of these is the infamous sheltering dragon. I recall walking one day by an open vacant lot that had rugged stones all about it on which children were playing. One little girl was ready to jump from a fourfoot rock onto the sandy ground and my immediate instinct was to protect her, to warn her not to jump for fear of her getting hurt. I caught myself, though, and kept my silence. Instead, I explored my feelings in this whole episode. What sort of a person would I be if someone had deprived me from my childhood right up to today of every skinned knee or hurt feeling or bloody arm each time I desired to "jump" literally or symbolically? What is this nursing instinct-like reaction that we have towards others' risky ventures? Does this caution clothed in sympathy too often prevail and so prevent the experience of extremes and even of God? Why don't we let each other be, including let each other suffer the consequences of our desires and decisions? Why, if I am willing (though uneager) to suffer some pain myself, do I want to deprive others of this real experience? Who are we to say what is best or better for a person, as if being sheltered from hurt is always and everytime the best thing? Perhaps the answer is most often found in our attitudes towards our own "vision of happiness"—a place, we imagine, where there would be no pain nor conflict. A perfectly sheltered existence; a sheltered society.

This freedom from pain may be the most expensive spiritual price we late twentieth century persons have had to pay for our culture's compulsion for security. But sheltering is not living and is therefore not a worthy goal for a people; as Rilke has put it: "Why do you want to shut out of your life any agitation, any pain, any melancholy, since you really do not know what these states are working upon you?" (70)

Just a few weeks after my experience with the child in the vacant lot, several adults and myself were sitting around discussing our various concerns and needs of the time. One woman, a mother of three and a fine friend, was talking of her father's serious illness and pending death (he being well along in years and having suffered several heart attacks). He had been raised a very strict Catholic in the old German school and was terrified both by the thought of death and by the "liberal" (a loosely-used term if ever there was one) changes of the Church of late, particularly regarding his well-preserved notions of heaven, hell, purgatory, and other explicitly medieval revelations on the afterlife. The daughter, though critical in her own spiritual life and in the lives of her children, was bent on sheltering her father from the death-bed anxiety of facing the fact that a lifetime of literal acceptance of all that Catholicism has taught might have been a mistake.

Now one can recognize the daughter's nursing instincts and sympathize with them. But I argued then as I do now that, in the long run, we have no more right protecting and sheltering our parents than we do our children or ourselves (or anyone else we love) from their necessary wrestling with despair and hope, loss of faith and rebirth of faith, death and life. We do not run our spiritual lives on sympathy but on courage and vision; therefore, why should we allow sympathy to dictate the kind of spiritual voyage our loved ones make? "The true body is a body broken," notes Brown. "To be is to be vulnerable. The defense mechanisms, the character-armour, is to protect from life. Frailty alone is human; a broken, a ground-up (contrite) heart." (LB184) Love hurts; life hurts; God hurts; experience pains. How can any of us be said to have learned love or life or experience of God apart from our bruises and bleedings, our losses and our broken dreams.

Once again we return to a basic question: What are the forces in our society that have educated us to even consider that sheltering ourselves or our children or even our parents is a worthy goal? Where have we learned to trust life—and the healing processes that are built into all that lives, from plant to animal to man and woman—so little? An experience of loss and finitude on one's deathbed might be the kindest and truest God-experience of one's lifetime. Without being paranoid, it almost smells of a conspiracy—this effort to talk and sell insurance and security so that it becomes not only a blanket to cling to but a blanket that smothers, stifling all experience and therefore God himself. On a college campus where I was teaching this past year, there *dared* to appear an insurance agent whose guilt-ridden pitch addressed to college students went something like this: "Have you given thought yet to buying life insurance (this for twenty-year olds!) for your parents' sake. For if you drop dead suddenly, they will miss you a lot, and your parents will have nothing to remember you by without a life insurance payment."

My reaction to this kind of salesmanship was of such anger that I really did hope that this gentleman himself had plenty of life insurance for should I have met up with him he might well have cashed in on it. (Or so I thought. As it turned out, he confined his preaching to the dorms, not daring—fortunately—out on campus in the light of day.) What we have here is a total misnomer. This is not life insurance; it is death insurance. To insure death instead of life; to insure sheltering instead of living; painlessness instead of Godliness; financial memory instead of ecstatic memories: to "guarantee" such results, all you have to do is get persons (especially vulnerable, young ones) to internalize this perverse mania for sheltering. That we should allow such dragons of death loose in our dormitories, into the privacy of our homes via television commercials and newspaper appeals, and, alas, into our very minds through attitudes they implant in magazine ads and in our culture as a body—this is conspicuous proof that we are close to becoming a sheltered society. A society sheltered from our deepest selves; our she and our he self; our moral as distinct from moralizing self; our id self—and being so sheltered from our truest selves, we are also sheltered from the experience of God. For a vulnerable God can only communicate with equally vulnerable persons. Protection does not signify strength; vulnerability does. Jesus did not learn to accept the crucifixion in an instant but through a lifetime of imitating the vulnerability of God. Our capacity to be vulnerable is not our weakness but our strength; for out of pain is born joy; and from despair, hope; and from being hated, love!

Vulnerability is a prize—beautiful, exciting, luring and tasteful. It deserves to be sought after with more abandon and zeal, more eagerness and full-heartedness than a boxer seeks a prize fight or an executive seeks to be number one. For with the prize of vulnerability and the consciousness it brings comes a life of *sur*-prises. A vulnerable person is a person full of surprises and ready for ever more surprises. Such a person prizes surprises. To be spiritual is to be vulnerable. Beware of the sheltering dragon! He will devour us with his promises of shelter. Beware of the dragon clothed in security and promising shelter. He will kill our very souls. And with them, God.

The English mystic Thomas Traherne warns us that "we infinitely wrong ourselves by laziness and confinement. All creatures in all nations and tongues and peoples praise God infinitely: and the more for being your sole and perfect treasures. You are never what you ought till you go out of yourself and walk among them." (Traherne, 91)

Another sinister and insidiously hostile dragon—one that prowls about seeking to waylay us from our everyday oath of spiritual experience—is the dragon of vicarious living. Like the sheltering dragon, this particular beast makes promises that at first sound generous of him and beneficial to us. Like all small but insidious dragons, he cloaks himself in ersatz ecstasies and nice promises. But to follow him is to learn, to our peril, that being nice is not being alive or being a lover. What is the particular promise the vicarious-living dragon makes? Since we are all prone to a certain self-pity, a certain weariness at our having to make such difficult spiritual journeys up mountains, down lonely, dusty roads, in rain and cold and sleet, seemingly by ourselves, this nice dragon steps out from behind the trees and promises, "Let me do it for you; let me take you there."

But there is a profound lie in any such promise. The lie is simply this: no one, no institution and no dragon, can experience God for me or for you or for anyone else but himself. Everyone has to grow into his own kind of creator; and everyone experiences ecstasy in his own time and own place and own manner. Sure, we can use and eagerly welcome guides along our journey, but the difference between a true guide and an enemy dragon in guide's clothing can usually be discerned at exactly this juncture: how much is being promised? For a true guide does not promise ecstasy, only assistance in the journey. A vicarious-living dragon, on the other hand, will promise the sun and moon to convince you to surrender your own need for experiences of God.

When such dragons seek to tempt us, we need to ask ourselves: Who can experience nature for me? or music? or love making? or pain? or the void? or dance? or the sea? or the quiet of the mountain top? or my own poetry? or my our children? or my own loving of a friend? or my own memory of these and other beauties? The answer is clear:

no one. Only we can experience God for ourselves and if we allow the deceptions of the vicarious-living dragon to become internalized into our own habits of responding to life, then we have allowed death into our very home; a lethal poison invades our soul. For no one, but nobody, can live another's life for him.

Now all this seems clear enough. Who would disagree? But whether we are aware of it or not, our society has built-in dragons of vicarious living that are constantly trying to seduce us willy-nilly into surrendering our own need to experience God. Some of them are introduced here. First come parents. Some parents (usually because they have not let themselves go to the gifts of life but cling to their sole role as parent) too often become victims of the all-devouring vicarious-living dragon. "Let me live your life for you" or "this is how to do it" is advice that is very far from healthy if children of whatever age (especially married ones) take such counsel too seriously. Parents, and especially older ones, have much experience of life to pass on to other generations; but it is valid only insofar as it is truly life experience, experience of the ecstasies of life. The surest test for the authentic guruship of parents is the following: are they still involved in searching out and experiencing the joys and ecstasies of creation? If they are not, then they are busying themselves with others' lives—something they have no right doing. For just as children need to resist vicarious living from parents, so parents need to resist living vicariously in their children or grandchildren. The test is always: what can they enjoy, create, take delight in when the children or grandchildren are absent? What set of symbolic toys have they learned to play with?

Other instances of dragons of vicarious living abound in our culture. Wherever our being spectators rather than participants in life is reinforced, there the dragon is at work. What Brecht observed of the theater can apply to movies, home, or church in our culture. "They sit together like men who are asleep but have unquiet dreams. True, they have their eyes open. But they don't watch, they stare. They don't hear, they are transfixed. They look at the stage as if bewitched." (in LB, 122) This is the essence of idolatry: staring; internalizing nothing but being satisfied, even sated, in the process. And it is surely our everyday experience in the very intimacy of our homes with television. How many lives are literally wasted away in staring at that one-eyed dragon as it offers us just enough diversions and promises by way of commercials to keep us continually seduced and mesmerized. Truly television is our culture's opiate of the masses, keeping people down as masses because it promises to live life for them. Let the actors do it for us—visit nature and have love affairs and suffering and laughter, too. This one-eyed dragon offers weeks full of adolescent sports competition that entices so many American males to pine nostalgically for a kind of competition they may or may not have enjoyed before they became family men. Vicarious ecstasy is always a pseudo and ersatz ecstasy. For there is no such thing. God is everybody's experience; such an experience cannot be done for us.

Not only is a dragon suspect for promising salvation (a promise no one can make for another), but also there are even dragons bold enough to promise the experience of God in shortcut form. These dragons are especially to be found lurking along the byways of North America, already so well known for TV dinners, instant communications, pocket calculators, and rapid conquest of time and space. If we can conquer time with face-lifts and miniskirts and space by jet travel and electronic communications, surely, the reasonable dragon argues, we can also conquer inner time and inner space (that is, spiritual time and space) with some prepackaged or frozen spiritual voyages. "Just thaw and go," promises this dragon. Just get high. That is all.

But this *Reader's Digest* way to God, the shortcut way, is doomed to failure. For ecstasy is not the same as emotional outburst or emotional high. Such highs leave out essential steps in authentic ecstasy, such as the ecstasy of sharing with others; it sidesteps the socially moral (justice) while reducing "morality" solely to private matters, such as sexual practices or imagination. It sidesteps the wasted time element that all authentic ecstasy, from friendship to stargazing to learning to dance or play the piano, implies. By eliminating creation's wasted times, it manipulates rather than respects creation. It is no wonder that such shortcut spiritualities tend to culminate in proselytizing and thus confusing "my" way of salvation with another's. The price one pays for such shortcutting is dear indeed, for one ends up not more vulnerable but less so; one ends up more dogmatic and controlled and desirous of controlling others than before one's instantaneous "conversion."

No, like any natural process, the growth of a rose or the development of a fetus, there is a certain time that creation needs for a true creation spirituality. Even God works in time. Every spiritual journey is just that—a journey—and the distance one travels is covered only in a certain time. The ways of plotting the distances and time lapses are multiple, and we shall present a variety of such maps in the Appendix. But what is common to each of them is striking: first, that there is no such thing as instantaneous shortcutting to God; and, second, that whatever map one cares to take on the journey, God is invariably the last, not the first, of the spiritual experiences.

What becomes dangerously lost sight of and one-sided in the spiritual perspective of the shortcutting dragon is that the true enjoyment of creation and Creator takes skills. There is an *art* to experiencing God. An art is not learned by shortcutting any more than it is learned by someone else doing it for us (vicarious living). An art takes time to develop, for it takes skill and effort and application and experimenting and mistakes. And all these things take time. In periods like ours, when the spirit of life enjoyment is lost, we need to train ourselves to enjoy life and to put the experience of pleasure of God first. One does not throw a "successful" party overnight and purely spontaneously but with some planning and deciding and preparation. Surely the party that is true spiritual joy and pleasure of God's company is not brought about any more easily.

Shortcutting dragons of all stripes and scales need not be confused with efforts to simplify and be spontaneous, for all such dragons are friendly to our spiritual journey, not inimical to it. How does one tell the difference between spiritual simplicity and pseudoecstatic shortcuts? One is natural; the other, forced. One is deep and derives its power from the depths; the other is superficial. One is so deep that it can afford to be quiet; the other is loud and noisy and continually talks about its favorite topic— itself. One is so deep at its roots that it mixes with other roots and thereby becomes socially conscious, aware of the We and not just the I; the other tends to be forgetful of injustice toward others. The one creates and reverences other creators of music and painting and dance and all; the other barely acknowledges art. Simplicity, then, is a real result of experience of God—the simplicity of a child; a capacity to laugh at oneself, others, and even God. Shortcutting, on the other hand, is not a laughing matter, as dragons who deceive us into such a path readily admit by their own lack of humor and perspective.

CHAPTER 13
Large and unfriendly dragons: institutions and institutional consciousness

The truly giant dragons, the ones that are capable of swallowing us whole without blinking an eye, are institutions. For the most part, institutions are far less subtle than smaller dragons in their effect on our journeying to God for they can afford to be. Their very bigness and the thickness of the scales on their enormous bodies ensures them that simple individuals (other than St. George himself) could barely hope to oppose them. In a simpler culture and time, dragons were natural phenomena and divine intervention through knighted heroes was sought after passionately. Today, nature fights us far less than do man-made institutions, and these become our people-eating dragons. That is why the spiritual voyager must be especially alert about these biggest and boldest of dragons along the not-easy trail of experience of God.

First of all devices of the institutional dragon is his alluring and appealing promises—for an institution promises so much and, generally, the bigger the institution, the greater the promise. What are some of these tantalizing promises held out by the institutional dragon? Not least among them is immortality. Yes, an institution promises a certain immortality. Oh, it may be of a vicarious kind (the "company" will continue to grow or our "government" will last forever) but it is immortality nevertheless. And most of us are interested in such a promise no matter from whom it comes. In America, the corporation not only promises immortality but can boast that it—alone among all human things—is itself immortal! Yes, that is a fact about corporate bodies; in America, corporations exist legally *in perpetuity*; unlike our own selves and bodies, they are not condemned to die. It is a slight transition to pass from seeing the perpetually lasting dragon to believing such a dragon when he says, "Come, follow me. I shall offer you everlasting life."

Salvation by institutions: that seems to be the American way as of the last twenty-five years. Whether it is salvation by education (which is so often institutionalized thinking and so rarely thinking at all); by the right church (even though Aquinas wrote, seven centuries ago, that religion is a "quality and habit of the soul" and fails to even mention religious institutions in his very definition of religion!); by the government (which, having begun as a servant of the people, now demands the people's servitude)—whatever it is our institutions are selling, there is a tendency to believe such large dragons as they promise salvation through "and only through" their auspices. ("How can bigness be all wrong?" we ask. After all, these dragons have survived through the centuries.)

Institutions promise power. That is surely a true claim, not a false one. Institutions not only promise power, they deliver on their promise. Consider, for example, how the ITT Company was able to be an effective force in toppling the duly-elected and constituted government of Chile. The power of the ballot box and of the country's own elected officers was cardboard compared to the power of the dragon ITT, headquartered an entire continent away. It takes spiritual power or what we call "courage" to stand up to such heavy dragons as institutions can be. Such was the kind of courage, for example, that some young men displayed in resisting the power of the U. S. government and army in America's undeclared war on Vietnam. The following observation was made not by one of these "rebels" but by a soldier who did indeed answer the call of the army and government dragons and fought in Vietnam; "It took a lot of guts to go against a machine as powerful as our government. And I just know, inside myself, that time has shown that the people who were protesting at home had a better concept of what was going on, and what was right, than I did at the time."[1]

With all these persuasive promises at the ready disposal of giant institutional dragons, it is clear why so many people are seduced by their enticements. But there are very great spiritual deficiencies in every institutional dragon, and all men, women, and children should be aware of how puny a soul a physically enormous dragon possesses.

We have already noted how every institution tends to seek its own immortality. Self-perpetuation is the goal of every institutional dragon. Now this kind of stubbornness to follow nature's ordinary cycle of death, fertilization, and rebirth is a hint of the monumental ego that an institution possesses. "Everyone shall die but I" is the motto. This can be a frightening prospect for it raises the obvious questions: What price will this dragon pay? Where are the limits to gaining its own immortality? Might an institution, even Faust-like, make pacts with the devil to assure its longevity? Will it whore after any way of survival at all, oblivious to the spiritual questions of *quality* of existence and of *why* survive at all and the moral question of justice? Robert Hutchins, whose entire life has been dedicated to the quality of higher education, apparently thinks that is the case in our large educational "service station" multiversities. The employees of these dragons are engaged in teaching "anything they can get anyone to pay for," observes Hutchins. Thus, Roszak comments, "The picture is clear enough: in the name of service (and, of course, in return for handsome fees and cushy appointments) universities and university men have been prepared to collaborate in genocide, espionage, deceit, and all the corruptions our government's sense of omnipotence has led us to." The university, he says, has surrendered "the indispensable characteristic of wisdom: moral discrimination" and thus has come to "resemble nothing so much as the highly refined, all-purposes brothel Jean Genet describes in his play *The Balcony.*"[2]

These intellectual brothels, in turn, spew out spiritual pimps who can be utilized by giant dragons to entice more and more persons into the dragons' network.

We have pointed out how the law grants institutional dragons the unusual gift of immortality. But what is an institution besides the "corporate person" status that our legal system gives it? First and most importantly, an institutional dragon is precisely *not* a person. Its definition in legal and financial circles as a person is a misleading if not an untrue and false definition for anyone on a spiritual journey. An institution is not a person. It is a *thing.* However, it is not a thing like a rock or a mountain is a thing of creation. It is not a God-made thing but a man-made thing.

Because the institution is a thing, it lacks the capacity for ecstasy or experience of God. This tremendous pleasure, open to all who call themselves men and women, is utterly lacking in the largest giants on earth, our institutional dragons. Imagine what this lack does to their bloated egos! Imagine how jealous one such dragon is of even the simplest human person! No wonder they have twisted our very language through legal and financial maneuvering, to be rebaptized as "legal persons," knowing all along that they were only things. How this must gall their pride, to know deep down in the bosom of their computer minds that these huge dragons are, in fact, *dumb* in the literal sense of the word. They are dumb things— silent and unable to speak. Incapable of ecstasy and spiritual memory, of ever forgetting themselves and standing outside of themselves, of being turned on by anything other than electrical impulses.

Their idols, in silver and gold, products of
human skill,
have mouths, but never speak, eyes but never
see,
ears, but never hear, noses, but never smell,
hands, but never touch, feet, but never walk,
and not a sound from their throats.
Their makers will end up like them,
and so will anyone who relies on them. (Ps.
115.4-8)

Even a cadaver responds to electrical impulses. And this is
what our giant dragons fear the most: they are lifeless. For
all the talk of their perpetuity, they have no life, no spirit.
They are spiritless.

It is no wonder such dragons are so often found along
the paths of spiritual voyagers, bent on making the route
even more treacherous than it is. For they are envious
dragons and want at least to seduce others into their state
of living without living; machine-induced activity; ego-tripping; and spiritual death. Indeed, it is a curious fact that
their envy and jealousy are so predominant in themselves
that they become the ruling forces for institutional
thinking. Is there not more energy exerted in jealousy in
almost every institution than there is in any act of
"service," no matter how proudly flouted? Jealousy makes
things turn in the dragon's belly. It is part of the
ego-consciousness that the dragon both appeals to and
encourages. For the dragon, we recall, has no id, no
imagination, no fun and games. Its only sport is the
seduction of egos.

If an institution is without spiritual experience, then
such a dragon is also without memory. Imagine living with
no link to a spiritual heritage, with no beauty that can be
recalled. No wonder a dragon is compulsive about tomorrow and continually proving himself today. No roots;
rootlessness, what a sad existence such dragons live!

Institutions, being things, are always nouns, substantives. They own the skyscrapers and the stock market. Such dragons are never verbs inviting caring and sharing, listening and laughing, like God does. God the verb vs. Institution the noun. What will the tactic of Institution be in this spiritual battle? It will be to convince other verbs for example, religion, law, family that they really are nouns. (Law as a verb it was once known as justice, long since faithfully departed; family where "staying together" as in "a family that prays together stays together" is as close to a verb as the late Western family was able to muster in its dying years.) By mesmerizing all other institutions, the institutional dragon stands a pretty good chance of hypnotizing the God traveler into its own nounlike image. If only the dragon can succeed in getting people to think more of buildings (e.g., "my church" or "the White House") and the people that guard them (commonly known as "churchmen" or "occupants of the Oval Office"), ecstasy and the experience of God will be forced out of the picture. For the dragon knows, even when everyone else forgets, that only people can experience God and that God depends on that experience. The dragon knows, for he, lacking this experience, is truly godless. How eager the dragon is to make us all over into his image.

And what means are at the disposal of these soulless dragons? One sure means is lying. After all, a *thing* is not capable of truth or falsehood; it cannot make a judgment. So what appears to be a difference to us mortals between what is and what is not is of no consequence to institutions at all. Dressed in the regalia of bloated human egos, these dragons can say and even convince others in saying just about anything. For example, two of this nation's most prestigious reports about underdeveloped countries, the appropriately named "Rockefeller and Peterson Reports," simply say nothing about the unemployment problem in these nations created, in great part, by multinational corporations that are eliminating jobs. Instead, the reports speak of the (fewer) jobs that the multinational corporations create.[3] Closer to home, more and more wage earners are seeing the truth of how large corporate dragons, while ostensibly paying a higher rate of taxes than individuals, in fact frequently do not. The facts are beginning to dawn on people—bloated incomes this past year of oil companies that confess to making from 100 to 300 percent greater profits while the people in the street pay out twice as much at the gasoline pumps and 20 percent more at the supermarket.

Prominent among institutions, we must include those large dragons known as "professions" which, as a rule, exist today more to assure their continued existence (which is, we recall, an institution's raison d'être) than to serve. One such profession was recently critiqued by one of its very own members. In the course of the Watergate hearings, Senator Howard Baker, himself a lawyer, while interrogating a witness who was also a lawyer, committed the following Freudian slip and unguarded revelation for us nonlawyers. "Now tell me what those liars—I mean lawyers—said next. . ."

Controlling the media, educational institutions, and, ultimately, our language itself, giant dragons are able to lie by sustaining myths that no longer (if they ever did) possess any validity. For example, the myth that there is a contented middle class in America that every hard-working citizen can attain and that "more and more" Americans partake of. In fact, "the people who call themselves middle class constitute a sort of voluntary buffer group between those who have nothing and those who have nearly all of it."[4] (The upper 1 percent of the population today owns over 40 percent of the wealth as compared to owning only 21 percent in 1949.) All those workers who earn less than $25,000 per year (95 percent of us) support the richest dragons, who are at the top. Or the myth that "socialism" is a foreign and dirty word to Americans—as if Lockheed and the chicken farmers of Mississippi and the AMA and the President himself were not subsidized on welfare gained from the pockets of the working people. Socialism exists in America but it is of a very selective kind: it exists for the powerful, not for the bulk of our citizens.

Having no souls and, therefore, no ecstatic experience of truth, institutions necessarily believe that what they control is truth (or enough of it). Such dragons shall continue to lie, bully, and threaten the people until spiritual people tame them like St. George did, putting them on a leash like a puppy dog, and make them accountable to creatures who are capable of discerning lies from truth.

One of the greatest achievements of our giant institutional dragons is their success (they love success and would like us spiritual travelers to love it equally) in getting spiritual voyagers to think like them—instead of like God. Thus, we meet more and more persons who have come under the spell of institutional thinking and, consequently, prefer memory that is sentimental to memory that is spiritual; a thing orientation to their lives rather than a playful and symbolic one; jealousy rather than cooperation with their co-workers; shibboleths and lies over truth; competition for immortality, status, and wages over developing more efficient ways of sharing ecstasies.

In addition, dragons have spawned two other kinds of consciousness whose consequences are equally lethal for us all. The first of these is a mentality of specialization. Gordon Liddy, a key though enigmatic figure in that event we now call Watergate, was described as being a lawyer capable of producing the "best quality legal memorandum—detailed and precise." "Detailed and precise"—there we have the epitaph for our super specialized institutions. "Specialize! Specialize! Specialize!" we are told and, like pursuing a carrot on a stick, so we do. But specialization means privatization and this kind of blindness seeing only the carrot offered to us and no other consequence of our and our dragons' work—is spiritual death. It is piecemeal instead of wholistic thinking. And acting. It is reducing the very nature of man from an animal capable of seeing wholly to one on the level of pure desire, chasing the carrot.

No less disastrous than a specialization-consciousness is the sign-consciousness that large dragons encourage. We have already discussed in Chapter 7 how much havoc such thinking can wreck on the spiritual voyager, but how is it that institutional dragons are involved? Institutions, not being capable of creative symbol making, are more than capable of sign manufacturing. Take a look at the inside of such dragons. Are they not experts at sign making? Sitting behind desks (the larger the desk, the more significant the sign of the person behind it); punching of buttons on one's phone (the greater the number, the more significant the sign); beckoning secretaries or nurses at will. Even brief-cases that are carried to and from work signify by their classiness or lack thereof.

Institutions not only deal inwardly in signs but also continually make signs for the rest of us in order to ingest us into their sign-conscious world. We call these signs "advertisements." Advertisers, the sign makers for great dragons, pursue us day and night, on our roads and in the privacy of our living rooms, consciously, unconsciously, and subliminally. It has been said that "some of America's most creative people are in advertising" and, unfortunately, that is true. The goal of the advertiser as advertiser is to get us to desire something that we did not previously desire. To attain this end, they will go so far as to manipulate symbols and reduce them to signs. For example, any number of ecstasies—sexuality, friendship, nature, music all become reduced to the boring level of sign-consciousness. Beauty is for selling, not enjoying. As a consequence, we become not a symbol-hungry people but a sign-hungry people. In this way, institutions incarnate literalism (instead of symbolism) and with this institutional mentality give birth to institutional people: a tired people; a spiritually energy-less people; victims of institutional dragons who have sapped their spiritual energy with as much vengeance as a vampire saps blood.

Do institutions instruct us to repress pleasure? To forget ecstasies? To avoid extremes and endorse mediocrity? To think of God as either absent or too transcendent to be in touch? To think of ourselves as creatures instead of creators and artists? To think sign and not symbol? So familiar are these patterns of consciousness to all of us today that it is no longer enough to caution about dragons in persons' clothing. Dragons so dominate our spiritual lives that we need to guard against persons in dragons' clothing! Persons capable of ecstasy and of being creators themselves have sold their souls to ecstatic-less institutions and, in doing so, become like them, urging the rest of us to follow suit. How it is that dragons can triumph and such a travesty can occur, we shall pursue further in the following chapter.

CHAPTER 14
Additional insights on tactics that unfriendly dragons utilize, such as how large dragons employ small dragons in their service

D ragons are exceedingly clever and they employ a variety of devices with which to beguile and then destroy spiritual pilgrims. Especially do the great and institutional dragons wisely employ smaller dragons for their purpose of attacking spiritual voyagers.

Big dragons truly are big and very, very powerful. This makes them and their wily promises especially appealing to the individual who senses his powerlessness and, in particular, to those with weak egos and those whose whole goal in life is ego building. You might even say that large dragons have a stake in promoting and prolonging an ego-consciousness. No one would deny how skillful they are at doing this, especially when spiritual travelers possess rather precarious adolescent egos. Why is it, for example, that ex-sports heroes fit so well into the corporate dragon's philosophy of life? To answer this question and derive additional insights, let us reflect on the following "success" story that was printed recently in a dragon-owned magazine (the kind you read on an airplane when you become bored watching liquor being dispensed). The title reads (complete with banner headline): "Frank McKinney's Formula for Success is Simple and Direct. You need ... SELF-DISCIPLINE AND THE DESIRE TO SUCCEED." (*sic*) And the article assures us, "achievement is something Frank E. McKinney Jr. has sought all his adult life .... His list of accomplishments in the past 20 years reads like Jack Armstrong ... captain of the Big Ten

Champion I. U. swim team; four gold medals in the Pan American Games of 1955 and 1959; a bronze medal in the 1956 Olympic Games at Melbourne, Australia . . . ." Then, when athletic achievements were accomplished, Mr. McKinney turned his eyes to banking and "in less than nine years became chairman of American Fletcher. Some will say, 'Yes, but his father was a power in American Fletcher before him.' True. But his father didn't win those gold medals."[1]

Mr. McKinney not only moved from one athletic achievement into another position but also moved *up* in the business world. He explains the philosophy of achievement he had learned as a champion: "The first is self-discipline. The second is the desire to succeed—the desire to become a professional in your own field—to reach the apex of that field." What is the goal he has in his new field of finance? "By the year 2000, instead of 14,000 banks in the country, we might have only 3,000 banks," he declares and, notes the interviewer, "at 34, Frank McKinney still has plenty of time to see and to help it all happen." To see what all happen? To see his team win and be champion. To achieve this goal, Mr. McKinney demands (as did any good coach he ever had, I am sure) dedication—not just dedication to a job but to (of all things!) a family! "We have an institution here—American Fletcher National Bank . . . 2600 people . . . have chosen to work here as their careers. Their motivation should be, then, to do anything possible, practical, feasible, and prudent to cause the American Fletcher family to succeed—to become the leader in its field." Now, we all admire excellence and striving for perfection, but people-excellence is one thing and thing-excellence (rah! rah! for the team) is another. Moreover, excellence for its own sake is profoundly human; but excellence as defined by beating up the opposition, as we have seen earlier, is the perversion of the sporting instinct. Are we to believe that Mr. McKinney truly believes that the institution American Fletcher is a family? Or is this a lie? Certainly it is a distortion of the English language marking the end of meaning to the word "family." Adolescent sports hero becomes capitalist hero. Is this a success story (as the magazine suggests) or a seduction story?

Another example of institutional appeals to adolescent egos is what religion, when it becomes institutional, can do to persons by appealing to their adolescent mysticism. Recently, in a large city in the United States, a cardinal of the Roman Catholic Church was held up on the street. His first and spontaneous response to the gunman was, "I am Cardinal so-and-so, archbishop of this city." The gunman, lacking the respect for his office that the cardinal obviously relished so highly, replied, "I know who you are, give me your money" and took his wallet anyway (which, incidentally, contained a few hundred dollars in cash). We have here an interesting instance of how a churchman can genuinely come to believe, through the wiles of the large dragons, that his institution's ego was on the line when he was held up—"l'institution, c'est moi." When religion concentrates on mystical experience alone, as when spirituality becomes one-sidely sacramental, then religion becomes dangerous indeed. For the sacraments—the God is here experience—are always meant to exist in opposition to social injustice or—the God is absent—experience. When one of the poles of this tension is removed, the first pole becomes pervertedly ego-appealing and such a sacramental spirituality becomes idolatrous, an end in itself that keeps persons from God rather than an occasion for inviting God and people to share company together.[2]

We have seen, then, how the adolescent quest for proving oneself and testing the ego, like the adolescent search for mysticism and power, is reinforced by large dragons. Large dragons employ the smaller dragon of ego-tripping for their own disastrous ends. When spiritual writers write (as they have for generations and from any spiritual tradition we can name) of the need to put to death the ego, of burying it so that from its ashes God might resurrect, they may not always have had in mind the putting to death of the institutional ego. But today, when such dragons are omnipresent and omnipowerful in our midst, a spiritual writer has to have this in mind. The putting to death of the ego (that is, a beginning stage to spiritual journeys) includes putting to death institutional egos and not just "private" ones. Indeed, the latter cannot be accomplished as long as the former roam about unmolested and unquestioned in their quest to seduce individuals.

Another instance of large dragons manipulating spiritual wayfarers through smaller dragons is the he-she exaggeration. In the interview referred to earlier, the young man who fought in Vietnam tells us: "I was like a lot of guys—I thought it was the manly thing to go and fight just because we were told to." "The manly thing"—a perfect way to seduce a young man is to appeal to his sexual ego. This young man and his comrades were so seduced. Sadism might almost be expected to be the result of such tactics. "I was firing mortar shells at a couple of North Vietnamese regulars. I had them in range. I could have killed them right away, at will. But I didn't. I played cat and mouse with them, made them run around to make it last longer before I did it. I was really warped." Like dragon, like son.

That the female sex is also manipuled sexually is clear to anyone observing the reasons that civil rights legislation was necessary. Advertisers, in the name of Freudian insight, somehow see some relation between a woman in a sheath dress hugging a refrigerator and the selling of the product; between bathing-suited beauties astride the hood of a car and the appeal of the car. Most women who have worked for any large-sized dragon at all can recount many a horror story of their experiences, so there is no need to dwell on so obvious a case of he-she dragonhood serving the needs of larger dragons.

Have you ever noticed how effective large dragons are at

producing guilt in persons? Dragons themselves are capable of neither guilt nor shame, being dumb as they are; but they are acutely conscious of how sensitive persons can be in this area. The arousal and accusation of guilt is necessarily part and parcel of a moralizing dragon, one that insists on private morality. Mr. Jeb Magruder, formerly employed by the White House, confesses his experience with that large dragon. "We had private morality but not a sense of public morality."[3] Isn't it striking how important a private morality—invariably a sexual one— proves to be to institutions who can afford to spend thousands of dollars hiring spies on an enemy's private life, as in the well documented case of Ralph Nader being pursued by General Motors' hired agents.[4] Or, in the case of the FBI hounding Dr. Martin Luther King.

At the same time, however, these same public dragons have no money to spend in self-criticism of their public morality. Instead, large dragons try to cover up their moralizing tracks by flourishing their own unique brand of public morality called philanthropy. "See what a good boy am I" shout our giant dragons with blood of their victims mixed with the fire of their breath. Since distributing the crumbs from a rich man's table (usually with tax deductions for the rich man) comes as close to morality as most large dragons are capable, it is clear that philanthropy may qualify as moralizing but never as morality.

It almost goes without saying that the great dragons called institutions appeal by way of offers of security. What, after all, are promises of immortality, salvation and power if not appeals to security? For the insecure (and surely every spiritual voyager is frequently insecure), the institutions seem a welcome home and place to rest one's head and aching body—and one's aching and eager ego. For they appear to have the power to order the chaos in which we live: God's power. And this is indeed an enticing promise.

A promise of security is a promise to shelter. We have

already seen how an institution is a noun. But a noun is also a shelter. Who ever heard of being sheltered by a verb? So an institution, with its size and power and ego-control and exaggerated he-ness is a perfect shelter—if that is what one wants, namely, to be sheltered. Our century of man-made catastrophes, of over 100 million human beings killed by other human beings in war, of atom splitting and population crowding, of profound social changes from migrations to cities to increased literacy, to American-Soviet hegemony: who wouldn't feel the need for some shelter? If from nothing else, at least from our man-made bombs. Our times have removed the belief in a providential purpose of creation to our institutions—the dogma that a Buick was something to believe in, preached by General Motors a short time ago, has now spawned a new one, "Datsun Saves." Our great dragons stress security and continuity in an otherwise insecure world (why is it that nine out of ten skyscrapers in our large cities are insurance companies?). It is a wise investment, this investment in sheltering.

Once a person consents to being sheltered from life, he is prone to letting someone else live life for him. The televison addict is born (is there "one every minute" as Barnum used to say?). "Let the pro football players live my life of sports heroics for me; I shall watch and get my jollies *vicariously*, as they say. Reliving my adolescence. Sweet time when the ego meant something; locker rooms; he-ness in the presence of other males. Don't get me wrong. This isn't anything queer, you know, or any of that new stuff they call "bisexuality"—I just mean that I, well, I enjoyed myself. Beating up guys; the crowds cheering; rubbing that tackle's nose in the dirt. Why shouldn't I relive it all here in front of my TV set Saturday afternoon and Sunday afternoon and Monday night and Friday night? It's a free world, isn't it?"

Are we free to let others live our lives for us? And by so doing to pervert our spiritual memories, dragging us back into an adolescent time (utterly distorted—the fact is that we weren't such important heroes then either) when we could be deeply enjoying ourselves, even God, right now? But vicarious living is very prosperous for our giant dragons. The air time costs for advertising men's deodorants (more sheltering?), for oil companies telling us how well they are caring for our environment (lying much?)—in short, for vicarious living time—are among the most expensive few minutes of time on earth. A great way to feed the dragons so they get bigger and bigger and, of course, so living becomes more and more vicarious. A great outlet for the dragon's jealousy that we human beings were (once) able to live, while he could not. Like likes like. Death attracts death. The dead are burying the living.

Yes, giant dragons are indeed clever to utilize the insidious ways of smaller dragons to carry on their business which so often waylays spiritual travelers. A concerted effort is carried on by all unfriendly dragons to deprive us persons (who are, after all, only people) from our enjoyments and pleasures of creation and Creator. If we feel deprived enough, then maybe we will look longer at what the dragons can offer us in terms of power and money and prestige and security. We might even begin to love these things and get a sort of joy from seeing them add up. (All this sort of thing can be added up, for it is quantitative—something that can't be said for sexual pleasure that is for its own sake and not for braggadocio; or a symphony; or a beautiful landscape.) Repress pleasure and substitute ours for it—that is the carrot at the end of the stick offered by the great and unfriendly dragons.

But death to the authentic pleasures of creation is death to ourselves. We people know this even if dragons do not. To refuse the repression offered by our institutions is to invite a dark night in our souls. A wondering and a doubt; a silence from God; an unromantic experience with nature and art; perhaps a lost job or slip in status. But the dark night is not meant to be a private horror; it is meant, as everything beautiful also is meant, to be shared. It is a public night, not a private one. The journey into hell that giant dragons can take us on (one valuable reason for their continued existence) is not Beatrice with Dante; it is all of us with the dragon. We are all victims; we are all being led by unfriendly giants. It can be a cleansing crucible to see face to face the realities of the ego and exaggerated he's and she's and moralizing and sheltering and vicarious living and shortcutting: to see the place where the dragons are born. Hell is its name. After all, we spoke in Chapter VIII of needing to touch the extremes to touch God. From hell, like Dante, we might (just might) be able to reach for heaven. All kinds of ordinary persons like you and me have done so: policemen (Have you seen *Serpico?*) and priests (Do you know what *kind* of priests have left the institutional priesthood? It is the kind who were willing to be beat up for a cause; who really *believed*, I mean believed, in life and the sharing of it) and principals and business executives and salesmen and fishermen and housewives and mothers and fathers and children (Have you seen Patty Hearst lately?). Conversion is ever present. Come, Beatrice. We have seen hell. There must be a better place than this.

There must be a place where death dressed in fancy clothes and riding big limousines and wielding crushing blows of power even from a scaly tail does not stalk; a place where people are people and do not think and walk and talk and act like dragons or machines; a place we can still recognize as living. So that we might commit ourselves to live and enjoy and share the enjoyment instead of letting dragons process life for us. It is better to become like God than like an institution, isn't it? And much more fun.

CHAPTER 15
Some dragon-bite kits and an observation on discerning friendly from unfriendly dragons

> You will tread on lion and adder,
>> trample on savage lions and dragons. (Ps. 91.13)

T he previous section exposed us travelers to a rather sobering picture of dragons large and small that lie in wait to deter us along the path of our spiritual journey. A spiritual journey is no time to be timid but to be alert and smart about the perils of falling under the spells of diverse kinds of dragons. Dragons do bite you know. Accordingly, one of the first requisites for a well-planned spiritual journey is to pack a dragon-bite kit such as the ones we offer in this chapter. There are several varieties of such kits available, so we shall offer a few that are, as they say, "guaranteed effective." Provided one keeps his cool in an emergency, the bite of even the largest and most fierce dragon need not prove fatal. Furthermore, the kits offered here will prove effective in actually preventing dragon bites if applied properly in advance. This is sure to be good news for each of us and for our traveling party (all of whom are our friends and whose seduction would offend each of us too) as we make our spiritual way through dragon-infested territory.

Our previous section dealt solely with unfriendly dragons. There are many of these. In fact, every dragon is potentially unfriendly, but there are times when dragons are friendly and helpful and useful. Of course, because institutions are always things, a dragon can never *be* a friend; only, at times, friendly. This means that a dragon is never an end—such as our natural ecstasies and their creator is—but only a means. The reason that friendly dragons appeal to us ultimately is simply that we need them. We depend on institutions to protect us from the cold or heat or rain like their buildings do. We need them to protect us from other dragons and other institutions. (Needless to say, this role is a particularly important and advantageous one that dragons can play for us.) We need them to go to work for us and to accomplish things for persons that persons could not accomplish by themselves, including bringing diverse people together. This happens, for example, in a school where different generations and different disciplines and different personalities and persons with varied experiences are brought together (supposedly) to think together about a commonly held interest in living. Dragons are known for making necessities for us that we cannot provide by ourselves, such as refrigerators and daily newspapers and soap and light bulbs and packaged foods—things few of us are able to accomplish alone these days. Yes, we do need dragons at times.

But in praising friendly dragons we must never lose sight of how they are meant to serve us people and not we them—otherwise, the tail will wag the dragon instead of our leashing and domesticating our dragons. Furthermore, dragons evolve—as do our personal and social needs, Thus, what was once a friendly dragon may one day evolve to be a dangerous and unfriendly one; and, vice versa, some unfriendly dragons can change to be friendly. (The United States Government, for example, was once a beacon of light to the oppressed and suffering of the world, a sign of joy to the young and to the hopeful; even the Christian churches were young and creative, questioning and serious at various periods in the West. As for enemy dragons turning friendly, one might point to socialism as a potentially friendly dragon for our future.) We can all appreciate now how crucial it is to remain alert in discerning friendly from unfriendly dragons. Therefore, to assist in this dragon discernment process (as well as to cure when once bitten), we offer the following wellproven dragon-bite kits. The first we shall call the 5-Question Dragon-Bite Kit.

This kit consists of five questions. The accompanying instructions prescribe that you apply each question rigorously and carefully to *any* dragon (the larger the better) you meet along your spiritual journey. The questions hit at the Achilles heel of the dragon world that we have discussed earlier; namely, the dragon's incapacity for life. That is why this kit has proven so effective for pilgrims of the past. It is simple and it gets at the heart not only of dragon values but also of every spiritual voyager: it begins with the acknowledgment that we each have a treasure, "where our heart is," and to discern the spirits is to determine whether the dragon will assist or seduce us in unfolding that treasure.

These are the five valuable questions to put to any dragon.

1. Do you celebrate life for its own sake? (Is life an end in itself for you?)
2. Do you seek to know injustices? human suffering? the neglected and the powerless? the weak and the innocent who suffer? Or is the term "injustice" a totally foreign word for you, one that portrays no feeling or arouses no compassion in you? The psalmist says, "Yahweh, who does what is right, is always on the side of the oppressed." (Ps. 103.6) Are you, Mr. Dragon?
3. Do you truly *serve?* This means, do you organize (yes, even, at times, institutionalize) attempts to relieve the pain and injustice that you sensed in question 2? Do you, Mr. Dragon, serve the authentically needy or are you self serving?
4. Are you hypocritical? This means, do you say you are doing one or another of the above things but in fact are not?
5. Are you manipulated and manipulating? That is, do you use the life or the suffering or the claim to service as a

means instead of respecting it as an end? Also, are you used by other dragons to attain their ends and do these ends qualify as authentic ones or as manipulated ones?

Application of this kit is simple, though of course one cannot take the dragon's word alone as the full answer. One must do research and examine where the dragon has left dragon prints and lessons from his past. One can, for example, apply this kit to a person's life. One's own or anyone else's. For the sake of example, let us apply it to the life of Martin Luther King, Jr.

1. Did be celebrate life for its own sake? Did he know how to enjoy life? It seems he loved his family and good times so the answer is affirmative.

2. Was he sensitive to injustice? Indeed he was. He never forgot the hurts and the pains of fellow blacks, whom he did not desert when getting degrees from status institutions but whom he assisted in unbalancing the injustices they had suffered.

3. He offered this assistance through organized boycotts, through the Southern Christian Leadership Conference (SCLC)—in other words, through institutions that were truly serving the suffering at that time in our nation's history.

4. He did not preach one thing and do another; his body and heart were where his mouth was for he went to jail and then even to his death for the sake of the injustice he had sensed.

5. He was not used. He was his own man to the end. We have concluded, then, that this man, who because he was a public figure was also an institution and a myth, passes the test as a truly friendly, because a truly life-loving and life-sharing, dragon.

This test can be applied equally to any institution or any person of your choice or chance encounter. But all five tests must be applied and passed (numbers 1 through 3 in the affirmative; number 4 and 5 in the negative). Otherwise, the candidate fails and we are in great peril if we ignore that failure and allow ourselves to associate with such dragons. A dragon that fails even one of these questions is truly a dragon of death and should be avoided at all costs; even quarantined.

A second dragon-bite kit that has also proven highly effective is the 3-question Kit. It includes the following questions:

1. Ideology. What does the institution or dragon *claim* to do? (For example, our schools claim to teach persons to think; our churches to encourage prayerfulness; seminaries to produce spiritual leaders for the culture.)

2. Political. How does this dragon accomplish what it does? What are its methods for doing what it wants to do?

3. Socioeconomic. How is this dragon supported economically and how does is support other dragons economically?

Like the previous kit, this one demands some hard thinking and research by persons who operate it, but it is effective indeed if so applied.

A third dragon-bite kit, called the Ecstasies Kit, guarantees effective results if the following steps are applied properly:

1. Return to Chapter 1 and the list of natural ecstasies.

2. Add whatever natural ecstasies you want to based on your own experience of creation.

3. Now, taking each ecstasy separately, put this question to the dragon at hand: How do you stand, that is, what do you accomplish and do, for the passing on of these ecstasies? This test will be very effective. For example, what are the psychological, financial and social facts regarding sharing of the arts in my country (or city or community)? Americans may find here how the Andy Hardy syndrome plus fears of lost masculinity prevent artistic ecstasies in a psychological way; how the price of tickets prevents it financially; how lack of distribution and financing of art companies prevents entire ethnic groups and neighborhoods from participating. Another example

would be nature: does this dragon (e.g., a particular mining company) respect the beauties of nature so as to pass them on to other generations for their ecstatic experience? Or does it use and abuse nature in the name of "more jobs" or "economic needs of a community" or of their own stockholders (often referred to, as we have seen, as a "family"). Is a community or a family a people who make money together? Or, better, a people who make ecstasy together? A dragon cannot be allowed to abuse the language at the same time that he destroys ecstasy. For a community without beauties to behold is already as dead as the dragon itself.

4. The next step in this dragon-bite kit is to organize with others who have reached your level of awareness to do something about taming the dragons in our spiritual midst.

Most of our lives we are subjected to being tested by dragons along our spiritual route. Some families; schools from first grade through grad schools; hiring for jobs; IRS; churches testing our purity of soul; etc. The list is endless. What these kits allow us to do is to get some perspective back into just who it is that is making a great and beautiful spiritual journey: is it any dragon or any bureaucracy or any institution? Never. That is impossible. These kits turn the tables and allow us, the spiritual voyagers, to discern once again whether dragons be friend or foe; it puts the dragons to the test for a change instead of ourselves. That is a good and holy thing, for "the sabbath is made for man; not man for the sabbath." Theologians call this turning of the tables on dragons so that they serve man and not man them *dominion*, and they derive the notion from the Genesis creation story where man is said to have been given the power to name, that is, control or have dominion over, the beasts of the earth (including dragons).

Every hostile dragon will have one malady in common. It is a disease that is inherent in the ego-world in which dragons operate and do their breathing and snorting of fire. This malady is repression. Every dying dragon represses life in order to make the rest of us over in its (and not the living Creator's) image. But this repression is subtle for it will build on the natural (and holy) ecstasies themselves. For example, sex will be defiled to become lust—and what is lust but repressed, instead of expressed, sexuality? Religiosity without politics will emerge, as it did in the repressive atmosphere of Jesus' time. "You are the very ones who pass yourselves off as virtuous in peoples' sight, but God knows your heart." (Lk. 16.15) God and those who are becoming like God will be knowers of hearts, and pietism and religiosity will prove no substitute for the "weightier" things of religon such as justice, integrity, and mercy. Sacraments offered as holy objects apart from respect for the whole sacrament, which is all of creation, will be suspect. For all of creation is an occasion for grace for those who are like the Creator. Any dragon's trick to repress creation's beauty for the sake of manipulating or controlling individuals will be immediately recognized by the symptom of repression. Repression always sires oppression. Oppression is to repression what smoke is to fire. Everyone who has met dragons knows this.

PART IV
Toward a Theology of a Sensual Spirituality

T he trip we have taken together in this handbook, a trip from the Age of Pisces to the Age of Aquarius, from an age of religion to an age of spirituality, has been enjoyable for me. And, as so often happens in fun experiences, I have learned much in the process. One does not write a book because one knows but because one wants to know. One point that I have learned only gradually in putting my thoughts to paper and that is now rising to a level of articulation as I complete the book is the following: how immensely *sensual* the spirituality is that I have presented in this book. I have spoken of skiing and love-making and Mahler's music and nature tripping; I have spoken of our experiences of ecstasy being, in fact, our experiences of God; I have urged a pleasure-loving, pleasure-seeking, pleasure-sharing spirituality. Clearly, I have, even without knowing it, been advocating a sensual spirituality.

I should have suspected as much (perhaps the reader did in picking up this book) from the title that came to me early in this study: "WHEE, We, wee." And from the nursery rhyme which inspired it:

> This little piggie went to market
> This little piggie stayed home
> This little piggie had roast beef
> This little piggie had none.
> And this little piggie said, 'WHEE! We, wee' all the
> way home.

Pigs, after all, are profoundly sensual animals, what with all that rolling around in the mud and all. Even their "oinks" sound sensual. And I really should have taken the lesson from my subconscious that was trying to tell me something (yes, even and indeed especially something theological) by whispering to me "WHEE, We, wee" as a title. In fact, I recently heard a feminist advise her audience never to compliment a man by calling him a "male chauvinist pig." Why not? Because he feels pride in his sensuality! (More often than not an act of self-flattery, according to the speaker!) Perhaps this book is nothing else than an exegesis of my (and most of our) spiritual "reading" as children. But then again, perhaps all living spirituality is of such a kind, an encounter with our childhood. Jesus suggested it was when he said, "Unless you turn and receive like children there will be no Kingdom for you."

This section represents an attempt to be a bit more adult and analytical in my approach to the theological implications of this book. In it I would like to explore, first, the sensual spirituality of the prophets; next, the resistance and support to this sensual spirituality in subsequent Christian history; and, finally, the future of this kind of spirituality.

CHAPTER 16
The sensual spirituality of the Hebraic prophets including Jesus

I would like in this chapter to explore the precedents—so easily forgotten—in Western religious experience for a sensual spirituality. While an obvious place to look is the Song of Songs (and I heartily recommend curling up with this sensual book at night or early morning, whichever you find more sensual whether alone or with another) or to the Psalms, that is not the route I am choosing to explore. I will instead explore the spirituality of the prophets of Israel and then of a more recent descendent of that same line, Jesus of Nazareth. Before we do this, let us consider the terminology for our exploration, or, better, some experiences on which the terminology is founded.

Elsewhere in this book I have used a negative methodology rather effectively for, as it were, creeping up on a definition of a spiritual term. I will do the same here, asking first: What is the opposite of sensual? For if the sensual deserves to be called spiritual, then it is itself a spiritual term, and we can approach it the way we do other definitions of spiritual experiences. It goes without saying that we are now (as we have been from the start of this book) speaking of experiences: the God of spirituality is the God of experience; God as verb. I ask then: What are our experiences of asensuality?

They are, unfortunately, legion. The reader will recall the complaint, cited in the introduction to this handbook, of W. B. Yeats, who dismissed most of contemporary society's "professionals" (the "pillars of society," you will recall) as being terrors to children and ignominious to lovers. Within this category are not only lawyers, scientists, and doctors, but (and deservedly so) theologians as well.

When I read theologians (and I do a lot of it), I can't help but second Mr. Yeat's observation. So many of them write, as Wilfrid Sheed comments, as if they have nothing to say or feel "that couldn't be translated into Latin." Latin, as we all know, is a dead language. And so is far too much theology ... and, I presume, far too many theologians. Reading certain theological books, then, strikes me as a profoundly asensual experience.

What are some other examples of asensual experiences? One of the most profound such experiences I ever had was, believe it or not, while dining one evening in a large city in the South. I came to eat, to discuss, to drink, to have a good, earthy time (arriving with the expectations that I suspect most of us bring to a dinner out). Instead, I underwent a shock of alienation. Sitting at my place at a plastic-covered tablecloth, I suddenly was presented with the most elaborate decisions to make: I counted eight (!) different pieces of silverware which I was destined to have to commit myself to throughout the meal; three different glasses I was going to have to make decisions about; four different plates that were destined to separate me from my food; and, sad to tell, the conversation reflected all too accurately the dinner setting. I guess we are indeed (or are not) what we eat (or don't eat). It was a harrowing experience; I was fortunate to escape with only indigestion. I learned there the value of eating sensually.

But I also learned to ask a question: What has our society done to ourselves (to say nothing of our stomachs) in so perversely alienating the mouth from the meat? How far have we gone in substituting man-made objects ranging from four different sizes of forks to plastic see-through cloths to glasses and tumblers and cups for every finger for the God-given pleasure of communing with wine and bread and other godly gifts?

When you consider other experiences of sensual alienation that we no doubt all share, you have to answer the above question with some sort of an exclamation like

"You haven't seen nothing yet, buddy!" How about our work conditions, for example? It was one thing for Karl Marx and Charles Dickens to complain of the filthy sweat shop and sleep-inducing monotony of assembly lines in factories in nineteenth century England, but at least this much can be said of those working climates: people *did* sweat and they did do manual labor (i.e., their hands got dirty and even worn in interaction with other material realities). But how about the bureaucrat in today's white collar (notice the title) jobs? Not only do they not sweat, they're not even allowed to sweat! (Isn't that the spirituality behind the waterfall of antiperspirant, anti-deodorant, antismell, antiliving commercials that so inundate us on television?) Shuffling papers and sitting under neon lights may not make workers cry, "Alienation!" but it should. (One doctor told me that he treats far more cases of hemorrhoids than slivers these days). But the amazing, and indeed alarming, situation in today's sensual alienation in work is that so few are objecting to it. Passively, unlike their sweat shop ancestors who howled till someone heard, do these workers—whether of academia or government, of bank or Pentagon or church—go to their sensual (and spiritual) deaths. Led like sheep, following their paychecks passively.

A repression of the sensual produces a perverse kind of pleasure-seeking, the kind of sado-masochistic sensuality that was relayed in the documentary film *Hearts and Minds*, when a bomber pilot of many sorties over Vietnam confessed that dropping bombs at 42,000 feet and watching them explode was a thrill comparable to Fourth of July fireworks as a child. Indeed, our asensual society has produced a sense-less people—people without senses or sensitivity; people in search of their kicks and jollies at the violent expense of others.

Surely there lies beneath all this asensuality some secret yearning for an awakening, for a sensual experience? If only some people or some person or even some religion were to say: "Yes, it's okay. Wake up. Be sensual."[1]

We have toyed now with some experiences of asensuality. It hardly seems necessary to elaborate or multiply examples since our lives are inundated in the asensual; we swim in it from our home television sets to our places of work and, far too often, in between as well (isn't every urban thruway, that triumph of technology and efficiency, also a triumph of treeless, peopleless, childrenless asensuality?) What are examples of sensual experiences? I suggest some of the following as starters:

> To walk barefoot in sand or grass is sensual.
> To laugh heartily is sensual.
> To burp is sensual.
> To get up at dawn and walk with the dew is sensual.
> To eat is sensual.
> To eat barbecued ribs in the hand is very sensual.
> To take a warm shower is sensual; to take a hot bath is very sensual.
> To make love is sensual.
> To throw pots is sensual.
> To give birth—to a child, to a picture, to a poem, to a song—is sensual.
> To sleep under the stars is sensual.
> To drink is sensual; to drink blood is very sensual.
> To swim is sensual.
> To ski is sensual.
> To lie in the sun is sensual.
> To dance is sensual.
> To hear opera is sensual.
> To watch dancers is sensual.
> To smell lilacs is sensual.
> To turn over dirt by hand in a garden is sensual.
> To be in darkness is sensual.
> A violin is sensual; a cello is very sensual.
> To cry is sensual.
> To pick corn is sensual.

To hug a baby is sensual.
To get a backrub is sensual
To be alive is sensual. Very, very sensual.

These are examples of sensual experiences. The reader can add her or his own. Included, I hope, in the reader's choices will be another look at our list of natural ecstasies from Part I of this book. Running down that list one can readily see that each ecstasy we have alluded to and called an experience of God is also deeply sensual. What do all sensual experiences appear to have in common? Are there common notes that we can draw out of them to reach an agreement on what we mean by the sensual?

First of all, they are all actions, activities, verbs. In a period when process theologians are considering the implications of God as verb,[2] our ears should immediately perk up when we hear this: here is a hint, perhaps, of God's activity and, indeed, personality in our midst. A second characteristic of these sensual experiences is their time aspect. They all happen (or can happen) in the now. There is no denial of time in the sensual mystical experience as there is in the idealistic mystical experience (Buddhists and Neoplatonists, Needham points out, feel "there is something unreal about time").[3] Time may be suspended or forgotten in these sensual experiences, but it is not repressed or considered unimportant.

Still another characteristic common to each of these sensual experiences is their bodiliness. They are not possible to angels or to those who want to strive to be angels. Dietrich Bonhoeffer, when he was subjected to the asensual life of prison (a life, I suggest, most of us in or out of prison are subjected to in large part today), expresses his need for the sensual:

> I should like to feel the full force of the sun
> again, making the skin hot and the whole body
> glow, and reminding me that I'm a corporeal

being. I should like to be tired by the sun, instead of by books and thoughts. I should like to have it awaken my animal existence—I should like, not just to see the sun and sip at it a litte, but to experience it bodily.[4]

The word "sensual" comes from the word "sense," meaning our bodily senses (do we have any other kind?) are put in motion in sensual activities.

What then is a sensual spirituality? A sensual spirituality is one that praises God for creating and continuing to create the sensual experiences of:

touch for holding; caressing; hugging; arousing; forgiving; healing . . . .

sight for drinking in colors of rainbows and paints and oceans and bodies black, yellow, red, white, brown and Renoirs and films by Fellini . . . .

hearing of birds chirping and leaves touching and voices speaking and music announcing and silence and waves lapping and . . . .

smell of lilac trees when you least expect it, of honey, of the sea, of freshly cut grass or hay, of roses, of bodies, of a winter day, of . . . .

taste of cookies, of rose d'anjou, of honey bread, of halibut, of lobster, of fresh salad, of Italian pasta, of Normandaise sauces, of . . . .

Thus, a sensual spirituality is not one that merely tolerates the experiences of the senses; much less is it one that tries to "put to death" the senses. A sensual spirituality praises the gift of one's senses—fingers and eyes, ears and olfactory nerves, tongue and imagination, nerves and brain waves and the Gift-giver. And it praises the Gift-giver neither abstractly by pious words or recited formulas nor asensually but in a decidedly sensual manner. That is, one celebrates the gift of these gifts by using them. Therein, as within any adult gift, lies the ultimate thank you or

Eucharist or prayer: in enjoying and using and developing and sharing the rich potential of the senses. One gives thanks for eyes by seeing and enjoying the looking; for the nose by smelling; for the ears by listening and developing the capacity to listen ever more richly. This Jesus taught in his parable of the talents, wherein those who bury their gifts (invariably out of fear, as the parable goes) are chastized; while those who invest them—multiplying them, using them, watching them blossom—are praiseworthy. For they are praisers of the Creator.

What more can be said of a sensual spirituality? It seems to me that the following qualities accompany a sensual experience that is radical enough to be called spiritual. First, *we become participants* not commanders, but in some way receivers and partially passive insofar as we receive gifts of color and touch, light and sound, through our senses. Here we can recognize how a mystery-oriented spirituality complements and indeed relies on sensual experiences of depth.[5] Participation in life's mysteries provides the core of this spiritual way of life and not a problem-solving, control-oriented attitude, on the one hand, or a mortification-oriented asceticism, on the other.

Second, such a sensual spirituality, because it relies on participation as distinct from subject-object control or dichotomizing, is profoundly *unitive.* It means we become the subjects we interact with in some way—the music we hear, the colors we ingest, the food we eat, the bodies we touch. Barriers of differences are broken down; unity is tasted, oneness is achieved. It is the essence of participation to unite with and to erase the boundaries of distinction between and among. This surely takes place in a sensual spiritual experience.

Third, matter is the beginning and end of the experience. We participate through our senses. The senses become doors and more than doors—the medium becomes the message. Our senses cannot be ignored, left behind, abandoned, or left to rot in the process. They are integral to the process and the keener and keener development of them leads to a deeper and richer, more senstive and more expansive spiritual experience. They need to be trained, disciplined, and even tested to develop to their untapped potential. Such development, then, is itself a spiritual exercise. What it is we are uniting with through our senses and with which we participate in a sensual spirituality is *matter*. Yes, good old material things. Like water or soundwaves or food or wine or a body or pigments of color. A sensual spirituality is a *material* spirituality. We praise the Creator of all matter and of all creation; indeed, we unite with that Creator's material creation.[6] To grasp the significance of this, it is necessary to recognize a distinction between matter (which is God-made and, therefore, glorious and to be praised and united with) and materialism (which is the onesided worship of what are usually man-made objects of literalism, such as dollar bills, Cadillacs, and other such idols). God is the author of matter; man, the erector of materialism. Celebration of the former is holy; worship of the latter is idolatry.

Fourth, it follows that a sensual spirituality is also a *feminist* spiritually—women are indeed related to matter in a special way. There is a truth to "Mother Earth" symbolism, to hills symbolizing female breasts, to the earth's fields giving forth vegetation and grain as the goddess Cybele reminds us. In Latin, the word for matter *(materia)* is from the same root as the word for mother *(mater)*. Even in our own language, "matter" and "mother" or "mutter" are not far off. A fear of the sensual is a fear of the mother. As such, those who construct their spiritualities on this fear (most usually men) fear women. A male spirituality fears the sensual. A feminist spirituality will embrace it. As a mother does.[7]

Fifth, a final characteristic of every sensual experience that is also a spiritual one is its memorableness. A sensual experience is a memorable experience: the beauty of it lodges in the imagination. From there it invites us to imbibe again, to go out to a new and future pleasure and union, to look forward and not backward.[8]

Our religious instruction from youth has often repeated that "God is Spirit." How we took this instruction, whether gracefully or ideologically, determines much of how we accept the sensual as integral to the spiritual. Some religion, wrapping itself in Greek philosophical notions which dictate that the spiritual must be the immaterial and asensual, would make us feel guilty or fearful to experience the sensual. Buttressed by rationalism and an impressive series of head trips, this kind of spiritual thinking calls the earthy and sensual anthropomorphism of the Bible inferior to its own abstractions. As if it is more likely that God is a paper-pusher or footnote-chaser than a lover, a farmer, a parent. The practical result ("by their fruits you will know" spiritualities) is a spiritual schizophrenia or at best a spiritual paralysis.

For the Hebraic spirituality, however, "God is Spirit" does not mean that God is the epitome of the immaterial. It rather means that God is the most alive of us all: the live-giver par excellence. It also means God is superbly passionate, filled with emotion and what Heschel calls "pathos" for human history. Thus, God is the most spirited of us all. "It is as non-biblical to separate emotion or passion from spirit as it is to disparage emotion or passion. . . . Emotion is inseparable from being filled with the spirit, which is above all a state of being moved."[9] God is passionate and deeply affected emotionally by the plight of humankind.

Because the Greek and not the Hebraic understanding of spirit has held sway so long in Western consciousness (particularly among Christians) I would like to go deeper into the emotional, even sensual, side of God as the Jews understood their God to be. Let us consider the God that the prophets of Israel knew so well. The prophet Hosea not only ponders God's relationship to Israel but also offers hints of the inner life of God. God, says Hosea, "will come to us as showers come, like spring rains watering the earth." (6.3b) The God whom Hosea experienced was no cold, distant ruler, no authority figure in the sky; rather, this God was sensitive and compassionate:

> My heart is turned within Me,
> My compassion grows like a flame.
> I will not execute my fierce anger,
> I will not again destroy Ephraim;
>   (11.8—Heschel's translation)

God is tender toward people like a mother who conceives a son; while the relationship is stormy, it will end lovingly: "When Israel was a child I loved him, and I called my son out of Egypt." (11.1) The love of God for Israel is like the love of husband and wife. Israel is the consort of God and Heschel points out that this insight constitutes "one of the most important ideas in the history of Judaism."[10] It is developed in the Song of Songs. A day will come, in spite of the infidelities of one of the marriage partners, namely Israel, when—

> You will call me, 'My husband,'
> I will betroth you to myself for ever,
> I will betroth you to myself with faithfulness,
> and you will come to know Yahweh (2.16, 19, 20)

Yahweh's love is compassionate and caring as is that of a parent or a lover, desirous of the pleasure of his beloved.

> I myself taught Ephraim to walk,
> I took them in my arms;
> I was like someone who lifts an infant close against
>   his cheek;
> stooping down to him I gave him his food.

> I was the one who was giving her

the corn, the wine, the oil,
and who freely gave her that silver and gold
of which they have made Baals. (11.3, 4; 2.8)

Not only does God perform the sensual acts of sharing the sensual and mothering her children, but also God even speaks sensually in Hosea. So deeply touching to humankind is the "knowledge of God" that the proper meaning of this frequently used phrase in Hosea is sexual union between God and his people. It means "the fulfillment of the conjugal intercourse between Israel and the Lord," comments one scholar.[11]

In the prophet Isaiah, the imagery for depicting the God of Israel is also memorably sensual.

Let me sing to my friend,
the song of his love for his vineyard.

My friend had a vineyard
on a fertile hillside.
He dug the soil, cleared it of stones,
and planted choice vines in it.
Yes, the vineyard of Yahweh Sabaoth
and the men of Judah
that chosen plant. (Is 5.1, 2, 7)

So God is a farmer, a planter of vineyards. One close to the soil. Earthy. And loving towards his crop.

That day,
sing of the delightful vineyard!
I, Yahweh, am its keeper;
every moment I water it
for fear its leaves should fall;
night and day I watch over it.

But the love of this vinekeeper can easily turn to anger.

> If thorns and briars come
> I will declare war on them,
> I will burn them every one,
> Or if they would shelter under my protection,
> let them make their peace with me,
> let them make their peace with me. (27.2-5)

The prophet Jeremiah also finds it necessary to describe the God of Israel in sensuous terms. God is a father and Israel a son and, like any father, God seeks Israel's pleasure.

> For I am a father to Israel,
> and Ephraim is my first-born son.
> And I was thinking:
> How I wanted to rank you with my sons,
> and give you a country of delights,
> the fairest heritage of all the nations!
> I had thought you would call me: My father,
> and would never cease to follow me. (31.9; 3.19)

Like Hosea, Jeremiah sees a marriage existing between God and his people. "I was their husband says the Lord." (31.32–Heschel's translation)

> I remember the affection of your youth,
> the love of your bridal days (2.2)

Indeed, the marriage's memory is of honeymoon days.

But this love, too, can turn to anger. "She roars at me ferociously; so now I hate her." (12.8) God's relationship to his prophet is of sweet enticement, on the one hand, and violence, on the other.

> O Lord, Thou hast seduced me,

And I am seduced;
Thou hast raped me
And I am overcome. (20.7—Heschel's translation)

It is a testimony to the sensual spirituality of the Jews that their prophet speaking of their God does not hesitate "to describe the impact of God upon his life" with words "identical with the terms of seduction and rape in the legal terminology of the Bible."[1][2]

Jeremiah's sensuality extends to images of eating and to sexual delights.

When your words came I devoured them;
your word was my delight
and the joy of my heart;
for I was called by your name,
Yahweh, God of Sabaoth. (15.16)

The four times the words "joy" and "delight" are used by Jeremiah are always in situations concerning nuptial festivities. This prophet saw his relation to Yahweh as one of betrothal to the God of hosts. In still another situation, Jeremiah refers to God's people as loincloths and God as loins: "For just as a loincloth clings to a man's waist, so I had intended the whole House of Judah to cling to me—it is Yahweh who speaks." (13.11)

Second-Isaiah, the prophet of comfort to a grieving people, also employs sensual imagery to understand the God of the Jews. He compares God to a potter. (Is there any vocation more sensual, more earthy, than the potter's?)

We the clay, you the potter
We are all the work of your hand,
Does the clay say to its fashioner, "What are you
    making?"
does the thing he shaped say, "You have no skill?"

> I it was who made the earth,
> and created man who is on it. (Is. 64.8; 45.9, 12)

Second-Isaiah uses an image that Heschel calls "the boldest figure used by any prophet." It is that of God as "a woman in travail."

> I groan like a woman in labour,
> I suffocate, I stifle. (42.14)

And God, in her care and compassion, handles humankind with the touch of a caring parent. "I hid you in the shadow of my hand, when I spread out the heavens and laid the earth's foundations and said to Zion, "You are my people." (51.16) Thus, as Heschel has put it: "The prophet very rarely speaks of God's face; he feels His hand."[13]

We have seen a profound difference between the God of the Jews and the God of the Greeks. The latter had to be asensual to fulfill the requirements of philosophical mysticism; the former was deeply rooted in the soil and the sensual, as were his foremost spokespersons, the prophets.

The prophets, in effect, take the sensual for granted vis-a-vis themselves, nature, others, childbirth, and God. Perhaps this facility with the sensual and the spiritual is understandable as being integral to a people of an agricultural economy who lived and survived so close to the soil. Earth, sun, water, babies were all integral to their human survival. Some would argue that the God of industrial society need not be sensual because humankind has lost its attachment to the soil. But I would say the opposite is the case. Precisely because we cannot take the sensual for granted, humankind is frantic with efforts to experience it—witness the insatiable appetites for "how to" books and erotic magazines for maximizing sexual pleasure. Our times are finally resisting the asensuality of so much of our attitudes and institutions. More than ever, then, do believers in a God of creation require a sensual God. And we have one.

But the sensual God of the Jews and the sensual prophets who announced this God were not trumpeters of the sensual in itself. The prophets' effort was profoundly historical; that is, to see the people of God develop into a people of justice and compassion, a people like their God. Sensuality was not a one-way pursuit for the Jews. The other root element to their spirituality, the overriding one, in fact, was historical. They were to carry on in their history the justice (i.e., judgment) of Yahweh. The sensual experience, then, serves political ends, which are clearly understood to be care, compassion and, above all justice for the people. "not mere feeling, but action" will accomplish Yahweh's justice. Prophets speak "not for the idea of justice, but for the God of justice."[14] For their God is a God, as we have seen, who can suffer. And compassion or sympathy, the ability to suffer with God, became "the fundamental feature of the prophet's inner life." This compassion can take the form of suffering with God in the sense of sharing the misery that God endures over the evil of injustice or of suffering for God, being moved by God's own pathos to act in God's name. "Thus the prophet is guided, not by what he feels, but rather by what God feels."[15] If *"ruah"* means passion, then a spiritual person is a passionate person. And a compassionate person.

The prophets' compassion urges them to act and speak concretely, threateningly, sensitively from an experience of injustice. They pull no political punches for they speak for Yahweh, not for political parties, personal gain or compromises. And for that reason their words, if hearkened today, are just as sensitive; just as threatening.

> Woe to you, ravager never ravaged,
> plunderer never plundered!
> When your ravaging is over, you shall be ravaged;

> when your plundering is done, you shall be
>   plundered. (Is. 33.1)

> Woe to those ensconced so snugly in Zion
> You think to defer the day of misfortune,
> but you hasten the reign of violence.
> Lying on ivory beds
> and sprawling on their divans,
> they dine on lambs from the flock,
> and stall-fattened veal;
> they drink wine by the bowlful,
> and use the finest oil for anointing themselves,
> but about the ruin of Joseph they do not care at
>   all.
> That is why they will be the first to be exiled;
> the sprawlers' revelry is over. (Amos 6.1, 4, 6, 7)

Notice that Amos is not departing from the Hebraic approval of the sensual in condemning luxurious living: The luxurious err because they do not care about "the ruin of Joseph"; that is, about other people. They lack compassion. It is one-sided hedonism; it is riches in the midst of suffering; it is unjust; therefore, it is an abomination to God who is a "God of justice." (Is. 30.18)

The historical struggle for justice presumes some sensual relationship to God and creation; more than that, justice itself might be understood as the very sharing of the fruits of the earth, the pleasures of spirited (i.e., spiritual) living. When the prophets look forward to the Day of Yahweh, a day when justice will reign as God desires, they find it necessary once again to fall back on the sensual for their richest imagery. Sensual joy and delight will prevail.

> Then the eyes of the blind shall be opened,
> the ears of the deaf unsealed,
> then the lame shall leap like a deer
> and the tongues of the dumb sing for joy;

for water gushes in the desert,
streams in the wasteland,
They will come to Zion shouting for joy,
everlasting joy on their faces;
joy and gladness will go with them
and sorrow and lament be ended. (Is. 35.5, 6, 10)

The days are coming now—it is Yahweh who speaks—
when harvest will follow directly after ploughing,
the treading of grapes soon after sowing,
when the mountains will run with new wine
and the hills all flow with it.
I mean to restore the fortunes of my people Israel.
they will rebuild the ruined cities and live in them,
plant vineyards and drink their wine,
dig gardens and eat their produce.
I will plant them in their own country,
never to be rooted up again
out of the land I have given them,
says Yahweh, your God. (Amos 9.13-15)

How sensual, how full of earthiness and wine, dancing and singing is this vision of the Day of Yahweh. How spiritual, too. For it is a vision of justice, the sharing of the sensual gifts of the earth. It is a spirituality of the God who is again a planter; this time a planter of people: rooting them in their homeland where delights and pleasures flow. A refreshing spirituality, this.

This spirituality was also Jesus' spirituality. Jesus was a Jew instructed in the sensual and prophetic tradition of his ancestors that we have considered above. He never read the Neoplatonists, the mystical philosophers who felt it necessary to squelch the sensual in order to feel the divine. He partied and drank wine; he engaged in Jewish sensual banquet meals; he walked with sandals and feet dirtied by the sandy earth of his homeland; he seldom slept in the city, preferring the outdoors, such as the park called

Gethsemane to spend the night in—usually, no doubt, sleeping on the earth; he frequently went out in nature—the desert, the lake, the mountains, the hills overlooking the lake—to be alone. He reveled in friendships with men and women alike, not feeling at all embarrassed or self-conscious (though the banker of the group was) when one woman of questionable repute poured perfumed oil on his feet and then dried them with her long hair. His friend John lay with his head on his breast.[16]

So sensual was he, and so far from being a platonic ascetic, that he was reproached by those who observed him as being a glutton and wine drinker! "The Son of Man came, eating and drinking, and they say, 'Look, a glutton and a drunkard, a friend of tax collectors and sinners.' " (Mt. 11.9 cf. 9.14ff.) His parables and preaching were the fruit of his compassion for persons and his intimate union with nature. Of seeds and rains he speaks; of lilies and leaven; of fruit and of fishing. All this was apt imagery for the Kingdom of God that Jesus announces.

What, if anything, does Jesus bring to the sensual spirituality of the prophets that is unique? Timing. Jesus announces that the sensuousness of the "Last Days," of the "Day of Yahweh," of the Messianic Age has begun. Jesus comes announcing the Good, sensual, News. And he does it sensually, as we have seen.

Jesus' message is an earthy one just as the prophets understood it would be. For example, he promises: "Blessed are the gentle because they will possess *the earth.*" (Mt. 5.5) In the Hebraic context of sensual prophecy, we recognize that this is not an etherial promise. It is an earthy one. Because if it is etherial, it "refers to the domain of the heart and everything continues peacefully as it was."[17] In fact, this very earthy promise is another sign that the Messianic Kingdom, a kingdom of pleasure and fullness, has begun, as the psalmist promised.

A little longer and the wicked will be no more,

search his place well, he will not be there;
but the humble shall have the land for their own
to enjoy untroubled peace (Ps. 37.10f.)[18]

Here no one can confuse the earthy promise with a spiritualized one.

Furthermore, the meaning of Jesus' farewell supper, which the Christian Eucharist celebrates, is the very "heavenly banquet" of the Messianic Kingdom. It is sealed with a sensual drinking of his blood. All three synoptic Gospel writers allude to the "heavenly banquet" theme in their retelling of the Last Supper. (cf. Mt. 26.29; Mk. 14.25; Lk. 22.15-18) Jesus anticipates a full messianic victory by way of a banquet, where the eating and drinking of body and blood is sensual indeed.

But for him, as for his prophetic ancestors, it all culminated in politics: in a sharing of the earth's joys, which also implies a criticism of the earth's manipulators. And so, attacking, retreating, being clever and being silent, being obtuse and being poetical, he could not escape in the long run the lot of the prophet. They caught up with him, these religious and professional pillars of man-made society. He had to die. A sensuous person who is in it only for his own pleasure is no great threat to society; but one who wants to share the joys, let us crucify him. Naked preferably.[19] And what, when he was asked about his task in life, did he summarize it to be? He needed Isaiah's help for that. "Go back and tell John what you hear and see: the blind see again, and the lame walk, lepers are cleansed, and the deaf hear, and the dead are raised to life and the Good News is proclaimed to the poor, and happy is the man who does not lose faith in me." (Mt. 11.4.5) To describe his mission he needed the sensual descriptions furnished by the prophets before him.

And so we learn that the Good News is sensual news. For it is an announcement about how the blind are seeing; the lame dancing and leaping; the putrifying feeling

comfortable and smelling clean again; the deaf hearing and
listening; the dead coming to life; the poor rich with this
and other Good, sensual, News. No putting to death of the
senses in this spirituality. Rather, a sharing of the joys and
ecstasies that the Creator intends by our sense experiences.

CHAPTER 17
Asensual vs. sensual spirituality during the Piscean Age of Christian history

We have seen how the Jews and a particular Jew named Jesus had no difficulty in building a spirituality on the sensual and sharing it. The obvious and very pressing question arises: What happened to this spirituality in the West and, in particular, in Christianity? First, I think it is imperative to take the *fact* of Western asensual spirituality very seriously. For it is a fact that the asensual and not the sensual has held sway in the theology of spirituality. To underline the factual basis of this observation, I would like to call the attention of the reader to the following religious phenomenon. It is a custom (I have been told) in Jewish households that the Sabbath celebration is to culminate in a husband and wife's making love together.[1] At the same time, manuals for Catholic priests were distributed and in circulation up to a few years ago in America which stated that the priest was to advise a married couple that if they want communion Sunday morning they should abstain from sexual relations Saturday night.

Lest, once again, we underestimate the pervasive influence and subtle power of this asensual spirituality in Christianity, I think it appropriate that we listen to certain influential preachers. The fifteenth century monk Thomas à Kempis gives the following spiritual advice in his influential work *Imitation of Christ*.

> The more violence you do to yourself, the greater
> will be your growth in grace.
> There is no other way to life and to true inward
> peace

save the way of the holy cross, and of daily
mortification.
Man must think of himself as he really is: nothing.
Truly to know and despise oneself is the best and
most perfect counsel.[2]

William James cites liberally from the fourteenth century
Dominican spiritual writer Henry Suso and concludes that
he was "distinctly pathological"[3] in his sixteen years of
bodily mortifications, which included (among others) the
following devices: a hair shirt and iron chain that he wore
until he bled; undergarments with 150 sharp nails in them
that ran up to his belly button and that he slept in at
night; two leather gloves with sharp-pointed tacks to wear
at night so that he would not in his sleep inadvertently
remove the lice that crawled on him from his body (this
way he would tear the flesh of his chest rather than relieve
himself of his lice). These are just some of Suso's
imaginative efforts to render himself less sensual. He
ceased this masochism after his fortieth birthday and has
been declared "blessed" by the Catholic Church. The
extremely influential French preacher of the seventeenth
century, Bossuet, gave the following sermon about sexuality.

Cursed be the earth, cursed be the earth, a
thousand times cursed be the earth from which
rises continually that heavy fog and those black
vapors which ascend from these dark passions
and hide heaven and its light from us and draw
down the lightning and rays of divine justice
against the corruption of the human race.[4]

Where did this worship of an asensual God arise from?
Clearly, we cannot examine each Christian spiritual writer
separately in this brief essay. Therefore, I will choose to
look at just two of them: Marcion and Denis the

Pseudoareopagite. The former is noteworthy because he appears to initiate in full force a Christian asensual spirituality for later generations; the latter is noteworthy because, without any doubt whatsoever, Denis' spirituality reigned supreme (though dissidents arose throughout church history) in Christian spirituality up to the sixteenth century.

Marcion was born about thirty years after Paul's death and insisted all his life that he represented the fullness of Paul's thought. That thought, as Marcion interpreted it, was virulently anti-Jewish. Quite logically, it was also anticreation—the world is "stupid and bad, crawling with vermin, a miserable hole, an object of scorn," said Marcion. He was also antisensual. In fact, so antisensual was he that he insisted that the God of grace and Jesus could not possibly have created "the disgusting paraphernalia of reproduction and nauseating defilements of human flesh from birth to final putrescence."[5] It followed from this that Marcion condemned all sexual experience and required a vow of celibacy for baptism itself. If already married, a Christian convert must refrain from intercourse after baptism and could not divorce. He actually tampered with Paul's letter to the Ephesians, which is so Jewish in its analogy of God's love to human sexual intercourse. Let us contrast the two texts:

> Paul: "He loves his flesh who loves his wife as Christ loved the church." (Eph. 5.28)

> Marcion: "He loves his flesh who loves his wife as Christ loved the church, that is asexually . . . . For the sake of her (the church) a man shall leave his father and mother and the two (man and the church) shall be one flesh."[6]

Not content with throwing out the Hebrew Bible and with altering Paul's own letters, Marcion draws a logical conclusion from his asensual spirituality: the Creator, who is the God of the Hebrew Bible, must be shunned. Instead, the God of Jesus, who would be "incapable of anger, entirely apathetic, free from all affections," should be adopted.

Needless to say, Marcion's spirituality was rejected. He was excommunicated from the Christian Church in 144 AD. Yet, his ideas did not disappear that readily. For two hundred years, Christian theologians continued to attack his works. This is evidence of how powerful a force his thought was in early Christianity.[7] The anti-Semitism of Marcion has endured to our time, most notably in the nineteenth century Christian historian, Adolf Harnack.[8] Unfortunately, as so often happens in prolonged battles, the two pugilists become to resemble one another more than they would want to think. The dualism between a God of creation and a God of grace was never breached in the mainstream of Christian spirituality. Marcion rejected the Jewish God for his passions—his capacity for anger as well as for affection. Clement and Origen taught that anger and affection must not be predicated literally of the God in the Bible. And Augustine agreed. The sensual God was effectively silenced.[9]

A second spiritual writer of lasting impact as regards a quest for an asensual God is Denis the Pseudoareopagite. We will call him Pseudo-Denis for short. Unlike Marcion, he was never excommunicated; rather, his works received a near canonization in both Eastern and Western churches—so much so that his authenticity (he was thought to be the Denis whom Paul converted in Athens) was not seriously questioned until the fifteenth century. Even at that time, entire schools stood by his authenticity (such as Cardinal Bellarmine, overseer of the saints lives in Catholicism—hagiography has remained profoundly asensual right up to the twentieth century). In fact, Pseudo-Denis was a sixth century Syrian monk. (Syria, by the way, was something of a hotbed for asceticism). It is to him that we owe the term "mysticism" to designate an interior experience of divine reality. Asceticism was recommended for the sake of a subsequent mystical experience. But such union first required a separation from all creatures and all of creation: a renouncement of self which Denis called "purification" but which had its antecedents in Clement of Alexandria's theory of *apatheia*. Apatheia was taught by the Stoics and it meant freedom from domination by exterior influences: a rugged individualism if there ever was one.

The philosophy underlying this spirituality (in addition to Stoicism) is the Neoplatonism of the last major Greek philosopher, Proclus, who lived 410-485. Proclus was a wealthy, handsome young man who underwent a profound conversion to Neoplatonic idealism and then committed himself to living out that philosophy as a way of life. (Philosophy still meant a spirituality or way of life at that time and not an esoteric, cerebral ego trip it so often means today.) He never married and was a vegetarian and semiascetic who was destined to be the last link between Platonism and the Western world. He did not fail those seeking a spiritual idealism. For Proclus, reality (what theologians would call creation) is not fundamentally material, but mental. The only true reality is the "one" and this he identified with God. In seeking consciously or unconsciously for union with the One, we need to renounce the appearances (for they are only that) of the body, including physical desires, social relations and political interests—all the misleading suggestions of the senses, imagination, and opinions.[10] Instead, we should devote ourselves to developing rational knowledge which prepares us to grasp eternal ideal realities like Mind, Power, Being.[11]

This is not such a far-out philosophy for a rich young man bent on mystical experiences as a life goal. But it is light years away from the Jewish sensual-political spirituality we have been considering which takes the poor and not just the priggishly wealthy into account. The fact that Proclus was not a believer hardly inhibited Denis the

Pseudoareopagite, of whom it has been said that "no other early Christian writer was so clearly influenced by a particular philosopher" as was Denis by Proclus.[12] Denis, like Proclus, Plato, and Aristotle before him, saw the order of the universe carried out in several hierarchies of beings descending from the orderly One and striving to ascend to them. The celestial hierarchy contemplates and shares in the divine perfection and consists of ranked members: Seraphim, Cherubim, Thrones, Dominations, Powers, Authorities, Principalities, Archangels and Angels. Each member becomes more corporeal as it descends (thus, less spiritual and close to the asensual God).[13] The earthly form of this hierarchy is none other than the church's hierarchy. Jesus is at the top post and in descending order we have chrism, communion and baptism; bishops, priests, and deacons; monks, laity and catechumens—three triads of each.

It seems to me that the real resistance to democracy in church structures today will be met at the level of spirituality. To become democratic, churches and their churchmen will have to surrender a hierarchical model of church structure that has become all the more hallowed and sanctified precisely because churchmen have internalized the hierarchical spirituality of Pseudo-Denis.[14] To alter this spirituality and its sociological projections onto institution will call for genuine *metanoia*, conversions in the fullest sense of the word from vertical to more horizontal spiritual and cultural models.

One result of this flight from the world of senses to the real world of God is that the soul, leaving behind the perceptions of the senses and of reason, falls into an obscurity. This is a holy obscurity for in it one knows God (*know* here is far from the biblical 'know': it means contemplation alone). God being unknowable, the ecstasy of union with him is done in darkness and a certain knowledge beyond reason.

As one might suspect, Denis does not even consider

Jesus of Nazareth. He is profoundly influenced by mono-physitism, a doctrine current in his time and area which, in fact, denied the human nature of Christ. No wonder Denis did not need the Hebrew Bible; his Christ had no historical, human lineage. Yet, Denis' influence through Catholic spirituality has been greater than that of Paul or even Jesus.

It should be noted that Denis, for all his claims to a union with a perfect one (whom he "Christianized" by calling it the Creator) and to being distant from this world, offers a definite political ideology. The question that I continually ask as a student of Western spirituality is: Why has Denis (and Marcion) been so frequently preferred in Christianity to the Jewish and prophetic, creation-centered spirituality? I can answer this only two ways. First, idealism attracts and especially it attracts the wealthy (like Proclus) who have leisure time, on the one hand, and who have a stake in keeping the status quo as it is, on the other. If guilt and fear over the sensual can be internalized in political upstarts, then all is well. The earthly hierarchies remain heavenly. Second, I am convinced that these spiritualities clearly are profoundly political. You cannot build an empire on justice (the prophets' spirituality) and the Christian Church did indeed inherit an empire in 312. Nor can you fight wars if sensuality is not carefully overseen and regulated, especially as regards the birth of children (i.e., warriors). The more you can sanctify this hierarchical and asensual spirituality, the more ideological and untouchable it becomes. Repression in the name of divinity becomes oppression from Marcion to Richard Nixon. Both repression and oppression are simple, efficient means for controlling others. They are as old as civilization.[15]

Thus, asensual spirituality, for all its claims to being otherworldly, is profoundly hierarchical and repressive. It is phallic in its compulsion to verticalism (God is up; we are down) and antiwoman. It is chauvinistic to an extreme, for example, to Tertullian's extreme that "woman is the gateway of hell" or Augustine's that "man, not woman, is made in God's image."[16] It is antiwoman because it is anticreation (women do bear children after all) and antimatter (since anything material changes and is not eternal or spiritual in the asensual sense). For all these reasons, it needs to be anti-Semite. Feminist theologians today are undermining the entire dominant history of Western spirituality with the deep questions they are putting to the chauvinism of the Fathers. The ordination of women in the sacramental churches (Anglican, Roman and Eastern Catholic) is the playing out of this struggle for the spiritual soul of Christendom.

I have said that Marcion's anti-Semitism and anti-creation spirituality as well as Pseudo-Denis' Neoplatonic flight to contemplation and hierarchical ascents has been the dominant theology of spirituality in the West. But there have also been exceptions to these asensual spiritualities, dissidents in the long line of Yea-sayers. They never prevailed in Catholic spirituality though they have had some impact. Let us consider a few of them briefly here.

Appropriately enough, one of the most outstanding proponents of a sensual spirituality in the West is a woman. Her name was Heloise and she lived a much-heralded life of study, romance and tragedy. Heloise was a famous woman in twelfth-century France who "far surpassed in knowledge all other women of her time."[17] She was lettered and under the guardianship of her uncle, Fulbert, a cleric and canon in that small but daring world of Notre Dame and the University of Paris. Fate changed her life when she was seduced emotionally and physically by the most acclaimed genius of that century. Abelard, who was a cleric, was the "undisputed possessor of the title of Master in the Schools of Paris,"[18] acclaimed in classrooms packed with eager students, and recipient of a generous income. Then came love and with it tragedy. Abelard and Heloise made love in the attic of her uncle's home; she became pregnant and was in rapture by the thought of it. Abelard sent her to his sister's home in Brittany to give birth, and there she delivered a son, Astrolabe. Abelard insisted that they get married, against the objections of Heloise, who saw therein a loss of Abelard's career—a career she envisioned as following in the noble line of Cicero, Seneca, Paul, St. Jerome, Theophrastus; namely, that a man cannot give himself both to philosophy and a wife at the same time. The philosopher was to be continent or at least single. He would have to resign his canonry to contract the marriage as well.

But Abelard, now nearing forty, could not bear to be separated from his Heloise, now about eighteen. The marriage would go through. And so, leaving the child with Abelard's sister, they returned to Paris and were married in a secret service. They tried to keep the marriage secret by living apart, but her uncle was boisterous and angry about it. Abelard, to spare Heloise the torments of her uncle, placed her in a convent of Argenteuil where they would meet in secret, making love at least once in a corner in the refectory when they could find no private room.

Fulbert fulminated at his niece being put in a cloister and, to avenge his wrath, arranged for a middle-of-the-night castration of Abelard. The deed done, Abelard withdrew to a monastery in Brittany and, in many respects, withdrew from the creation-centered philosophy he had always espoused and even lived. He replaced it with a kind of guilt, remorse and Neoplatonic spirituality that characterizes Augustine and other Western male theologians. Thus he writes:

> My love, which involved us both in sin, let us not call it love but concupiscence. In you I cloyed a wretched appetite, which was all I really loved.

> I, who had led up to then a life of continence, yielded my loins to lust.

Abelard spiritualizes his feelings for Heloise in the best Platonic tradition.

> To Heloise, his dearly beloved sister in Christ, Abelard, her brother in Him . . . . Sister, once so dear to me in the world, now exceedingly dear to me in Christ.

> I must address as *Ma Dame* the spouse of my Lord.

Thus Abelard enthrones Heloise. She is part of the spiritual hierarchy, à la Pseudo-Denis perhaps. "What greater praise than that she who was once the wife of a mere man should be called now the spouse of the sovereign king?"[19]

So much for Abelard, whose castration proved to be more than just physical but intellectual and spiritual as well. What about Heloise? Heloise, unlike Abelard, never whitewashed her sensual experience; never internalized guilt about it; never surrendered to an asensual spirituality. She built her spirituality on a commitment to human friendship and she never wavered. She stood by the consequences of her actions, even when "all the accepted values were to undergo a radical transformation."[20] Being a mistress, a lover, a mother was no shame to her; it was no sin against God. But marrying Abelard and thus bringing about his demise was a crime for which she chastised herself. She was convinced that her love was unselfish: "I sought not my own pleasure but yours." And when Abelard insisted on spiritualizing their relationship following his monastic conversion, Heloise responded: "To God, in species, but to Abelard as individual." Her love was hard as hell and would not be repressed for the sake of a platonic spiritual flight.

She accepted her lot to be prioress in the Abbey of the Paraclete but only because there seemed no other way out in medieval society. There, she still loved Abelard, and she refused to be deceived or to forget.

> I am still young and full of life; I love you more than ever and suffer bitterly from living a life for which I have no vocation.

> The pleasures of lovers which we have tasted together have been so sweet that I cannot despise them nor even efface their memory without great difficulty. Wherever I turn, there they confront me with their eternal longing.

Heloise boasts that out of love she would follow him, even in his physically mutilated condition, to hell itself. Just as she gave herself up totally to him out of love, now she enters the convent solely because he advises it. And this will demonstrate the fullness of her love.

> Whatever the state of my life, God knows I still fear more to offend you than to offend Him. It is you rather than He that I desire to please. It is not out of love of God, but at your request that I entered religion.[2][1]

We find in the story of Heloise so much ready-made drama and fateful tragedy that she is seldom considered from the perspective of a theological thinker. But I am suggesting that she is. In her spirituality (which is always as much a way of living as a theory of living) she rejects an asensual God; she rejects the pseudo-Dionysian flights to an immaterial universe or to the One (i.e., the Species). She insists to the end, and in spite of wretched suffering, on opting for the individual; i.e., material Abelard. She trusted her experience of love with him and built her life on it: she was possibly the first and profoundest existentialist. She rejected the temptation (urged on her by Abelard and others) to internalize fear or guilt though she admitted guilt consistent to her spirituality; namely, the guilt of accepting Abelard's overtures to marriage against her better judgment and thus jeopardizing his position (in this she was proven 100 percent accurate).

In the living out of this sensual spirituality she was very much a victim of her culture and period. Her pregnancy, for example, was surely a turning point leading to her denouement, and many couples are able to love her and Abelard's precastration spirituality today thanks to the pill. Sociologically, there were not many options open to a young woman who wanted love but was under the guardianship of an uncle save convent life. Thus, in a real sense, Heloise, a victim of a culture built on asensual spiritual assumptions as well as of her own sensual spirituality, is a historical figure to reckon with. For she was true to her chosen spirituality; she paid untold consequences for it; indeed, she is critical of the demands of monastic spirituality and points out how it is a male, not a woman's way of life—even the clothes have been designed by and for men, not women, she complains. In her own way, then, she is prophetic in her spirituality. Generous to share her love; willing to enter history; a harbinger of a feminine consciousness.

A second example of a creation-centered, sensual spirituality is that of Francis of Assisi. Though vowed to celibacy after his conversion, he was not vowed to asensuality as is clear from his deep friendship with Clare, his rapturous relationships with nature in terms of sister sea, brother fire, sister birds. His political sense and symbolic consciousness unite: he goes out to the poor and lepers and outcasts of his day, on the one hand, and surmises the repressive consequences should his band of followers yield to the political opportuning of Rome, on the other. "Never," this saint wrote in his will composed between May and September, 1226, "ask for any privilege from the Roman curia, either directly or through any intermediary—for a dwelling-place, the authority to preach or for protection from persecution."[22] He always made "the least possible compromise with the social system," observes Yves Congar.[23] The political and cultural exigencies of Medieval Society and the Church did not heed Francis' spirituality that was at once sensual and political. But we need not forget it. Indeed, we should pursue it.

A third example of a spiritual dissident in the asensual spiritual suppositions of Christianity is Thomas Aquinas. For Aquinas, "asensuality is a vice."[24] His spirituality was never adopted by Catholicism; "in fact his doctrine never really penetrated the depths of Christian thinking."[25] Chenu points out that the reason for this was Aquinas' "theology of matter", a creation-centered spirituality which clashed invariably with the pseudo-Dionysian suppositions of matter as an anchor dragging us down from ascending on high. But, for Aquinas, there is no such goal as separating oneself (in medieval language, one's soul) from one's body: to do so would be to destroy the person. "Just as neither a hand or a foot can be said to be a person, likewise neither is the soul a person."[26] He rejected the dualism of the mind that taught there was a "superior reason" dedicated to attaining perfection and divinity and a secondary "inferior reason" devoted to study of nature. He insists that the human being is one, a unity that includes "sensation, imaginations, passions, and even concepts."[27] He denies that instincts and sensual energies are to be eschewed. On the contrary, they are the "seat" of virtues and "share in the dignity of reason and love." It is virtuous to enjoy sensual pleasures.

It follows that in striving to perfect human society, a person perfects herself. Unlike Augustine, Aquinas based his spirituality on matter and the Creator's presence in it and not on the flight to a world of ideas. But, for this very reason, Aquinas became prophetic, and "roused the anger and disdain of intellectuals and religious people by proclaiming the importance of matter in the metaphysics of the universe, in the constitutions of man and in the evolution of society." Plato and Augustine and Pseudo-Denis fled from time: time is nonreal for it is associated with change and with matter. The truly spiritual for them is eternal. Not so for a sensual-political spirituality. "To possess a body is also, and by that very fact, to exist in time." We are not pure, atemporal spirits; nor need we pine to be such. Augustinian Neoplatonism discounted 'becoming' as Plato did—it implied corruption and degeneration. "Becoming is proper to non-being" for them.[28] The spiritual goal of Augustine and Pseudo-Denis is to escape time; not, as in the prophetic view, to change the times, making them more just in their sharing of ecstasies. It is curious that Aquinas recognized the historical dimension only when he was commentating on the Scriptures. But he recognized the personal aspect to time in his sense-oriented philosophy. "There is no knowledge that does not come through the senses." "No science of man is totally true which does not find its object among the material realities in which his body is immersed, both in its being and in its operations." Because Aquinas saw human perfection in the perfecting of the matter of humankind and the cosmos, his is an "optimistic vision of man and of the world."[29] Creation is good and from a good God; it continues still.

Aquinas is not afraid of pleasure. In fact, he divides one's choices in life styles (active or contemplative) along one issue: which direction provides the greatest pleasure for the individual. "The life of any man at all seems to be that in which the enjoyment is the greatest, and that which he finds most attractive." Interestingly, he cites the Hebrew Bible in this discussion of pleasure, "When I go home I shall take my ease with her." (Wis. 8.16) "The goal of the contemplative life is pleasure, which is in the affective appetite." A person shares in God's company "by way of a certain regeneration or recreation."[30] Ecstacy with God is our recreation (being re-created) with God, our enjoying the divine playmate with whom we have chosen to pass our time. "The divine person himself is enjoyed" by graced persons and all persons are capable of such profound participation with God. The ultimate end of humans is enjoyment. "The fruit of man is said to be the ultimate end of man, *which he should enjoy."* Pleasure constitutes the very definition of the "fruit of the spirit." A spiritual fruit is "something having the nature of an ultimate and pleasurable experience." And the root of them all is love, "the first perfection and the root of all of them."[31]

While Aquinas, then, clearly put forth a matter-oriented, time-oriented spirituality, one that took the senses and the sensual far more seriously than did the Neoplatonic school, he was by no means free of the prejudices regarding women and sexuality that so characterized the male mind of Greek philosophy and medieval thought, or of an ahistorical vision of human destiny. At least, unlike Augustine, he did insist that both man *and* woman are made in God's image and likeness. And, his spirituality did not repress time.

A fourth example of a dissenter from an asensual spirituality is the Italian humanist Lorenzo Valla. (1407-1475). Valla was a modern thinker insofar as he insisted on analyzing and criticizing what others took for granted. He developed tools and methods for this critical work and his methods were to influence Erasmus who followed him. He exposed as fictitious the supposed correspondence between St. Paul and Seneca and, above all, he demonstrated that Denis the Pseudoareopagite's works could not possibly have been those of a contemporary of St. Paul.[32] In this and in his criticism of the Vulgate edition of the New Testament, he anticipated Luther.

Valla's best-known effort was a highly political (read: prophetic) one. He underminded once and for all any speculation about the possible authenticity of the Donation of Constantine. Legendarily, this document recorded

Emperor Constantine's bequeathal of Rome and its territories to the Pope. In fact, it was fabricated by the Papal Chancery in the ninth century to provide a legal precedent for the temporal powers of the Pontiffs. Valla was scornful of the perpetuation of such a fraud. "A Christian man who calls himself the son of light and truth ought to be ashamed to utter things that not only are not true but are not even likely."[33] He railed against idle metaphysical speculations, preferring a return to the spirit of the Gospels and Paul to the decadent scholasticism of his day.

His first published work was a dialogue originally entitled "On the True Good" but popularily known as "On Pleasure." Though this treatise has earned the eminence of a "major Renaissance document," it might prove something of a disappointment to persons looking for a quick sensual fix. In it, he pits a Stoic against an Epicurean and himself plays a third or "Christian" role of mediator. He endorses pleasure but, still very much under a medieval influence of life-after-death spirituality, postpones it to heaven. Thus, his work on pleasure is in no way a breakthrough regarding spirituality; but it is a revelation of how near to the brink of sensuality an honest thinker came—endorsing it fully though putting it off for a future life. It was a short step from this postponed eschatology to the *joie de vivre* of Renaissance living that was to happen. By his critical demythologizing of papal power (for this he was hired as a pontifical secretariat and finished his life in Rome) and of Pseudo-Denis' works and by his endorsement of the scientific, critical method, he opened the door to prophetic spirituality, on the one hand, and to a Gospel spirituality that was not Neoplatonic, on the other. The latter he never lived to share in.

In the twentieth century, the paleontologist and priest Teilhard de Chardin has found a welcome hearing from many persons seeking to unite matter and spirit in their deep lives. He taught that matter and spirit need not be distinct entities in nature or in human experience and that salvation was not to be sought in "abandoning the world" of sense but in active "participation" in building it up. True to much of the twentieth century's scientific and evolutionary suppositions, he saw the whole cosmos and humankind as a piece of it in constant process and evolution. The fierceness of the acrimony leveled against his thought from dualistically-trained religious authorities is evidence of how to the quick he touched the spirit of twentieth-century persons. Apropos of our subject, he writes:

> In their struggle towards the mystical life, men have often succumbed to the illusion of crudely contrasting soul and body, spirit and flesh, as good and evil. But despite certain current expressions, this Manichean tendency has never had the Church's approval. . . . Asceticism deliberately looks no further than the first aspect (the gravity of matter). . . . and it recoils, exclaiming 'Flee!' But what would our spirits be, O God, if they did not have the bread of earthly things to nourish them, the wine of created beauties to intoxicate them, and the conflicts of human life to fortify them?[34]

For his taking of matter seriously (so seriously that he calls it "holy matter"), for his acceptance and eagerness of the temporal and the coming of a future brought about by a re-energized humanity, for his uncompromising position against Manichean dualism, Teilhard is surely to be commended. He represents a turning point in the history of Christian spiritual theology no less significant than that of Aquinas seven centuries previous.

However, there are weaknesses below the surface of Teilhard's thought that prevent his contribution from being anything more than a bridge between one spiritual epoch and another. The first of these pitfalls is that he only partially overcomes dualism in his thought. If one examines his language carefully, one finds that with him the anima is too much on a pedestal and, consequently, his thought is intensely chauvinist and phallic. Consider, for example, these expressions from his *Divine Milieu.*

> make us shoot up higher and straighter . . .
> God . . . is finally to penetrate into us. . .
> human life opens on a road . . . that *climbs upward* (sic)
> The Christian is . . . to climb in the light of the Cross
> All the paths . . . have this in common: that they lead always upward.[35]

Ultimately, then, Teilhard is afraid of the sensual and the pleasurable and he confesses as much. "Renunciation gradually gains mastery over pleasure, death consummates life."[36] His is no resurrection-oriented spirituality in the long run.

A second serious deficiency in Teilhard's thought logically follows. That is that he remains always *de* Chardin; that is, a son of the aristocracy. His politics (including his near romanticism with war in his First World War experience) remain aristocratic and uncritical; his thought entertains little awareness of political evil in social structures. For this reason, certain authors have called him the "Mary Poppins of theology." He is a victim to some extent of the progress supposition in nineteenth-century evolutionary thought (as if because we are always in process we are also necessarily progressing). His spirituality retains something of the priggish, asensual, chauvinistic suppositions of a person who is unfamiliar with body and body politic. For all his efforts at building a world of *hominisation* (humanization) and love, I do not think his way is the way to do it.[37]

A third and necessary criticism of Teilhard is that, like so many other Christian mystics before him (beginning with Paul, whom he admires so fully), Christ becomes a symbol and almost a sign for him. But the Jesus of the Gospels, with his own Jewish cultural and spiritual heritage, remains almost entirely unknown to him. Teilhard fails to break with the docetistic tendencies of so much Christian mysticism. (Docetism teaches that Christ is divine and anything human about him is strictly by chance.) He is far more apt to cite Paul in favor of his mysticism than Jesus from the Gospels.

For these three reasons—because he is chauvinistic, dualistic and ultimately afraid of the sensual; because he is unaware of political evil; and because he ignores Jesus for the Christ—Teilhard's contribution to a sensual spirituality is severely limited.

We have seen that the spiritual God of the Jews is also a sensuous God; indeed, the creator of all that is sensuous, including senses, desires, appetites, memories, sexuality, the earth. In fact, this is the theological meaning of sensuality: it is God-given and God-made (not man-made). Furthermore, we have seen that the prophets' spirituality was steeped in the sensual and, I submit, that it is for this reason above all that Heschel[38] consistently resists all attempts to apply Platonic or Neoplatonic categories of ecstasy to prophets (as Philo in fact did). Prophetic spirituality is, in fact, incompatible with Neoplatonic, asensual mysticism and flight from matter, history, time and social justice (or injustice). Pleasure is sinful only when it is one-sided; that is, when it is death-oriented or at another's expense (cf. sadism) or when it implies a giving up of hope and life, as in cynicism.[39]

We have examined how Jesus, in entering human history, did so as a sensual, alive, feeling person in the prophetic spiritual tradition of his ancestors. But Christianity, for the most part, succumbed to anti-Semitism and aprophetic, asensual spiritualities throughout its history. These spiritualities (including Marcion's and Pseudo-Denis') put more stock in Plato and Proclus than in the prophets and Jesus of the Gospels. While exceptions arose in the West in the Middle Ages in terms of Heloise, Francis, and Aquinas and certainly in the Renaissance and Reformation, the real fruitful contribution had to wait for two more recent western thinkers, each from the Hebraic tradition of prophetic, sensual spirituality: Karl Marx and Sigmund Freud.[40]

Christian spirituality has been, for the most part, involved in a flight from sensuality. A business of "saving souls" with all that implies as distinguished from inspiring persons to love life and to share it. Amos (6.1-7) castigates those who seek their own pleasure at the expense of justice. Is it possible that today, with the aid of technology and law, humankind might be able to build an earth where both pleasure and the equal sharing of pleasure are possible? When Jesus speaks in John's Gospel about "the works of my Father," he is speaking of political works of relieving the pain of others. "To know Yahweh" does not mean mystical flights of private rapture; it means "to *do* justice" as the exegete Jose Miranda demonstrates. (M, 293) And therein lies profound, divine pleasure. We need to be about these same works no matter how they wrench us from the comforts and private satisfactions of asensual mystical flights. Marx understood this when he bluntly accused Western philosophy of its "chief defect"; namely, "the thing, reality, sensuousness, is conceived only in the form of the object or of contemplation."[41]

Some persons, slightly but not profoundly familiar with theological terminology, will raise an objection to a sensual spirituality in the name of *concupiscence*. Concupiscence is a technical theological term coined by Augustine to depict the basis of humankind's gravity toward evil. It does not mean, however, in any primary sense[42] a gravity toward the sensual, although the asensual, Neoplatonist Church Fathers such as Augustine projected this limited sense onto it. What it does mean is one-sidedness. The fact that we have a ready-made term in contemporary American vocabulary for "concupiscence" shows how significant an experience this is for many: "concupi-scence" means, in everyday jargon, "being hung-up." To be hung-up is to be a victim of one-sidedness or concupi-scence. We see then that Augustine, whom no one could accuse of not being hung-up about sex and the sensual, was deeply involved in concupiscence. No wonder he became the theological father of concupiscence. Unfortunately, we have inherited his hang-ups and concomitant guilt until we break out of his asensual spirituality. To be concupiscent is to be hung-up and up-tight instead of ecstatic (i.e., turned on). It is to be one-sided. It is one-sidedness and not sensuality that draws human persons into evil. According to Isaiah, the root of all evil is "man's false sense of sovereignty" that displays itself in lack of compassion or, in biblical terms: "stubbornness of heart"; "hardness of heart"; "brazen-faced and stiff-necked"; "uncircumcised heart." It is this callousness that is the root of sin in the Hebrew Bible, as Heschel insists.[43] As distinguished from their Mesopotamian neighboring religious beliefs about sin, the Jews did not see sin as a noun or a state but as an adverb. "To the prophets, sin is not an ultimate, irreduc-ible or independent condition, but rather a disturbance in the relationship between God and man."[44] Sin is relation-al. And the God sin offends is a God of justice—Yahweh is "the liberator who brings justice." (Ps. 7.12)

Evil, for the Jews, is political—far from being the metaphysical reality it is to Augustine and Pseudo-Denis who, like Plato, see evil as "an absence of good." The theme of the Last Judgment is a theme of salvation from the oppression of injustice. For the Hebrew word for "judge," *mispat*, means "the defense of the weak, the liberation of the oppressed, doing justice to the poor." (M,114,137) "Sin", in the biblical tradition, far from being carnality and bodily awareness,[45] means to remain un-moved, passionless, at another's misfortune or injustice. To be without compassion, to be hard of heart, is to be a sinful person. And the word "hatred," as Jesus uses it, follows perfectly the prophetic tradition insofar as it means, ultimately, "lack of compassion." Sin, then, is a concrete choice to follow the gravity of a one-sided, uncompassionate existence. Thus, we see that an asensual spirituality is itself a product of sinful concupiscence, for it is one-sided regarding the gift of the body and senses and regarding justice, about which it is always silent.

One reason for the silence in Christianity regarding justice on earth is the projection of the Last Judgment into another time and space, called heaven or life-after-death. Deep commitment to this kind of eschatology results in justifying a great deal of asceticism or mortification of senses. Such is always the case when one conjures up the idea that the end is very, very near or very, very important. "Intensified exhortations to asceticism in St. Paul are to be explained by the expectation of an imminent parousia."[46] Bringing about a world of justice that Yahweh could recognize and love does not count in such a spirituality. And theologies like Marcion's (or Irish or French Jansenism), which all too readily equate Paul's word *sarx* (flesh) with sensual aberrations or sexual temptations, arise easily in such a nonprophetic spiritual context. Yet Paul meant by *sarx* only weakness or concupiscence in the sense of one-sidedness.[47] Again, those who shout "concupiscence" the loudest are themselves guilty of its primary meaning which is one-sidedness. To be asensual is to be guilty of the sin of concupiscence, as Aquinas suggests.

A sensual spirituality, to keep from being concupiscent, has to be two-sided, not one-sided. Compassion as well as passion; sharing of the pleasure as well as enjoying the pleasure. Christianity has failed to develop a two-sided spirituality because it forsook the prophets of the Hebrew Bible. Either the parousia (in the early church) or heaven (in the medieval church) distracted believers from the task of making this earth shareable by way of justice. In the name of God, Christianity has frequently killed the godly in our midst: nature, sex and one another. Self-mutilations and masochism and sadism in the form of crusades, inquisitions, witch-burnings are as integral to Christian spiritual history as lofty heights of mysticism. When you repress authentic, justice-oriented prophecy and pleasure, its opposite will assert itself.[48]

Christian spirituality has been a victim of Neoplatonism in all its forms for long enough. Paul rejected the wisdom and philosophy of the Greeks (1 Cor. 1.22; 2.4f.; Col. 2.8). It is time we did the same. These Greeks, who lack a category for prophecy and changing history in the name of justice and who fear the sensual, should be rejected for the sake of the Hebraic, prophetic spirituality that unites the two in the name of the Creator of both. How dare we of the West ignore the spiritual experience of doing justice any longer.

A sensual spirituality, then, *is* a political spirituality: it is about enjoying and sharing the joys of the earth, of creation. It is not—it cannot be—about owning or accumulating power, immortality, control or rewards. It is sharing the pleasures of the earth by way of justice.

CHAPTER 18

Prophetic re-incarnation spirituality: a Jewish-Christian spirituality for a post-Piscean Age

T he end of the Age of Pisces, an age of conflict between body and soul, the sensual and the spiritual, is occurring. What will the future spirituality need to be? I can best categorize it as prophetic re-incarnation. The word "reincarnation" can mean, as it does for Neoplatonists and some Eastern religions, a "solution" to life after death and wickedness in this life.[1] I reject this notion of reincarnation as being tied up with other-worldly pastimes and the fantasizing of immortality that are such an escape from this life. Its flight from prophecy is similar to that which so characterized the spiritualist spiritualities of Neoplantonic Christianity.

No, what I mean first by re-incarnation is far more Jewish. I mean the need to become fleshy (incarnate) again because we have lost this sensuality, this sense. We have settled for non-sense, asensuality, other-worldliness. Such a re-incarnational spirituality will be a prophetic spirituality not only, as we have demonstrated, because the prophets lived it, but also, and in a special way, because our senseless culture needs it so desperately. To preach it, to offer a home for sensual spiritual voyagers, to offer encouragement for the sensual—all this will be the actual doing of prophecy, "knowing the Father" (who is also a mother). Restoring justice insofar as every creature of this sense-loving Creator has a right to the enjoyment of the sensual. And, as is readily apparent, it means entering fully once again into human history and human flesh and sensuality as Jesus did. Jesus, whom Christians know as, the "event of the Incarnation." This event has been lost sight of in the Greek and rationalistic efforts to suppress the sensual. We need — God needs — a re-incarnation. And she is depending on us to bring it about.

A second meaning to re-incarnation that I can assert with confidence as a theologian operating from a Jewish and Christian background is the matter of timing. Eastern theories of re-incarnation emphasize the cyclical nature of existence: how one's current level of existence reflects one's previous spiritual state. A Christian theology of reincarnation brings a loud and extravagant claim to this sense of cyclical timing; that is, that this time around is the last time around. For the freely baptized Christian, the message is: "This is it. Your last and final opportunity." Is this not a reasonable understanding of Paul's theology of baptism when he claims that "our former selves have been crucified with Christ" (Rom. 6.6) and that we, like Christ, "will never die again." (6.8) Thus, as far as believers are aware, the present time is the only time for them. Eternal life is the last reincarnational time around for them. For them eternity has begun and a birth to a new and final (eschatological) self is taking place. This sense of Christian re-incarnation makes our present lives not only an incredible challenge but a divine occasion. An occasion for divine ecstacies and the sharing of them. "World without end..."

What does this re-incarnational spirituality mean practically? It means that we take the route that Freud dreams of when he talks of sublimation as being the "way out." "Sublimation is a way out, a way by which the claims of the ego can be met without involving repression." What does he mean by *sublimation?* It implies the conscious "sacrifice of instinctive pleasures for the common good"; it is turning energy "aside from its sexual goal" and diverting it "towards other ends, no longer sexual and socially more valuable."[2] As Marcuse puts it, citing Freud along the way, "sublimation means a change in the aim and object of the instinct 'with regard to which our social values come into the picture.' "[3]

Brown wants to discount sublimation as "the way out"—suggesting that it, in fact, "leads to an aggravation of the human neurosis" rather than salvation.[4] What is the way out for Brown? The resurrection of the polymorphously perverse human body. A Dionysian consciousness "which does not observe the limit, but overflows." A non-negating, "perfect body"—the body of humankind, the body politic rising as one. (LB 68) I am not so sure that Marcuse and Brown are wholly at odds since Marcuse, while accepting sublimation as integral to the process of human salvation, makes a distinction between repressive and nonrepressive sublimation. The latter is sublimation without desexualization and in the social context of repression it takes the form of "the negation of all accepted productivity and performance."[5]

In Freud as both Brown and Marcuse understand him, we have the basis for a sensual, prophetic spirituality as I have outlined it in this book. First, regarding the sensual, I agree with Brown and have presented a polymorphous sexuality in the first chapter of this book in the form of natural ecstasies. Nature and sex, friendship and thinking, music, dance, other arts, and sports are indeed ends in themselves. In Chapter II, I have dealt with how wisdom might sort out the repressive sublimations of fasting, celibacy or formal meditation and see that, given the exigencies of spiritual survival in a repressive (i.e., anti-spiritual) world, such practices might prove useful *as means only.* Means to what? To ecstasy, of course. With Brown, in Part II of this book, I have suggested that the spiritual mutation that one undergoes by restructuring existence around ecstasy will indeed be extremist, "overflowing" in his words. Compassion, growing into an awareness of the integral relationship between one's own ecstasies and others, is the culmination of a person changed by ecstasy. And it leads directly to politics, to the ecstasy of the whole body politic.

What are examples in our midst of sublimation experiences that are at hand for all of us to engage in or take heart from? Work can be one such form of healthy sublimation—provided, of course, that it is nonalienating and sensual. It is especially in work that we find our spiritual expression. Not compulsive and productive work but work as the prophets worked—work of consciousness-raising, of sharing words of encouragement and support, of destruction and of fire. This work, work for others, which today is always done with others, is the only work worthy to be called "spiritual work" or nonrepressively sublimated work. It is the work of the prophets, which is the work of all of us. It will take as many forms as peoples' newly released imaginations will allow. Some are in circuses, some in hospitals, some in classrooms, some in homes working as parents, some in counseling, some in dancing and music-making and in study, some in the woods and others in child care centers. There is a collective body (is this what 'church' once meant?) growing gradually of worldwide spiritual workers. They are not repressed and buttressing their faith with pious shibboleths (those who are part of the oppression true prophetic workers work to remove); but are growing, ever growing out of repression into expression. And sharing. And enjoying. And rejoicing. And being alive. And sensual. And sharing. There is great pleasure in this. There is resurrection even. For all.

This spiritual work (as distinguished from spiritualized work) is the task of sharing the sensual, becoming spiritual and enjoying the process. It is not a "good work" that justifies a person's enjoyment of pleasure. The former, for a spiritual person, needs no justification. Prophecy is itself, in the last analysis, a pleasure; a fun time, albeit frequently a suffering and a hard time. "The reward of *mispat*," as the rabbinic saying goes, "is *mispat*."

As Einstein put it, "The most important motive for

work in the school and in life is the pleasure in work, pleasure in its result and the knowledge of the value of the result to the community . . . a joyous desire for the highest possessions of men, knowledge and artistlike workmanship."[6] Joy, the fruit of passion and Spirit, underlies all prophetic hard times. Thus, we arrive at a notion of service as a spirituality. Service when it is prophetic in its impetus qualifies as spirituality. It is a way of life and of responding deeply to life.

It seems to me that the fundamental issue today is not jobs—though jobs are important. It is not work; not pay. The more fundamental issue—the one lying behind jobs. work and pay—is *pleasure*. Where will our race enjoy itself? lose itself? spend money to pay workers who bring ecstasy to others? If our nation were to put its 10 percent unemployed to work at jobs of beautifying life—making artistic centers in our neighborhoods and discovering the untapped resources in young and old alike for music, dance, theater, film-making—instead of fret about putting more automobiles on our highways to secure jobs—would we not all be better off in every possible way? There is something impotent about a nation that can sell $11 billion worth of jet fighters and put persons to work that way, but will not or cannot subsidize the beautifiers of life.

To be effective, this sensual, prophetic (and therefore spiritual) work will require a new kind of society with new economic goals and political means. A society where people are the goal, not the means. People are the only ones who can enjoy the sensual or share it—institutions are asensual. A society where profits are means, not ends. It will mean new kinds of educational, familial, religious institutions ones that are dedicated primarily to the sharing of the sensual fruits of the earth. They will be inspired by this uniquely Jewish but long forgotten contribution to culture: that sublimation takes a natural course not in loving pleasure the less but in loving the sharing of it as much. Such a spiritual society will learn its lesson well from mistakes of past, other-worldly spiritualities (which were so effective in keeping certain persons in control in this world). Namely, that the belief in an "imminent parousia" requires sublimation—not out of duty or moral obligation but, rather, out of a noncaring that arises from loving one's vision so fully. This was Paul's experience. Though he was mistaken about the parousia's arrival, he was not mistaken about living it unconditionally.[7] So with us: our parousia is justice on earth. It is coming. It is coming as soon as we truly fall in love with it. And out of that love will be born a burning, chilling, God-like spiritual service; a dedication to making it happen.

What will prevent this parousia from happening? All the evil spirits that currently possess and haunt us and our institutions: Sexism, racism, agism, literalism, militarism, fascism, sado-masochism, capitalism, materialism often expressed as consumerism. St. Paul speaks of two states of existence: the "in the law" and the "in Christ." In the first state, we are subject to the wiles of law, suffering, death, sin, flesh (meaning weakness), Adam, world; in the second, we are freed. Diessmann[8] pictures the process in this graphic way.

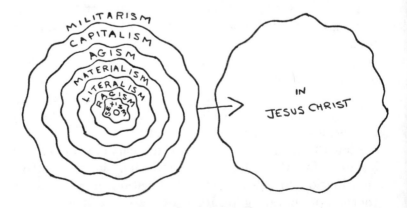

I propose re-doing the picture in accordance with our experiences of evil. Our freedom will look like this:

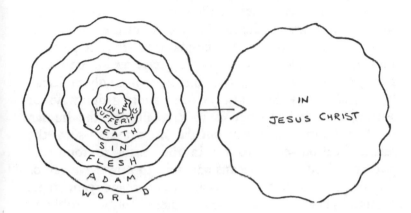

Instead of the circles of unfreedom that were experienced by Paul and represent his technical vocabulary, we see our prophetic future in language appropriate to our experiences. Our freedom is freedom from sexism, racism, literalism, materialism, agism, capitalism (especially in its advanced, corporate stages), militarism. Freedom from these "isms" is indeed "our way out." Every effort at every level of self, others or institutions, to purge these evil spirits is prophetic, is nonrepressive sublimation, and is spiritual service. This nonrepressive sublimation in work for the sake of others' liberation is not exactly the Dionysian mysticism that Brown calls "our way out." It is that—ecstasy is that—but it is also something more. It is the necessary dimension of sharing the ecstasy as well. It is not pure mysticism but prophecy as well. Like the prophets practiced; and Jesus did.

Who will support and encourage us along our spiritual, re-incarnational way? Certainly artists will. The reason artists have had such a heavy role to play as spiritual gurus the last few centuries is surely because they are sensual.

Their service and work is to alert, arouse, excite and even flatter the senses.

And the artist accomplishes this effort at goose-bump-making or moving of others by skillful manipulation of matter—bodies for dancers; oils and color for the painter; sounds and beats for the musician; clay for the potter. The artist's materials are matter; her goal is to sensitize persons, rendering them sensible and feeling once again. Artists are also, because they arouse the sensual, profoundly political. "Art and poetry have always been altering our ways of sensing and feeling—that is to say, altering the human body."[9] Political issues of our day are sensual issues—the relation of ourselves to oil in the earth, to food and potential food in the oceans and soil; to power we can or cannot harness from the earth; to war and gang rape. Asensual persons are surprised by there being a "problem" as regards the distribution of the earth's sensual goods. The artist or the sensuist in each of us would not be.

Religious traditions are another place to look for possible assistance in living a re-incarnational spirituality. I do not mean, of course, religions that imagine themselves to be inextricably married to a Neoplatonist, asensual spirituality and which are, for that reason, dying and being replaced by eastern traditions of spirituality. I mean religions that are alive enough to be able to abandon the Greek for the Hebraic spirituality. Since I am a child of one of these traditions, namely, Roman Catholicism, I would like to comment on some potential contributions it might well make.

First of all, I am struck by how sensual Catholicism is. While this sensuality is a heritage of European Catholicism (Who enjoys life with the abandon of the French, Italian, Spanish, Bavarian, Austrian?), American Catholicism should be catching up soon (or else giving up its spirit). One observer of the American scene, film critic Pauline Kael, sees this happening. She points out how "almost every interesting American movie in the past few years has been directed by a Catholic." Why? Because their Catholicism offers "a certain sensual richness in their background."

> There was more sensuality around them in their formative years, because their religion was itself more sensual, more suggestive, providing more material for the imagination.[10]

Nor is Pauline Kael alone in her recognition of sensuality and Catholicism. Two persons as different as Wilfrid Sheed and Thomas Mann agree. Comments Mr. Sheed: We Catholics "were raised on extremes, real flesh in the host and a real God in heaven; we had beliefs and not opinions .... We brought much animal exuberance to the simple fact of being Catholic."[11] And Thomas Mann observes:

> An art essentially sensuous, based on symbolic formulas ... must lead back to church celebration; and indeed I do believe that the secret longing and ultimate ambition of all theatre is to return to the bosom of the ritual out of which—in both the pagan and the Christian world—it sprang. The art of the theatre is in itself already baroque, it is Catholicism, it is the Church.[12]

The blues of Chartres' stained glass and the reds of Sainte Chapelle are not just beautiful; they are so sensual and delicious in their richness of color as to make a person, in Henry Adams' words, "drunk with the passion of youth and the splendor of the Virgin. No words and no wine could revive their emotions so vividly as they glow in the purity of the colors."[13] Is there some nonrepressive sublimation (and not merely repressive sublimation, the presence of which in Catholicism no one could possibly deny) in Catholic tradition that rendered it so sensual? I can think of at least two such elements. The first is its regard for sacraments. As Sheed says, Catholics not only eat appearances of body and blood, they eat body and drink blood. The Eucharist is a profoundly sensual event—at least in theory. So is baptism in water; oily consecration of church ministers in ordination and the sick in the Sacrament of the Sick; sex in marriage. If Catholic churches find themselves barer and duller these days, I suggest it is because the sensual has been lost.

Thomas Aquinas took his basic symbolism for the sacraments from the very physical and sensual life of the human body. The human body with its birth, puberty, eating, disease, injuries and sexual activity becomes the proper symbolic image of sacrament for him.

Sacraments presume the sensual; while medieval Catholicism and much of current-day Latin Catholicism can presume the sensual, American Catholicism, because it is a victim of so much asensuality in our culture and in its Jansenist bias, cannot. The need, then, is to once again arouse the expectations of participants in the potential sensuousness of sacraments.

For example, are priests at all sensuous? Fr. Burtchaell[14] suggests that no priest should be allowed to celebrate Eucharist who has not been a host at a meal. But what life-styles do most priests live with their hired help and asensual passing of the day? "Of the earth, earthy; of the soil, soiled" was the litany-like refrain that a priest served up for a year to me and my novitiate class. Most priests have been taught, by seminary repression, to forget the sensual; or, in Ignatius of Loyola's words, "live like an angel." Surely the ordination of women priests, provided they are not victims of the same repression, augurs well for a more sensual sacramental experience.

It strikes me that Protestantism, with its devotion to the word, also has much to learn from the more sensual, symbolic expression of God's presence that re-incarnated sacraments could bring. Luther, prophet and biblical man that he was, was a profoundly sensual person. He utterly rejected the asensual mysticism of the discredited Pseudo-Denis. However, his followers very early became uncomfortable with Luther's prophetic re-incarnational spirituality. Pietism replaced both sensuality and prophecy.

Another spiritual tradition in Catholicism is celibacy. Discounting the perverse celibate option, which is one of flight from ecstasy, sensuality, sexuality and the world, is there still something non-neurotic and indeed creative about voluntary temporary celibate decision? Surely there can be. For a celibate, by refusing to concentrate the libidinal energies on genital activity as such, sets out in search of alternative outlets for humankind's sensual energies. A true celibate is a dreamer, a dreamer about alternative forms of sensuality who explores alternative forms of sublimation in a primarily nongenital life-style.[15] Being a sensual celibate who is prophetic is a possibility, at least, and possibly a sign of hope for others.

The theological setting for celibacy, after all, has nothing whatsoever to do with "witnessing for virginity or making an idol of virginity." The reference to celibacy in the Gospels refers to witnessing "for the sake of the Kingdom." What kingdom? We have discussed it at length above: a kingdom of just distribution and enjoyment of the earth's ecstasies and sensual pleasures. A kingdom where sharing of the fruits of the earth is celebrated. Contemporary, asensual society can little afford to draw *a priori* any repressive rules about what diverse ways the polymorphously perverse human body might discover to express itself. The prophets found new possibilities in the human psyche, even undreamed of ones. So might some few celibates.

Marriage, too, though by no means the only alternative to sexual expression, might prove to be for some persons a nonrepressive rather than a repressive sublimation. Living together; working if not together at least in support of one nother; in some instances, giving birth and rearing a child together all this takes sublimation. Indeed, the example of parental love still endures as archetypal of a genuinely healthy sublimated activity. The parent who gets up in the middle of the night to care for a sick child; parents who continually educate their children, even seeking new and creative avenues for their ecstasies of every kind—here lie our most enduring examples of healthy sublimation. There is never any need to engage in sentimentalizing or romanticizing the facts of parenthood so long as theirs remains a freely chosen service—a service of ecstasy, one another's ecstasy—and not an idealistic goal or sanction set by society. The Hebraic image of God and Israel making love together harbors some profound truth about it. And perhaps it is a hint, even a "revelation," that God relates to humankind through nonrepressive sublimation—the kind young lovers dream of; and humankind (that means us!) respond in kind to God. Our nonrepressive sublimation is, then, our adult prayer. As is our ecstasy and the sharing of it.

According to latest figures, at least 10 percent of American adults are living a gay or bisexual life-style. Are such persons to be excluded from a prophetic re-incarnational spirituality? By no means. Just the opposite is the case. The ultimate hang-up (read: concupiscence) for those threatened by gay persons is, it seems to me, that gay love is nonproductive love. There is no baby-making when a man or woman makes love with one of their own sex. There can only be the pleasure, the fun, the sensuousness and the expression of love as a goal. It makes love-making *now*-oriented; sensually oriented; nonjustifying. Thus, the gay life has often in literature been a symbol for the pleasurable life. And well it should be. For this very reason, then, because gays should be expert at sensuality, this life-style needs to come out in the open; gays need to refrain from hiding their light under a bushel. Not only for their own pride and sense of personal worth (which is a first step), but also for our society's sake. Our senseless, asensual, sadistic society needs all who can return us to our senses. And gays have a special vocation to play in this respect, it seems to me.

It goes without saying (though I'm saying it anyway) that the gay who wants to make a spiritual contribution to society will do it the way all others do: by the nonrepressive sublimation of working for others' pleasure and service. In other words, prophecy will play just as important a role in the gay's life-style and consciousness as will the sensual. Because gays are so often excluded from society's institutions (like women are), we can hopefully depend on them to offer alternative institutions—ones that are more sensual, more alive and quickening than those we have inherited.

Another tradition in Catholicism is monasticism. Need all monasticism be repressive sublimation or neurotic? Of course not.

> The difference between a neurosis and a sublimation is evidently the social aspect of the phenomenon. A neurosis isolates; a sublimation unites In a sublimation something new is created - a house, or a community, or a tool— and t s created in a group for the use of a group [6]

Catholicism once put its considerable cultural weight and influence behind the monastic movement that was based on a platonic spirituality. Why can churches today not do the same behind a prophetic movement based on sensuality? The encouragement of communities that are a prelude to an earth where monogamous, heterosexual persons, gay persons, bisexual persons and celibates rejoice together, dancing before their God. So that, like islands in an otherwise asensual sea, places of sensual spiritual refreshment might be found. Where play is the activity, but creativity is the result. Catholicism was once big enough to invite and encourage extremism in life-styles, from monastic and celibate to the eremitical life, to raising families of two dozen children. Need churches today be any less imaginative and adventurous than were their ancestors once they are freed (as I have tried to do in this book) from the hang-up (read: concupiscence) of the asensual spirituality?

Sensual sacraments and liturgies, church leaders and schools, life styles and working conditions—there lies the re-incarnational church for a post-Piscean Age.

Because the potential in Catholicism for sensuality is so great, the potential for prophecy or the sharing of the Creator's pleasure is equally great. I am personally convinced this is the primary reason that in the Latin Catholic countries of Latin America, Portugal, Spain, France and Italy a special appeal to Marxism exists. (And surely in the theologians from these cultures also.) As we have seen, to abandon oneself to the love of life is also to render oneself vulnerable to abandonment to share it. Karl Marx offers sublimation instead of repression. (I am not speaking of the USSR's interpretation of his thought.) Marx, in his youth, was a mystic—as numerous Catholics are. Marx did not repress his mysticism; though he did learn to express it (that is, to channel it or sublimate it) in prophetic work. He thus becomes an archetype of nonrepressive sublimation. One would not expect less of a Jewish prophet.

It is clear then that the times require not only a sensual-prophetic spirituality that can be called re-incarnational, but also that in the process of living out such a spirituality the very meaning of sensual will be rediscovered. For we have lost its meaning. It has come to signify hot-tempered orgies to some; and libertinism to others. And to the middle class it means more of the "good life," implying more consumerism, more materialism, more hoarding and devouring of the earth's riches by a few at the expense of the many. We shall come to an experience, and after that to a reunderstanding, of what sharing the ecstasies the Creator intended for all can possibly mean.

CONCLUSION:
"WHEE! We, wee
all the way home"—
a summing up and a sending off

This little piggie went to market.
This little piggie stayed home.
This little piggie had roast beef.
This little piggie had none.
And this little piggie said . . .
      "WHEE!
        We!
           wee"
              all the way home.
          (from everyone's childhood)

While this book has been about a pleasure-oriented, sensual spirituality no one should think that the author or anyone else knows yet what pleasure means or what the sensual spirituality will come to mean. What we are sure of is that we do not experience it fully enough yet. And surely we know what spiritual sensuality will *not* mean: it will not mean luxurious living, yachts, six-inch deep carpets, and T-bone steaks for the few; it will not mean more hoarding of the earth's goods of energy and food at the expense of the many for the pleasure of the few. One certain criterion for a spiritual sensuality will be the sharing dimension to it. This is the dimension of realism and insight the Hebraic prophets bring to the entire discussion. Surely such a spirituality will include the natural ecstasies discussed in Chapter I as a focal point for cultural and institutional living. What else is involved awaits our living of it. We are en route to learning by experiencing the meaning of sensuality. And with it the meaning of a creation-centered, creation-praising and creation-sharing spirituality.

There is an extremely important *Caveat* and *danger* sign that looms on our journey. That is the warning not to look back. The reader will recall how, in the Introduction, I relayed the story of the Age of the Bull and the Age of the Ram as comparable in the depth of change of human consciousness to today's Age of Pisces yielding to the Age of Aquarius. There was one side to the story I left out until now. If you recall, when Moses came down from his experience with God on the mountain top, he was so infuriated by what he saw the Israelites doing that he broke the commandment tablets. What were they doing? They were whoring after the past gods! They were worshipping the religion of the previous age, the Age of the Bull. They refused to face the new spiritual consciousness that Moses ushered in, that of the Age of the Ram.

So we, too, on the verge of breaking into a new spiritual age, need to beware of the Gods of the past. They will continue to haunt us and attract us by nostalgia and other temptations into their seductive, safe, secure, familiar wiles of dualistic mysticisms with their consequent repressions and oppressions. We need to be brave, standing and moving together, into a new spiritual age. We should not delude ourselves by underestimating the newness of this age and what new demands a justice and prophetically-oriented spiritually will make on our former mystical lives. We need to remember Dietrich Bonhoeffer who called for today's holiness to include a giving up of our own holinesses. Nor should we underestimate the power the former age still possesses with which to seduce us. We have a clear lesson from the Israelities: to look back piningly is to commit idolatry.

Instead of looking back, we are invited to look

deep—deeply into ourselves for our ecstasies and deeply into ourselves, others, and our culture for our pain. In particular, it seems, the pain of boredom. As I have been writing this book of meditations, a murder has occurred in a Chicago suburb not far from where I type. A family of five has been murdered in their home in the midst of a residential, middle-income suburb and the home set on fire over a weekend. Both parents worked: Mr. Fuchs as a purchasing agent for a company; Mrs. Fuchs as an administrative assistant in the high school where two of their three children slain with them went to school. A neighbor girl, soon to be a sophomore in high school, comments on the event. "It's kind of a neat day. Nothing like this ever happens around here."

When the experience of "WHEE!"or ecstasy is lacking in a people or in a culture, I guess we just have to expect that ecstasy and the reason it lends to living will be sought elsewhere—in violence, in the thrill of murder, in drugs, in more and more violence. It is strange how far the West has come: it used to be that churches provided ecstasy for people. (The purpose of liturgy is to "excite devotion," insisted one renowned medieval theologian once.[1]) Is there anyone, any institution involved in "exciting devotion" toward life and living in these last days? Is the greatest ecstasy our society offers us truly our weekly trips to the bank with a paycheck?

As we come to our true home, we will recognize it as a place where WHEE! is learned and appreciated. It is a place where ecstasy is passed on. The joy of living, instead of the thrill of death in all the violent and vicarious ways it raises its head on the television news or nightly programs.

But a true home is also a place where the I, while it experiences the joys and true ecstasies of living, learns to forget itself. To think symbolically. Politically. We-ly. To think with the *We*, not the *I*. To learn the meaning of sharing, of sharing water with a thirsty person and knowing that it is more than water; and the person more

than that person; and you are more than you; I more than
I. That we are we; and we are God. A place where the
boundaries of the ego are blasted through with the spirit of
We think and We act and We share. A sharing of the
ecstasies. Plenty of pleasure to go around. If only we
defined pleasure we-ly and less in ego's terms. The WHEE!
teaches us that the goal is pleasure, the pleasure of
ourselves and the pleasure of God—which are the same
thing. But the pleasure is not only mine or yours but our
neighbors' as well. Thus, our true home is a *We* home as
well. The We's—and not the I's—have it!

And, finally, there is the weeness of us all. The ugly and
the beautiful both stop us short, get us outside of
ourselves, are bigger than we are. We are small, truly small,
before Chartres Cathedral or Beethoven's Last Quartets or
a ripe sunset over' the sea; and we are small, also, standing
on the soil of Dachau, hearing of FBI, CIA and Presidential
abuse of the people's power, or kneeling when hearing of
the assassination of a beloved leader. And there is some
very great truthfulness in this—that we are small. That
life—and its extremes—are borne through but not by
ourselves. That we are, in a word, wee-ful folk.

How little we all are! And how surely we all know it.
How many years shall anyone of us wander this earth or
any other planet? As a race, we have only been around a
few million years. A speck. A drop. An easily forgotten
event. A forget-me-not. And all the monuments that we
attempt to erect for ourselves, from siring children to
building pyramids to starting companies to writing books
to writing the newpapers and on and on: what is all this
quest for immortality, for being remembered, for leaving
something behind if not a confession that each of us
knows, deep down, how puny we are. For all the vastness
and divinity and touching of skies and sea and power and
love of which we are capable, we are still but a spark in a
live wire, destined to last as long as the flash of a firework.
Though we be creators and revel in it, we are created

creators, not self-made creators. First we have received. To recognize the *weeness* of us all is to recognize our responsibility to pass on the *WHEENESS* and the *Weness* of us all. What more dare we ask for, beg for, even pray for than to be an instrument of something bigger than we are: instruments of ecstasy.

"Where are we going? Always home," says the poet Novalis. Home is a part of our deep past and our deep future. Home is where we have tasted ecstasy and will taste it. Home is where we first experienced the profound relationship among the sensual, others, and God. I suppose home began for most of us in the womb. Where it will end depends on us. Home is far too spiritual an experience to be a literal place—"a house is not a home," the song says. Home is resurrection and re-incarnation. Some adults experience home in marriage; others in a hermitage; some in communes; others in gay alliances; still others as celibates; others as wanderers. All can experience home in their prophetic works. Because home is ecstasy and the sharing of ecstasy in play and work and because the sharing of ecstasy has been so retarded in human history, home is still a dream. A vision of our future. Home is still to be discovered and sought after and received with overflowing joy: a kingdom of God being born from the depths of our ecstasies and pains.

Going "WHEE! We, wee all the way home" is going past and forward, going where we have already been and where we most have our heart set on going. And going together. It is almost as if Plato was right when he suggested that . . . trailing clouds of glory do we come from God, who is our home.

REFERENCES

PREFACE

[1]Thomas Merton, *No Man is an Island* (Garden City, NY: Doubleday Image, 1967), p. 40.

[2]James W. Fowler, "Perspectives on the Family from the Standpoint of Faith Development Theory," (unpublished paper: n.d.), p. 10.

[3]Karl Rahner, *Theological Dictionary* (NY: Herder & Herder, 1965), p. 432.

[4]Ernest Becker, *The Denial of Death* (NY: The Free Press, 1973), p. 50.

[5]Ashley Montagu, *Touching* (NY: Perennial Library, 1972), p. 184.

[6]Erik H. Erikson, *Childhood and Society* (NY: Norton, 1963), p. 319.

[7]Robert E. Ornstein, *The Psychology of Consciousness* (San Francisco: W.H. Freeman, 1972), p. 67.

[8]Wendell Berry, *The Unsettling of America: Culture & Agriculture* (NY: Avon Books, 1977), p. 98.

[9]Elsewhere I have discussed the violent exegesis done by certain Christian mystics on Jacob's dream. The issue comes down to whether believers, on reading the Scriptures, see therein a story of earthiness as blessing or as curse. See Matthew Fox, *A Spirituality Named Compassion* (Minneapolis: Winston Press, 1979), chapter two, "From Climbing Jacob's Ladder to Dancing Sara's Circle."

[10]Cited in Claus Westermann, *Blessing in the Bible and the Life of the Church* (Philadelphia: Fortress Books, 1978), pp. 20f.

[11]See Helen Kenik, "Toward a Biblical Basis for Creation Theology," in Matthew Fox, ed., *Western Spirituality: Historical Roots*, Ecumenical Routes (Santa Fe: Bear & Co., 1981), pp. 27-75. Translation hers.

[12]Andrew Weil, *The Natural Mind* (Boston: Houghton Mifflin Co., 1972), p. 96.

[13]Cited in Lionel Salter, *The Illustrated Encyclopedia of Classical Music* (NY: Harmony Books, 1978), p. 36.

[14]Emil G. Hirsch, "Compassion," in *The Jewish Encyclopedia*, Isidore Singer, ed. (NY: Funk and Wagnalls, 1903), p. 202.

[15]See Is. 22.14. Cf. Thorlief Boman, *Hebrew Thought Compared with Greek* (NY: Norton, 1970), p. 108f.

[16]Claude Tresmontant, *A Study of Hebrew Thought* (NY: Desclee, 1960), p. 103.

[17]Paul Tillich, *Systematic Theology, III* (Chicago: Harper & Row, 1967), pp. 412, 410.

[18]Gerhard Von Rad, *Wisdom in Israel* (NY: Abingdon Press, 1978), p. 168.

[19]Roland E. Murphy, "Wisdom Theses," in *Wisdom and Knowledge,* II (The Villanova University Press: n.d.), p. 191.

[20]Roland E. Murphy, "The Understanding of Revelation in Prophecy and Wisdom," *Chicago Studies* (Spring, 1978), p. 57.

[21]Marvin H. Pope, *Song of Songs: A New Translation with Commentary* (NY: Doubleday & Co., 1977), pp. 115f.

[22]Roland Murphy, "Interpreting the Song of Songs," *Biblical Theology Bulletin* (July, 1979), p. 104.

[23]Roland Murphy, "Un Modele Biblique d'Intimite humaine le Cantique des Cantiques," *Concilium* (1979), p. 96.

[24]Alexander Jones, ed. *The Jerusalem Bible* (Garden City, NY: Doubleday, 1966), p. 991.

[25]Aabraham J. Heschel, *The Prophets* (NY: Harper & Row, 1962), p. 258. Edward Schillebeeckx, *Jesus: An Experiment in Christology* (NY: Seabury, 1979), has developed the thesis of Jesus as convivial guest and host at table—a sensual spiritual theme. See pp. 200-218 and *passim.*

[26]Adelgundis Führkotter, OSB, *Hildegard von Bingen: Briefwechesel* (Salzburg; Otto Müller Verlag, 1965), p. 14.

[27]Magna Ungrund, I.C., "Grundlegende Voraussetzunge," in Ildefons Herwegen, OSB, *Beitrage zur Geschichte des alten Monchtums und des Benediktinerordens* (Munster: Aschendorffschen, 1938), p. 19. Subsequent references in the text are to this study.

[28]*PL* 377c.

[29]*PL* 764.

[30]*PL* 818 c/d.

[31]Cited in Matthew Fox, *Breakthrough: Meister Eckhart's Creation Spirituality in New Translation* (NY: Doubleday, 1980), p. 209. All references to Eckhart's words are from this edition unless otherwise noted.

[32]Reiner Schumann, *Meister Eckhart: Mystic and Philosopher* (Bloomington: University of Indiana Press, 1978), p. 15.

[33]Thomas Aquinas, *De divinis nominibus expositio,* #430. See also, #427-437, 706, 739.

[34]Titus Szabo, "L'Extase chez les theologiens du XIIIe Siecle," *Dictionnaire de Spiritualite,* vol. IV, col. 2130.

[35]See Matthew Fox, "Meister Eckhart and Karl Marx: The Mystic as Political Theologian," in Richard Woods, ed., *Understanding Mysticism* (Garden City, NY: Doubleday, 1980), p. 557.

[36]M.D. Chenu, "Body and Body Politic in the Creation Spirituality of Thomas Aquinas," in Fox, *ed. cit.*, pp. 193-214.

[37]M.D. Chenu, "The Spirituality of Matter," in Chenu, *Faith and Theology* (NYU: Macmillan, 1968), p. 108.

[38]G.K. Chesterton, *Saint Thomas Aquinas, "The Dumb Ox,"* (Garden City, NY: Doubleday, 1956), p.29.

246

[39]Julian of Norwich, *Showings* (NY: Paulist, 1978), p. 186.

[40]Dietrich Bonhoeffer, *Letters and Papers from Prison* (NY: Macmillan, 1967), p. 120.

[41]Walter Brueggemann, *The Prophetic Imagination* (Philadelphia: Fortress, 1978), p. 38.

[42]Cited in "Body Pleasure and The Origins of Violence," *Script* (June, 1977), p. 1.

[43]E.F. Schumacher, *Small is Beautiful* (NY: Perennial Library, 1975), p. 149.

[44]M.D. Chenu, "Profit and Christian Principles," in Chenu, *op. cit.*, pp. 168-184.

[45]Jose Miranda, *Marx and the Bible* (Maryknoll, NY: Orbis Books, 1974), p. 31. Interestingly, a pastoral worker in Peru, Father Ernest Ranly, has compared *Whee, we wee* and liberation theology of Latin America, in "Revolutions in Spirituality," *Spiritual Life* (Summer, 1980), pp. 74-79.

[46]Rosemary Ruether, *Faith and Fratricide* (NY: Seabury, 1974), *passim*.

INTRODUCTION

[1]C. J. Jung, *Aion* (NY: Pantheon Books, 1959), p. 87.

[2]Peggy Constantine, "Way of Women," *Chicago Sun Times*, Nov. 2, 1975, § 4. p.7.

[3]Susan Brownmiller, *Against Our Will: Men, Women and Rape* (NY: Simon and Schuster, 1975).

[4]James Baldwin, *The Fire Next Time* (NY: Dell, 1970), p. 45.

[5]"U.S. Cynical, may need war, Nixon says," *Chicago Tribune*, Nov. 18, 1975, p. 1.

[6]Cf. M. D. Chenu, "The Human Situation: Corporality and Temporality," in *Faith and Theology* (NY: Macmillan Inc., 1968), pp. 116-137.

[7]Thomas Aquinas, *Summa contra gentiles*, Bk. II, § 3.

[8]Arthur Schopenhauer, *On the Fourfold Route of the Principle of Sufficient Reason*, trans. by Karl Hillebrand (London: Bell & Sons, 1891), p. 4.

CHAPTER 1

[1]*Chicago Sun Times*, March 12, 1974, p 38.

[2]Rollo May, "What is Our Problem?" *Review of Existential Psychology and Psychiatry*, III (May, 1963), p. 111.

[3]Friedrich Nietzsche, "Thus Spake Zarathustra: A Book for All and None" in *Ecce Home*, ¶ 3. In *The Philosophy of Nietzsche*, trans. by Clifton Fadiman (NY: Random House, 1954), p. 896.

[4]"Meanings of 'Roller-Ball' " in *Chicago Sun Times*, June 22, 1975, P-1, p. 1.

CHAPTER 2

[1] "The practice of oral repetition is widespread in the form of mantras and litanies, in recitation of sutras, in kirtan (chanting of divine names in Hinduism), the Nembutsu, the practice of pure land Buddhism, and in certain forms of prayer." (N, 47)

[2] Arthur J. Deikman, "Deautomatization and the Mystic Experience," in Charles T. Tart, ed., *Altered States of Conciousness* (NY: Anchor Books, 1972), pp. 26, 40.

CHAPTER 3

[1] Cf. Ronald Müller, "Poverty is the Product," *Foreign Policy* (Winter, 1973-74), pp. 71-103.

[2] C. H. Dodd, *The Parables of the Kingdom* (London: Fontana, 1961), pp. 20f

CHAPTER 4

[1] William Hocking, *The Meaning of God in Human Experience* (New Haven: Yale University Press, 1912), p. 439.

[2] Thomas Aquinas, *Summa theologiae*, I, q.8, aa. 1-4. Translation mine.

[3] *Ibid.*, I-II, qq. 109, 110, 114.

[4] *Ibid.*, I, q. 43, a.3.

[5] *Ibid.*, ad. 1.

[6] *Ibid.*, I-II, q. 112, a.1.

[7] Josef Pieper, *A Guide to Thomas Aquinas* (NY: Pantheon Books, 1962), pp. 146, 143, 142.

CHAPTER 5

[1] Davis Sutor, "Lessons for the Living in Death and Dying: An Interview with Elizabeth Kubler-Ross," *National Catholic Reporter* (April 20, 1973), p. 11.

[2] Gore Vidal, *Two Sisters* (Boston: Little, Brown, 1970), p.41.

CHAPTER 6

[1] Aquinas, *Sum theol.*, I, q. 43, aa. 3,6; II-II, q. 180, a.1; I-II, q. 70, aa. 1, 3.

CHAPTER 7

[1] For further ideas on symbols and spiritual education see Matthew Fox, "Religious Education as Symbol-Making," *Notre Dame Journal of Education* (Summer, 1974), pp. 237-244.

CHAPTER 8

[1] Jung, *op. cit.*, p. 44.

[2] Hanna Colm, "The Demonic in Love and Sex," *Review of Existential Psychology and Psychiatry, ed. cit.*, p. 155.

[3] Vidal, *loc. cit.*

[4] Wilfrid Sheed, "America's Catholics," *New York Review of Books*, March 7, 1974, p. 18.

[5] Dodd, *op. cit.*, p. 16.

CHAPTER 9

[1] Cf. Matthew Fox, "Panentheistic Spirituality: Religious Education for the Future?" in *Living Light* (Fall, 1974), pp. 357-367.

[2] C. H. Dodd, *The Founder of Christianity* (London: Fontana, 1971), pp. 70f.

CHAPTER 10

[1] William A. Clebsch, *American Religious Thought: A History* (Chicago: University of Chicago Press, 1973), p xvi.

CHAPTER 11

[1] Jacobus de Voragine, *The Golden Legend*, trans. by G. Ryan (London: Longmans, Green & Co., 1941), pp 233f.

[2] In Kurt Blaukopf, *Gustav Mahler* (NY: Praeger, 1973), p. 119.

[3] Cf. Mary Daly, *Beyond God the Father* (Boston: Beacon Press, 1973).

[4] David Murray, "Questions Still Hover Around the Mayaguez," *Chicago Sun Times*, May 26, 1975, p.6. See Brownmiller, *op. cit.*, for more on the relation between war and gang rape.

[5] Aquinas, *Sum. theol.*, I-II, q. 63, a.8.

CHAPTER 13

[1] Marvain Scheffler in Bob Greene, "The Killing Ends, the Healing Starts," in *Chicago Sun Times*, May 14, 1974, p. 16.

[2] Cited in Theodore Roszak's, "On Academic Delinquincy," in Roszak, ed., *The Dissenting Academy* (NY: Pantheon Books, 1968), p.12.

[3] Muller, *loc. cit.*, pp. 80f.

[4] William Raspberry, "The Middle Class Myth in America," *Chicago Sun Times*, Oct. 13, 1973, p. 32.

CHAPTER 14

[1] *Allegheny Airlines Magazine*, May, 1974, p. 22

[2]Cf. Paul Tillich, *Systematics*, III (Evanston: Harper & Row, 1967), pp. 182, 184; and Fox, pp. 153-6.

[3]Jeb Magruder, *One Man's Road to Watergate* (NY: Atheneum, 1974).

[4]Thomas Whiteside, *The Investigation of Ralph Nader* (NY: Pocket Books, 1972).

CHAPTER 15

[1]Other observers of the American cultural and religious scene who have recognized this same vice of asensuality include: Walter Kerr, *The Decline of Pleasure* (NY: Simon and Schuster, 1962); Theodore Roszak, *The Making of a Counter Culture* (Garden City, NY: Doubleday, 1968); Lucien Richard, *The Spirituality of John Calvin* (Atlanta: John Knox Press, 1974). Eastern religions do indeed sport traditions of sensual spirituality although the limited purpose of this book does not allow our going into that tradition here. In Hinduism, for example, *Kama*, the desire for pleasure through love especially constitutes a perfectly legitimate (through not definitive) spiritual way. An erotic aspect exists in many Hindu cults and in the Tantric movement a man and woman "embody a divine condition" in sexual union that symbolizes the union of Shiva and Shakti. Cf. M. Eliade, *Yoga* (London: Routledge and Kegan Paul, 1958), p. 267; Sidney Spencer, *Mysticism in World Religions* (NY: A.S. Barnes, 1963), pp. 59f., 95f., 336; John B. Noss, *Man's Religions* (London: Macmillan, 1969), pp. 191f.

[2]Cf. Daly, *op. cit.*

[3]Joseph Needham, "Time and Knowledge in China and the West," in J. T. Fraser, ed., *The Voices of Time* (NY: George Braziller, 1966), p. 96.

[4]Dietrich Bonhoeffer, *Letters and Papers from Prison* (London: SCM Press, 1967), p. 187.

[5]For more on a mystery-center spirituality see Fox, chapter two.

[6]For obvious reasons I find the term "spirituality of matter" redundant in a creation-centered spirituality. Yet the term is necessary in some situations in our asensual culture. For more on spiritualities of matter, see George Santayana's essays in *Animal Faith and Spiritual Life*, Lachs, ed., (NY: Appleton-Century Crofts, 1967); M.D. Chenu, "The Spirituality of Matter"; "Christian Reflections of the Truth of Matter," "The Human Situation: Corporality and Temporality" in *Faith and Theology*, *op. cit.*, pp. 106-36. Chenu is one of the few Christian theologians who has never succumbed to asensual, aprophetic spiritual ideologies.

[7] Cf. Rosemary Ruether, *New Woman New Earth: Sexist Ideologies & Human Liberation* (NY: Seabury Press, 1975).

[8]These criteria that I recognize in a sensual spiritual experience appear to correspond amazingly to William James' criteria for a mystical experience. See his *Varieties of Religious Experience* (NY: Mentor, 1958), pp. 292f.

[9]Abraham J. Heschel, *The Prophets* (NY: Harper and Row, 1962), p. 316. The same scholar explains that *"ruah"* ("spirit") frequently means passion, a state of the soul, in the Hebrew Bible. I am much indebted in this section on the prophets' spirituality to this monumental study by Heschel. His work has opened my eyes to the paucity of any Christian spirituality that, out of anti-Semitism or any other motive, divorces itself from   properly Jewish roots. Anti-Semitism *is* anti-sensuousness.

[10]*Ibid.*, p. 50, note 7.

[11]E. Baumann, "Yada und seine Derivate," *Zeitchrift für die Alttestamentliche Wissenschaft*, XXVIII (1908), p. 125.

[12]Heschel, *op. cit.*, p. 114.

[13]*Ibid.*, p. 444.

[14]*Ibid.*, pp. 309, 219.

[15]*Ibid.*, pp. 313, 314.

[16]Some exegetes suggest that Jn. 13.23 implies lying near to Jesus; Raymond Brown, *The Gospel According to John XII-XXI* (Garden City: Doubleday, 1970), p. 577, says John "is resting on Jesus' bosom, just as in 1.18 Jesus is described as in the Father's bosom." In any interpretation, intimacy is the message.

[17]M, p.36. Cf. p. 217. This and other critical works of exegesis are so terribly important for a recovery of biblical (as distinct from Neoplatonic) spirituality because they demonstrate the intrinsic connections between the Hebrew Bible with its prophetic spirituality and the New Testament. The mystification of the Scriptures in the name of spiritual allegory and the allegorical method of interpreting Scripture that reigned so many centuries in Christian spirituality under the influence of Philo, Pseudo-Barnabas and others, can now reap the burial it so well deserves.

[18]W. F. Albright comments on this Psalm, "possessing the earth is parallel to being admitted to the Kingdom." In Albright, *The Anchor Bible: Matthew* (Garden City, NY: Doubleday, 1971), p. 46.

[19]There is much more to the sensuality of Jesus' spirituality but the key to it is to understand how profoundly Jewish he was and the consequences of his being a poet as a parable-teller. See Matthew Fox "The Prayer and Spirituality of Jesus: A vision from the Gospels," in *Living Light* (Summer, 1975), pp. 179-92.

CHAPTER 17

[1] For this and many other insights on Jewish spirituality, I am indebted to Ron Miller of the theology faculty at Lake Forest College, Lake Forest, Ill.

[2] *The Imitation of Christ*, trans. by A. Croft (Milwaukee: Bruce, 1940), Bk. I, § 25; Bk. II, § 12; Bk. I, § 24.

[3] James, *op. cit.*, pp.241f. Norman O. Brown observes that "Chris tian asceticism can carry punishment of the fallen body to heights inconceivable to Plato." In *Life Against Death* (Middletown, Ct Wesleyan University Press, 1972), p. 309.

[4] Bossuet, *Traite de la concupiscence*, Cited in Jordan Aumann *The Theology of Christian Perfection* (Dubuque, Iowa: Priory Press, 1962), p. 265.

[5] Cited in Heschel, *op. cit.*, p. 299.

[6] Cited in Wayne A. Meeks, *The Writings of St. Paul* (NY: Norton, 1972), p. 193.

[7] *Ibid.*, p. 186.

[8] See Adolf von Harnack, *Marcion: Das Evangelium vom fremden Gott* (Leipzig: J. C. Hinricks, 1924; rp 1960). One shudders in considering the political consequences of anti-Semitism in Nazi Germany, Harnack's home territory.

[9] Cf. Heschel, *op. cit.*, pp. 301-303.

[10] Proclus, *Commentary on First Alcibiades*, in Victor Cousin, ed., *Opera Inedita*, 2nd ed. (Paris, 1864), col. 518.

[11] Proclus, *The Platonic Theology*, trans. by Thomas Taylor (London, 1816), Bk. IV. Cf. Proclus, *Chaldean Philosophy*, trans. by T. Johnson (Osceola, Mo., 1907), Bk. II, IV.

[12] E. F. Osborn, "Pseudo-Dionysius," *The Encyclopedia of Philosophy*, vol. VI (NY: Macmillan, 1972), p. 510.

[13] Cf. Dionysius the Pseudo-Areopagite, *The Ecclesiastical Hier- archy*, trans. by Thomas L. Campbell, Catholic University of America Studies in Sacred Theology, Second Series, No. 83 (Washington: Catholic University of America Press, 1955). For more on Pseudo-Denis and his influence in the spiritual tradition of Eastern Christianity see: Vladimir Lossky, *The Mystical Theology of the Eastern Church* (London: James Clarke & Co., 1968).

[14] Consider the very title of Pseudo-Denis *The Ecclesiastical Hierarchy* often referred to as The *Celestial and Ecclesiastical Hierarchy of Dionysius the Areopagite.*

[15] Cf. Freud's definition of culture or civilization as repression in his *Civilization and its Discontents* (NY: W. W. Norton, 1962).

[16] Julia O'Faolain has collected the chauvinistic spiritualities in her *Not in God's Image* (NY: Harper Torchbacks, 1973). See, too,

Rosemary Ruether, ed., *Religion and Sexism* (NY: Simon and Schuster, 1974).

[17] Etienne Gilson, *Heloise and Abelard* (Ann Arbor: University of Michigan Press, 1968), p.4.

[18] *Ibid.*, p. 1.

[19] Cited in *ibid.*, pp. 74, 3, 73f.

[20] *Ibid.*, p. 58.

[21] Cited in *ibid.*, pp. 62, 73, 76, 94.

[22] Cf. J. Joergensen, *St. Francis of Assisi* (Garden City, NY: Doubleday, 1955), p. 269. My translation of Francis' will is from Yves Congar, "St. Francis of Assisi: Or the Gospel as an Absolute in Christendom," *Faith and the Spiritual Life* (London: Darton, Longman & Todd, 1968), p. 42.

[23] *Ibid.*

[24] *Sum. theol.*, II-II, q. 142, a.1. Cf. Pieper, *Guide to Thomas Aquinas, op. cit.*

[25] Chenu, *op cit.*, p. 107

[26] *Sum. theol.*, I, q. 75, art. 4, ad 2.

[27] Chenu, *op. cit.*, p. 110.

[28] *Ibid.*, pp. 113, 117, 126.

[29] *Ibid.*, pp. 133, 136.

[30] *Sum. theol.*, 1, q.43, aa. 3,6.

[31] *Ibid.*, II-II, q.180, a.1; I-II, q.70, aa. 1, 3.

[32] Roberto Weiss, *The Spread of Italian Humanism* (London: Hutchinson University Library, 1964), p. 43.

[33] From his "Treatise on the Donation of Constantine," cited by Neal W. Gilbert, "Lorenzo Valla," in *The Encyclopedia of Philosophy*, VIII, *ed. cit.*, p. 226. Still in the twentieth century Louis Bouyer, *The Spirituality of the New Testament and the Fathers* (London: Burns & Oates, 1963), p. 415 can claim that Pseudo-Denis "transcends Neo-Platonism in a wholly Christian Way." It is difficult to imagine how such scholars can justify a spirituality that lacks Hebraic prophecy and sensuality as "Christian." Bouyer clings to Denis' world-view as if Denis were indeed a contemporary of St. Paul; such spiritual fundamentalism in Catholic spirituality that resists critical scholarship and its distinction between Hebraic spirituality and sixth century monastic spirituality resembles Protestant fundamentalism's attempts to deny evolution in order to save a six-day creation. One wonders how great a role latent anti-Semitism plays in this enthusiasm for Denis over the prophets. It is certainly politically comfortable to talk as if "hierarchy" were a biblical term. Reading works on spirituality like Bouyer's makes one wonder if all the wrong questions have been asked from a Neo-platonic rather

than a Hebraic, prophetic perspective, in spirituality for centuries.

[34]Teilhard de Chardin, *The Divine Milieu* (NY: Harper Torch-back, 1968), pp. 105f.

[35]*Ibid.*, pp. 87, 89, 102, 104, 139.

[36]*Ibid.*, p. 139.

[37]Daly, *op. cit.*, offers justifiable criticism of Teilhard's "Christolotry" and anti-feminist spirituality (pp. 190ff.) and Ruether (R. 25ff.) offers an insightful analysis into why it is that male celibates so readily enshrine female virgins as objects of adoration.

[38]Heschel, *op. cit.*, p. 363.

[39]*Ibid.*, pp. 90f.

[40]For other dissenters from an asensual spirituality, see Anders Nygren, *Agape and Eros* (Philadelphia: Westminster Press, 1953).

[41]Karl Marx and Friedrich Engels, *On Religion* (NY: Schocken Books, 1964), p. 69.

[42]Karl Rahner and Herbert Vorgrimler, *Theological Dictionary* (NY: Herder & Herder, 1965), p. 432.

[43]Heschel, *op cit.*, pp. 165, 191, n. 3.

[44]*Ibid.*, p. 229.

[45]Cf. M, 128 and Ruether on Augustine's sin-as-sex spirituality, (R, 53ff.).

[46]Rahner, *op. cit.*, p. 38.

[47]See J. T. Robinson, *The Body: A Study in Pauline Theology* (London: SCM Press, 1961).

[48]Cf. Susan Sontag, "Fascinating Fascism," *New York Review of Books*, Feb. 6, 1975, pp. 25ff.

CHAPTER 18

[1]Unfortunately this is the case in Quncy Howe Jr.'s *Reincarnation for the Christian* (Philadelphia: Westminister Press, 1974).

[2]Sigmund Freud, *Leonardo da Vinci: A Study in Psychosexuality*, trans. by A. A. Brill (NY: Random House, 1947), p. 49; *A General Introduction to Psycho-Analysis*, trans. by, J. Riviere (NY: Perma Giants, 1953), p. 27.

[3]Herbert Marcuse, *Eros and Civilization* (NY: Vintage Books, 1962), p. 188.

[4]Norman O. Brown, *Life Against Death*, *op. cit.*, p. 307.

[5]Marcuse, *op cit.*, p. 190.

[6]Albert Einstein, *Out of my Later Years* (Secaucus, NJ: Citadel Press, 1974), p. 35.

[7]See Albert Schweitzer, *The Mysticism of Paul the Apostle* (NY: Seabury, 1968), who demonstrates once and for all how unhellenic and how Jewish Paul's mysticism was though it was distorted by his

early conviction of an imminent parousia. The question for the Christian is: What does Paul's mysticism mean when parousia is *not* imminent (as now, for example)?

[8]Adolf Deissmann, *Paul: A Study in Social and Religious History* (NY: Harper and Row, 1957), p. 297.

[9]Brown, *Life Against Death, op. cit.*, p. 312.

[10]In *Chicago Sun Times*, April 27, 1975. Sec. i-C, p. 2.

[11]"America's Catholics," *loc. cit.*, p. 20.

[12]Thomas Mann, *Freud, Goethe, Wagner* (NY: Alfred Knopf, 1937), p. 107.

[13]Henry Adams, *Mont-Saint Michel & Chartres* (Garden City, NY: Doubleday Anchor, 1959), p. 151. The twelfth-century theologian Alan of Lille answers the question why humankind was created, "Because it was fitting that corporeal as well as incorporeal nature should come to participate in the divine goodness, should relish that goodness, and live happily " In *Contra haereticos*, i. 14 (PL, CCX, 319.)

[14]James Burtchaell, *Phileman's Problem* (Chicago: ACTA, 1973), p. 141.

[15]Donalds Goergen's, *The Sexual Celibate* (NY: Seabury, 1974) is a bold attempt to help free celibates from concupiscence; i.e. hang-ups. It is the most candid work and therefore the best I know of to look at celibacy with more than medieval superstition.

[16]Geza Roheim, *The Origin and Function of Culture* (NY: Johnson Reprint, 1943), p. 74.

CONCLUSION

[1]Aquinas, *Sum. theol.*, III, q. 66, a.10.

NOTES